on nature

on nature

GREAT WRITERS

ON THE

GREAT OUTDOORS

EDITED BY lee gutkind

ASSISTANT EDITOR, kate luce angell

JEREMY P. TARCHER/PUTNAM

A MEMBER OF PENGUIN PUTNAM INC.

NEW YORK

A list of permissions appears on pages 255–56.

Most Tarcher/Putnam books are available at special quantity discounts for bulk purchase for sales promotions, premiums, fundraising, and educational needs. Special books or book excerpts also can be created to fit specific needs. For details, write Putnam Special Markets, 375 Hudson Street, New York, NY 10014.

Jeremy P. Tarcher/Putnam
a member of
Penguin Putnam Inc.
375 Hudson Street
New York, NY 10014
www.penguinputnam.com

Library of Congress Cataloging-in-Publication Data

On nature : great writers on the great outdoors / edited by Lee Gutkind ; assistant editor, Kate Luce Angell.
    p.   cm.
ISBN 1-58542-173-1
1. Nature.   2. Natural history.
3. Outdoor life.   I. Gutkind, Lee.   II. Angell, Kate Luce.
QH81 .O674   2002   2002020002
508—dc21

Printed in the United States of America
10 9 8 7 6 5 4 3 2 1

contents

on nature

outward bound

LEE GUTKIND

Earlier that day, we dropped our backpacks and food at the base of a mountain and bushwhacked with day packs (water, windbreakers, and gorp, only) upward to the top. It had been very rough going from the beginning, and our leaders were playing games with us. The Outward Bound experience is often manipulative; leaders periodically decide not to lead (sometimes they will suddenly disappear!) in order to see how—and if—participants bond under physical and social stress, a common Outward Bound theme. In fact, our expedition actually began in a storeroom area where ten strangers from throughout the U.S. were asked to choose the food they would like to eat for the duration of the trip and then to divide the food and hundreds of pounds of equipment for which they would be responsible to carry amongst themselves. Everyone is usually on their best behavior at this point. Few debates over canned mackerel and/or tuna or carrots and celery versus raisins and Grape-Nuts will occur, although the identity of minimalists, those satisfied with daily diets of peanut butter and "bikkies" (crackers) and those obsessed by eating (these people discuss food—sushi, milkshakes, french fries, favorite restaurants—nonstop) will quickly emerge.

During the first few days, the stronger members of the group might also help those taxed by the initial shock of the physical demands by assuming greater responsibility for cooking and cleaning up, finding water, or setting up sleeping tarpaulins. Rallying around one or two less able or prepared members serves as a bonding and solidifying vehicle. We range in age from 23 to 55. Surprisingly, older members are more likely to be physically prepared for the experience, while younger people err by assuming that their bodies will compensate for a lack of self-discipline and training. Outward Bound was originally developed in response to the experiences of the merchant marine during World War II, when German U-boats decimated British merchant shipping. The frigid waters of the North Sea claimed hundreds of seamen, the greatest number among younger sailors, who, seemingly, were more physically fit. Studying the situation, German-born educator Kurt Hahn discovered that the younger, inexperienced seamen weren't as well oriented—psychologically—for the rigors of survival in the open sea as were older and more seasoned sailors. Invariably, the younger people panicked; fear led to exhaustion and eventual capitulation. Hahn introduced a program of rugged physical training designed to help young recruits develop mental toughness. The name Hahn chose for the program, Outward Bound, referred to the moment when a ship leaves its safe harbor for the unknown of the open sea.

That day, the dynamics of the group had not worked well. Everyone took a turn reading the terrain map and following a compass during the bushwhacking, but we were not making good progress to the elusive peak. It was frustrating because we could see the peak off in the distance, and we could also see ribbons of trail leading up to it, but we always seemed to be getting sidetracked, picking the wrong path. Even when we were moving in the right general direction, the constant appearance of false summits became increasingly irritating. Although we experienced a momentary feel-

ing of satisfaction when we finally did find our way to the top—
much later than planned—we were tired, hungry, thirsty, and testy.
The sun was going down, and our instructors suddenly informed us
that if we did not quickly return to our original point of departure
with all of our camping and sleeping gear within the next hour, we
would have to sleep on the ground in our clothes and without food.

Ordinarily, I would not have cared about where and under
what conditions I might be sleeping on any given night. Outward
Bound is by no means supposed to be a luxury camping experience.
You are issued very basic equipment and expected to carry sixty- to
seventy-pound packs from before dawn to after dusk, sometimes
hiking in unrelenting heat. Except when it rains, you will not
shower; you carry only one change of clothing—no wallet or wrist-
watch—and a few toiletries. At the end of the day, your pants and
shirt are glued with perspiration to your skin. In Outward Bound,
there's usually no toilet paper; you use flat rocks, dry sticks or leaves
to wipe yourself. You carry out trash, scrub cooking pots and pans
with dirt, and drink your dishwater—all hardships I usually consider therapeutic, at least in small doses and in contrast to my normal life in the city.

But that early evening, I was tired, dirty, sweaty. Listening to
the bickering of my companions, I was becoming increasingly annoyed. Throughout most of the day, I had removed myself from the
decision-making process because no one could agree on any single
direction; one of the reasons I had signed up for this Outward
Bound was to disconnect myself from the hostile bickering of a failing marriage. The more I listened to the ongoing debate, the more I
was reminded of the life I was attempting to forget. And although I
did not have a terrific sense of our present location or of where we
had stashed our gear, I realized the absolute futility of the present
situation if someone, *anyone*, did not assume a strong leadership position. (An important Outward Bound concept is not only to function as a member of a team, but also to assume leadership at an
appropriate time.) I further realized that it was far better to be on

the bottom of the mountain at night where it was warmer and where water and shelter would be much more readily available than at the rocky, wind-whipped top. So when I stepped forward and asserted myself with a loud and authoritative "follow me" and moved out with a strong step and in a definite direction, everyone fell in behind and followed my lead. At some point during our descent, I began to realize, based on the general familiarity of the terrain, that I was probably going in the right direction. This I believe was a bit of luck, combined with my own natural instinct for survival—a spontaneous reaction to the threat of danger or aversion to unnecessary discomfort.

Over the years, I have learned that instant and instinctive responses to difficult decisions are usually the most advantageous; even when I invest the time to painstakingly weigh and agonize over my options, I will usually return to my initial, spontaneous feelings. This is the way in which athletes compete, with body and mind acting in unison, analyzing a backhand or jump shot or decision to run rather than pass the ball, retrospectively, if ever. I have a friend who calls this the "go with the flow" philosophy of living. Allow the river of life to chart the course of your existence. Personally, I prefer thinking about it as the ultimate exercise in self-trust. If you follow the natural spontaneity of instincts, you will usually make the right decision for yourself—not necessarily for anyone else. In this case, the best decision for me was to be at the foot rather than the peak of the mountain. That day, everyone in my group seemed seduced by my aura of sudden self-confidence. I, in turn, could feel the snowballing momentum of their faith fueling my own uncanny self-trust. Buoyed by this feeling, I visualized our mutual destination. I lacked all awareness of how fast I was traveling, who was traveling beside and behind me. Deep in the recesses of my mind, I could actually see the gear we had stashed under a clump of bushes, the exact spot where our bags and supplies were waiting for us. The weight of the group, now silent under my spell, hanging on and being dragged by my aura as if I were a magnet and they were flakes of metal, was exhilarating. I don't know how much time passed, but at the point the sun was about to tuck itself down behind the largest mountain and night was about to fall, all of our gear, our sleeping bags, our tent and food were at my feet—like magic! This was one of a few rare triumphant experiences of a lifetime in which I, normally a very deliberate and careful person, allowed myself to be guided wholly by my own interior psychic machinery.

In some respects, creative nonfiction writers undergo ordeals as demanding, difficult, and subsequently rewarding as Outward Bound every day. Books and essays are mountains of mystery, causing inconceivable struggle and great bursts of physical and intellectual energy. Because the genre is so demanding, requiring story (a narrative framework), scene (dialog, description, characterization, etc.), action (drama, suspense), *and* information (factual content), a creative nonfiction writer is constantly bushwhacking through unfamiliar and frustratingly elusive terrain. Most of the time the struggle is worth the effort, and both writer and reader are rewarded, as in my instinctive odyssey down the mountain, leading my partners to food, water, and gear. But writing about nature also makes such breakthroughs more precious and memorable. Something special—primeval—seems to happen when human beings find themselves out-of-doors (and deep in the wilds), and for some writers, the feeling is nothing less than intoxicating, even if the experiences they are describing have been as difficult as Outward Bound—or worse.

Writing about nature also presents daunting challenges, beginning with a basic understanding of biology, ecology, wildlife, and related sciences such as astronomy and anthropology. Writing about nature requires a deep knowledge and respect for history and an ability to present the factual information in a broad and illuminating context, as essays in this anthology by John McPhee and Barry Lopez, among others, masterfully illustrate. Writing about nature usually also requires travel, sometimes to faraway places, as in Sherry Simpson's "Killing Wolves," which takes place in the Arctic tundra, or to nearby backyards, as in Lucy Wilson Sherman's "Learning from Goats," or Mark Doty's "House Finches."

Despite the protestations of Bill Bryson (excerpt from "A Walk in the Woods") and SueEllen Campbell ("Misery"), this travel and the physical involvement it necessitates—wherever the destination—provides an emotional and/or intellectual transition that allows the writer to reflect, not only about what they see, hear, or learn, but also about life itself—from the deepest roots of creation to the zigs and zags of their own existence. Because of this aspect of reflection, which is often so natural and necessary, it is easy to understand how some writers become overindulgent and one-dimensional when dwelling on the subject of nature. Or, as Joyce Carol Oates puts it in her aptly titled essay, "Against Nature," nature writing "inspires a painfully limited set of responses . . . REVERENCE, AWE, PIETY, MYSTICAL ONENESS." The essays in this anthology demonstrate the potential spectrum of the subject—from the fearful respect illustrated by Paul Lindholdt to the irascible annoyance shown by Oates.

But Lindholdt, Oates, and McPhee also demonstrate that the best writing about nature as represented in *On Nature* begins and ends with a story—quite classical in structure—with a character or set of characters, a plot or scenario, powered with action, suspense or intrigue, along with a sense of timing and creative judgment that evoke significant emotions, such as laughter, awe, or tears. The essays appearing in this anthology were selected around those standards—by which all good creative nonfiction writing should be judged.

edward hoagland

Hoagland considers the delicate balance of nature, and that the laws governing this balance may be more powerful than we give them credit for. Observing his animal neighbors in the New England woods, the author notes that even human interference can have its place in the eternal give-and-take.

nature's see-saw

I live at the top of Vermont, next to Canada, and moose leave their tracks in my garden occasionally, investigating the vegetables out of curiosity without eating them, in the same way that they may emerge from the trees onto the lawn to stare at my crowing rooster to see what he is. With no wolves around, they are increasing by 15 percent a year, though the pioneers had wiped them out, along with the wolves. But caribou, which originally share that old-growth forest, have not come back because the caribou's mossy, lichenous diet was destroyed along with those virginal woods.

Instead, deer (called "Virginia" deer at first) moved north, thriving on the cutover vegetation. So I have deer, too, around my place, which are periodically thinned back by a severe winter, when the snow gets taller than their legs. Moose, being bigger, don't mind the snow, but will die from a brainworm that deer carry (and seem immune to) if the deer get too thick. In other words, the two animals are in balance here. The moose can't move too far south because of the deer and the deer can't go much further north on account of the snow.

Opossums also migrated up, finding the new habitat to their liking—in old books they too boast the sobriquet "Virginia"—but they stopped short of my latitude simply because their naked tails froze in Vermont north of approximately the White River. Raccoons and skunks are similarly opportunistic creatures but have no such problem with frost, so I do see them. My rabbits are snowshoe rabbits, however. The cottontails' northward swarm stopped near the White River because of the depth of our snow and our mean winters.

8

Canada lynx, like the caribou, had disappeared when our primeval forests were felled for charcoal. But bobcats, which are more versatile, moved up from cottontail country to fill the lynxes' ecological slot, toughing out the cold weather by ambushing a deer in a snowdrift, perhaps, or strangling it, then camping for a month by the carcass. In the summer they eat rodents, birds, everything, and I hear them scream from the mountain ledges above my house. Or my dog may tree one, growling from a spruce limb above my head in the dark of night.

The balance between predators and prey—bobcats and rabbits, fisher and porcupine—is different from the relationship between parallel species, such as moose and deer, fisher (a large form of weasel) and fox, fox and coyote, or coyote and bobcat.

Red foxes thickened to fill the void in predators as nineteenth century sheep farming and twentieth century dairying replaced the charcoal industry, and hedgerows, underbrush, and woodlots grew back. Foxes eat what cats eat, plus impromptu berries, nightcrawlers, slugs, grasshoppers, woodchucks, and cows' afterbirths, while combing the meadows for voles. I've had them so bold that, chasing that rooster of mine, they've slammed right into my knees. Even southern gray foxes, a slinkier, nocturnal, tree-climbing species, have recently materialized in the north country.

And turkey vultures have begun to follow the interstate north every summer to compete for carrion with our wilderness ravens and farm-field crows, which are resident all year. Ravens nest on my cliffs, driving off the crows, though they are very much shyer toward people than crows. Nor do they mob hawks and owls as boisterously as crows do.

Red-tailed hawks and barred owls patrol the notch where my house is, but if I walk downhill for an hour or so to the swamps along Willoughby Lake, I will see red-shouldered hawks instead, or hear the five-hoot tattoo of a great horned owl at dusk.

Though the trout-fishing will probably never equal the prodigality of pioneer times, the crash in fur prices has brought beaver and even otter back, while bears—an estimated two thousand inhabit Vermont's nine thousand square miles—are making out fine, fattening in derelict orchards on defunct farms and upon old-field budding aspens in early spring. One bear tried to hibernate in my hayloft, after climbing an apple tree next to the garage and biting apart a birdhouse that a mother deermouse was nesting in, after the swallows had gone south. After I repaired the box, a flying squirrel settled in.

When mice colonize my house, I can't bring in a bear to stop their scuttling, but what I'll do is catch a three-foot garter snake and inset him through a hole in the ceiling to eat the babies. During the summer, this stratagem works. In winter an ermine moves in and does the trick.

Less tractable was the problem of the porcupines that for years kept chewing on the floor of my garage in their hunger for salt. Fishers had preyed on porcupines on the frontier, as martens had preyed on red squirrels, but the fishers and the martens had been trapped out. The marten's demise was a boon to goshawks, Cooper's hawks, horned owls, bobcats, and other enterprising hunters that can grab a quick squirrel. But the porcupines, equipped with quills, had no such effective secondary enemies, at least after country people stopped eating them (and squirrels), around the 1950s. In 1957, the state of Vermont, responding to complaints, started to release the nucleus of a new population of fishers, 124, acquired from Maine. One site happened to be close to my house, and quite soon I began finding porcupine skins inside upon the ground and picked clean, until their numbers were in reasonable balance again.

Fishers, like bears and beavers, in taking to civilization, have spread throughout New England, prompting the recent reintroduction of sixty marten, too, in central Vermont. Vermont alone has perhaps one hundred thousand deer, and wild turkeys, reintroduced to the state in 1969, are nearly all over—so that, altogether, the New England region is richer in wildlife than when Henry David Thoreau was writing *Walden* 150 years ago.

There are exceptions, of course. Loons (which require an undis-
turbed lake to nest on), wood turtles (which frequently try to cross
roads), warblers and other songbirds that winter in Latin American
rainforests, are stymied and gradually vanishing, even as more pro-
tean actors elbow in. The busy coyote, which has migrated east
through Ontario from the prairie Midwest in the past forty years,
eating housecats, road kills, wild grapes, leopard frogs, coon pups,
and whatnot, may be the most notable of these. Though the settlers killed off the wolves and "catamounts" (mountain lions), they
didn't shut off the future need for a middle-sized predator, and the
"brush wolf" or "trickster" of nineteenth century lore turns out to
fill the bill.

Flux itself is balance of a kind; and along my stream, which
feeds eventually into Lake Memphramagog and the St. Lawrence
River, the local pack of coyotes has thrown the foxes and the bobcats
into a tizzy. Coyotes will kill and eat grown foxes (as they did the
cocker spaniel next door), so the foxes simply withdraw from our
mountain notch in years when I hear the coyotes' flamboyant howls.
The coyotes also answer my harmonica, and may sneak into the
garage and drag a twenty-five-pound sack of dog food into the
woods. They search the stream back for fishermen's discards, flush
and leap high for a woodcock, then eat its eggs, or discover a fawn.
They can't kill a bobcat, but will sweep through in January and devour the bobcat's hoarded winter larder, creating a very grim situation for the bobcat. Being as versatile as African jackals, coyotes
prosper in the tracks of humans in the way that jackals follow lions—and we're doing better than lions.

In the years when coyotes den on the mountains above, my
fields aren't scoured for meadowmice as thoroughly as they would
be if the foxes were at work. Coyotes range further out, so there is a
surplus of rabbits and mice close in. Marsh hawks and red-tails then
take over some of the foxes' micromanagement role, as well as the
owls, fluttering like gigantic butterflies in the moonlight, as I sit outside watching them and the bats. Coons, too, help take up the slack,

afraid of the coyotes but at least able to scramble up a tree if they have to.

One banner noontime in Augusta a flock of real butterflies descended upon my goldenrod—hundreds of Monarchs fattening for their autumn flight toward Mexico. Half a dozen snakes, safe from any hawk because they were next to the house, and my special garden toad who has swelled so big that no snake can swallow him, were basking in the sun.

A few years before I had paid $110 to have a pond bulldozed; and already a great blue heron was frogging in it; bear, moose, and deer tracks marked the margins; and the sky's mysteries were reflected on the surface.

I could see all these things because I had just paid fifteen thousand to have my vision restored—a cheap price for new eyes that, with plastic implants, saw as I did fifty years ago.

Plastic eyes—and more wildlife running around in New England than when Thoreau was alive? Nature is complicated.

václav havel

Even before he was elected president of Czechoslovakia in 1989, Václav Havel was a vocal opponent of the
economic policies that had made his country among
the most polluted in the world. In this speech, originally
given at the University of California in 1991, Havel argues that the problem his country—and the world—
now faces is not economic or political, but the troubling
tendency of most humans to consider themselves the
"masters of Being."

the quiver of a shrub
in california

In my country forests are dying, rivers resemble open sewers, people are sometimes advised not to open their windows, and television advertises gas masks for children to wear on their way to and from school. Mine is a small country in the middle of Europe where the borders between Welds have been destroyed, the land is eroding, the soil is disintegrating and poisoned by chemical fertilizers that in turn contaminate the groundwater, where birds that used to live in the Welds have lost their nesting places and are dying out, while agronomists are forced to combat pests with more chemicals. My country supplies the whole of Europe with a strange export: sulfur dioxide.

For years I was one of those who criticized all this; now, I am one of those who are criticized for it.

When I think about what has brought about this terrible state of affairs and encounter on a daily basis obstacles that keep us from taking quick action to change it, I cannot help concluding that its root causes are less technical or economic in nature than philosophical. For what I see in Marxist ideology and the communist pattern of rule is an extreme and cautionary instance of the arrogance of modern man, who styles himself the master of nature and the world, the only one who understands them, the one everything must serve, the one for whom our planet exists. Intoxicated by the achievements of his mind, by modern science and technology, he forgets that his knowledge has limits and that beyond these limits lies a great mystery, something higher and infinitely more sophisticated than his own intellect.

I am increasingly inclined to believe that even the term "environment," which is inscribed on the banners of many commendable civic movements, is in its own way misguided, because it is unwittingly the product of the very anthropocentrism that has caused extensive devastation of our earth. The word "environment" tacitly implies that whatever is not human merely envelops us and is therefore inferior to us, something we need care for only if it is in our interest to do so. I do not believe this to be the case. The world is not divided into two types of being, one superior and the other merely surrounding it. Being, nature, the universe—they are all one infinitely complex and mysterious metaorganism of which we are but a part, though a unique one.

Everyone of us is a crossroads of thousands of relations, links, influences, and communications—physical, chemical, biological, and others of which we know nothing. While without humans there would have been no *Challenger* space shuttle, there would have been no humans without air, water, earth, without thousands of fortitudes that cannot be fortuitous and thanks to which there can be a planet on which there can be life. And while each of us is a very special and complex network of space, time, matter, and energy, we are nothing more than their network; we are unthinkable without them, and without the order of the universe, whose dimensions they are.

None of us knows how the quiver of a shrub in California affects the mental state of a coal miner in North Bohemia or how his mental state affects the quivering of the shrub. I believe that we have little chance of averting an environmental catastrophe unless we recognize that we are not the masters of Being, but only a part of Being, and it makes little difference that we are the only part of Being known so far that is not only conscious of its own being but is even conscious of the fact that it will one day come to an end.

Yet anyone who has said "A" must also say "B." Having recognized that we are no more than a tiny particle in the grand physical structure of things, we must eventually recognize that we are also no more than a speck in the grand metaphysical structure of things. We must recognize that we are related to more than the present moment, the present place, that we are related to the world as a whole and to eternity. We must recognize that, by failing to reflect universal, superindividual, and supertemporal interests, we do a disservice to our specific, local and immediate interests. Only people with a sense of responsibility for the world and to the world are truly responsible to and for themselves.

The communist rulers of Czechoslovakia acted according to the principle of *"après nous le déluge."* Hoping that no one would notice, they secured absolute power for themselves by bribing the entire population with money stolen from future generations. Miners extracting low-quality brown coal from open-face mines—coal that was then burnt without filters or scrubbers—were satisfied because they could easily buy VCRs and then, tired from work, they sat down to watch a video, not noticing that the children watching with them have pus flowing from their eyes.

Their wives noticed. Glad as they were that their husbands were earning relatively decent wages, they began to suspect what those wages represented; they began to realize that had the wages been lower and the difference invested in cleaner, more efficient means of generating power, their children would not have chronic conjunctivitis. *"Après nous le déluge"* is the principle of a man who is related to no order but that of his own benefit. It is a nihilistic principle of a man who has forgotten that he is only a part of the world, not its owner, of a man who feels no relation to eternity and styles himself a master of space and time.

I believe that the devastation of the environment brought about by the Communist regimes is a warning to all contemporary civilization. I believe that you should read the message coming to you from our part of the world as an appeal to protect the world against all those who despise the mystery of being, whether they be cynical businessmen with only the interests of their corporations at heart, or left-wing saviors high on cheap ideological utopias. Both lack what I would call a metaphysical anchor, that is, a humble respect for the whole of creation, and a consciousness of our obligation to it.

It is not my intention to lecture anyone, but I have felt it necessary to share with you the philosophical experience that I, like so many of my fellow citizens, have gained in the environment I come from. I would say that this experience is the principal article that we can and should export from my country at this time.

Were I to encapsulate that experience in one sentence, I would probably phrase it as follows: If parents believe in God, their children will not have to go to school wearing gas masks, and their eyes will be free of pus.

sherry simpson

Simpson is from Alaska, a place where it is common—
even necessary—to kill animals for their fur and meat,
but as she reminds us, "in the real world . . . nothing is
that simple." With a sharp eye for contradictions, Simpson examines the world of the wolf trapper and his
curiously intimate relationship to his prey, posing questions about death, survival, and cruelty that have no
easy answers.

killing wolves

At the Goldstream General Store just down the road from my house, three creamy wolf pelts dangle from the log beam above the dog food section. Their paws brush my cheeks as I walk the narrow aisle, the wood floor creaking beneath my feet. My fingers drift across the fur. A single paw covers my entire hand.

When it's cold, as it often is in Fairbanks, I wear a dark blue felt hat trimmed with toffee-colored muskrat, and a down parka thinly ruffed with coyote. The plain animal softness warms and comforts me in the harshness of winter. Sometimes I covet thicker, more beautiful furs—the flaming fox hats and luxurious wolverine ruffs that others wear. I bought a glossy black fox hat in Vladivostok once, but it's too fancy for everyday use. It hangs in my closet and tickles my arms when I reach for my more sensible hats.

Usually I try not to dwell on how these animals died, or who killed them. Even though I was raised in Alaska, I was also raised on Disney, in that fantasy world where creatures sing and talk, foxes and hounds play together, and only mean people kill animals. I cried the first time I saw Bambi's mother die. I was twenty-nine. In the real world, of course, nothing is that simple. I acknowledge my own contradictory notions. I don't hunt, but I enjoy a tender moose roast. I dislike state-sponsored wolf control, but I'm irritated by people from Outside telling Alaskans what to do. I want to wear fur, but I don't want to kill animals for it, least of all the appealing, doggish wolf. Deep in this ambivalence, I recognize a moral blind spot, a deliberate turning away from the way life and death proceed.

I know I will never kill a wolf. Still, I wonder what goes on out there in the wilderness, where wolves kill moose and caribou, and men kill wolves, where something happens that is more cruel and honest and frightening than most of us can bear.

Ben Hopson Jr. stands on the frozen lake thirty miles northeast of Fairbanks and sweeps his hand across the scene. "Pretend this is a wolf trail," he says, gesturing to a snowmachine track waffling the snow. A Nunamiut Eskimo from Anaktuvuk Pass, he wears snow-pants, a wool hat pulled over a baseball cap, and a white anorak ruffed with wolf. His eyeglasses darken as the wan morning light of February seeps through the trees and washes away the blue shadows. In the ten-below chill, our breath frosts.

We shuffle closer, our boots squeaking in the feathery snow, and strain to hear Hopson's soft voice as he points beyond the fringe of black spruce and birch trees. "There's a herd of caribou ten miles that way," he says. Now we're trying to picture the Brooks Range country he knows near his village, where constant wind lathes the snow into a hard crust and the wolves grow long, silky coats.

Just when I think I've fixed the picture—the line of wolves loping against the snow, moving as silently as smoke—Hopson drops a 750 Helfrich trap on the snow. To me, it is a clanking, rusty contraption, a metal puzzle that will somehow resolve into something that can seize a one-hundred-pound wolf by the leg and hold it fast. With his feet, Hopson carefully spreads the square steel jaws apart and sets them into an instrument of kinetic desire that cannot be satisfied until it springs free and claps shut.

We are learning how to catch imaginary wolves, here at Wolf Trapping School. Everyone else is catching them better than I am, because they are trappers, and I am not. Going to Wolf Trapping School is like attending graduate school in catching animals, the organizers tell me. A certain level of outdoor skill is presumed here; you cannot simply saunter into the woods and expect to hoodwink the fabled Alaska wolf, a clever and elusive animal with more claim to the territory than we have.

Our instructor, Ben Hopson, learned what he knows from his wife's brother and uncles, and from all his time on his Arctic trapline. As he shows us how to catch phantom wolves with a blind, or concealed, set, he moves and speaks deliberately, as if first considering every act and word. First, he anchors the trap's chain by freezing it into the snow with steaming hot water poured from a Thermos. Scooping a trap-size hollow into the trail, he lines the bottom with six-inch lengths of slender willow branch to prevent the trap from freezing to the bed.

With a few hundred caribou nearby, he says, wolves will circuit through his traps once a week, following the same trail, often stepping in their own tracks.

"Sure, it's like going to the store," someone says.

The men laugh. "7-Eleven for caribou," someone says.

Gripping a long knife in his bare hands, Hopson begins paring snow from a rectangular slab until he's shaped a square pane an inch or two thick. Gently, he lays the snow pane across the trap. "A lot of times I have to do this four or five times when the snow conditions are too soft. While I'm shaving these I've had them fall apart right on me," he says with a slow smile, acknowledging all the things that can go wrong. Hopson trims the lid until it drops evenly across the trap, flush with the trail surface. He scrapes his fingers across the snow until the edges blend, then with the knife tip grooves the surface to match the snowmachine track.

Now the trap lies unseen, waiting. Trappers describe the situation like this: Out of 365,000 square miles in Alaska, the wolf must step onto a 4-inch circle. I start to understand something about wolves and trappers, the intricacy of effort that leads to their encounters.

As the sun tops the trees and illuminates the snow, Hopson demonstrates other techniques. How to disguise a trap with moss common to his area. Where to set traps around a caribou kill—here he uses a partial carcass to demonstrate. What scent lures to use—"Bear fat. Puppies really like it. You'll have them all lined up in your traps there." (I blanch until I realize he means full-grown but inexperienced wolves, not little puppies.)

My mind lingers on the trap cloaked beneath the snow. When the session ends for lunch, Hopson presses his foot carefully against the surface and then slides it back quickly. The trap erupts from below with a metallic gulp, spraying bits of snow and moss into the air.

There have always been trappers in Alaska, beginning with the Natives who caught furbearers for clothing, meat, and a score of vital needs. In the old days, Inupiat Eskimos wrapped fat around sharpened and bent pieces of whalebone; when the bait thawed in the wolf's stomach, the bone sprang open and pierced the animal's gut. Once whites moved into the country, wolves were generally considered vermin that ate up all the game that men desired. Trappers were often solitary men like old Oscar Vogel, who guided and trapped in the Talkeetna Mountains for decades and wrote things like, "Time and suffering mean nothing to wolves," and "Intelligence and compassion go hand in hand, and wolves are without compassion," never recognizing his own lack of compassion for a fellow predator.

Beginning in the 1920s, the Territory of Alaska paid a bounty on wolves, first ten dollars, then fifteen, then twenty. Trapping wasn't the only way to kill a wolf. Some bounty hunters poisoned them. Others bludgeoned pups in dens. Somehow, despite episodic pogroms—aerial wolf shooting, state-sponsored predator control—the wolves survived. Today, biologists guess that between 6,000 and 7,000 wolves exist in Alaska, swallowed up somewhere between the mountainous southern coasts and the tundra plains of the North Slope.

Hardly ever does anyone see a living wolf in the wild. I have a friend who grew up in Ruby, a Native village on the Yukon River. He trapped marten and other animals to put himself through college, though, as he says, it's a helluva way to make a living, relying on what rich women in Paris and New York feel like wearing that year. One winter he called to tell me something about wolves. He'd been sleeping in his trapline cabin when a stirring outside awakened him. Peering through the single small window, he saw a pack of wolves slipping through the trees and circling the cabin before they disappeared again. From his mystified but pleased tone, he could have been telling me about a dream he'd had, a dream that might signify nothing, or everything.

The unknowable wolf hunts along the edge of our vision, never allowing a clear view of itself. Imagination, fear, and longing fulfill what experience cannot. And so a wolf is no longer just a wolf. It's a vicious, wasteful predator. Or it's the poster child of the charismatic mammals, the creature that stands for all that's noble, wild and free. A wolf is social, family-oriented, intelligent and communicative—like humans. A wolf kills because it can, for the sheer pleasure of it—like humans. It's either/or, the sacred or the profane. Inevitably, the wolf becomes a distorted reflection of the human psyche, a heavy burden for one species to carry. We can hardly bear the burden of being human ourselves.

In Alaska, people are always fighting about wolves, and I knew the trappers wouldn't be happy when I asked to attend their school and write a newspaper story about it. Pete Buist, the head of the Alaska Trappers Association, is deeply suspicious of reporters, mostly because he regards the Anchorage newspaper that hired me as a stronghold of liberal greenies who have never written one true word about trapping. But the trappers understand how bad they'll look if they refuse, and so they agree with false cheer. Nevertheless, when Buist addresses the gathered students before we begin, he warns them that I am present with a photographer. "I have no reason to distrust Sherry Simpson," he announces loudly in his blustering voice. "But don't feel you have to talk to her if you don't want to." I try to look trustworthy and sympathetic, even though I know and they know they probably won't like what I write.

Luckily, trapping interests all kinds of Alaskans, most of them individualists who don't care about party lines. They want to look good in the newspaper, but more than that, they want to be understood. Nearly three-quarters hail from southcentral Alaska. Among them are weekend trappers from Anchorage and Fairbanks, bush trappers from Coldfoot, Bettles, and Nabesna, a chiropractor and a commercial pilot, a father and son, middle-aged and young men. Trappers are mostly just guys, guys who hunt and fish and like doing what they want when they want.

My group includes Mike Johnson, a friendly fellow who traps alone along the southern edge of the Brooks Range. He figures if he learns one trick that catches him one wolf, the $125 fee will be worth it. Jim Farrell, a lean, bearded guy with a Western drawl, comes right out and announces he's a novice at wolf-trapping, though until he moved to Wasilla a couple of years ago, he trapped coyotes as part of Wyoming's predator-control program. Phil Rogers of North Pole is burly and talkative; he traps marten, wolverine, wolf, and other furbearers to earn money in the winter. A Delta River man, he hardly says anything, not even his name, but he pays close attention to the instructors and lets me drive his snowmachine. He wears a beaver hat the same coppery shade as his moustache; I never see his hair because he never takes off his hat. Two young Norwegian exchange students from the University of Alaska came because they're just interested in trapping, or so they say. They scribble notes and snap photographs and speak to each other in low voices, and some of the hardcore trappers regard this warily, as if the handsome youths might actually be animal rights infiltrators.

It's hard to imagine the mountain men of yore registering for seminars in killing and skinning. When I signed up, organizer Steve Potter told me that for many years, wolf trapping in Alaska waned as trappers concentrated on easier, more lucrative furbearers such as marten and lynx. The body of lore gathered by old-time wolfers began fading away, like many skills of Northern living. But in recent years, interest has grown as pelt prices began to improve and wolf populations increased. The Alaska Trappers Association founded the wolf trapping school to encourage new trappers and teach them the right way to go about it. In most parts of the country, people want to preserve wolves. In Alaska, some believe in preserving wolf trappers.

It's not an easy life. Fur prices and market demands can be fickle. The weather can work against you. Animal populations fluctuate. The European Union threatens to ban imports of fur caught in leghold traps. Trappers don't get rich. And people who regard wolves as symbols of the wild don't appreciate seeing their symbols shot, trapped, and strangled in snares. Against all this, the trapper struggles to hold on to something that seems almost as elusive as the wolves they pursue: the chance to make a life out of wilderness.

Smart wolves and smart trappers share certain traits. Both must be exceptionally cautious and alert to the world around them. To outsmart the other, each relies on natural attributes—the wolf its superior sense of smell, the trapper his opposable thumbs and large brain. Technology is not enough to catch wolves. Instinct is not enough to evade trappers. Among wolves and trappers alike, the most successful individuals learn from their mistakes. But, as instructor Jim Masek reminds us, wolves risk far more than people do.

"Humans—we take lots of lessons to learn things," he says, unloading his trapping gear from his snowmachine. "Wolves, it's life or death for them. If they don't learn it once, it'll be something that kills them."

Masek, 39, is not much interested in educating wolves. Long acknowledged as an expert trapper, he earned legendary status among his fellows in February 1994 by capturing a dozen wolves in one set of snares and traps on the Minto Flats near Fairbanks. This act prompted the editor of The Alaska Trapper to suggest establishing a new unit of measure: a "Masek" of wolves. I remember feeling dismay and anger when I studied the newspaper photograph of Masek kneeling within a semicircle of dead wolves laid out like trout. It seemed so excessive and unnecessary. The article included Masek's account of how he lured the pack toward a boobytrapped moose kill. The young, inexperienced wolves stepped into traps first; the others panicked, bolting away from the scene and into other snares. Masek figured eventually he'd catch the few who escaped, since they were deprived of their leaders.

Now that I see his boyishly rosy cheeks, blue eyes, and straw-blond hair, Masek seems less like a bloodthirsty killer and more like what he is, a country boy who hails from Nebraska and South Dakota. His face, other trappers joke, is probably enshrined in wolf dens throughout Minto Flats. Masek is consumed by the hard work, the contest of wits, the outdoor life. This is a man who buys snare cable in ten-thousand-foot rolls, who owns a hundred wolf traps, who learned the feeding call of ravens so he can locate wolf kills. He lives alone out on Minto Flats, northwest of Fairbanks, in a log cabin he built on the Chatanika River. In winter, he rides his snow-machine thirty miles to the nearest road, and then drives another twenty miles to reach Fairbanks. In summer, he works for a big construction company, but you can see that the trapline embraces his true existence.

On this snowbright afternoon along the icebound Chena River, we double up on snowmachines and skim along the river for a mile or so before stopping here. Sundogs hover in the hazy sky above us. Spruce and birch trees crowd the riverbanks, some of them tipping gradually into the river. Once we leave the road, we enter a largely unpeopled wilderness that stretches east for thousands of miles to the other side of the continent. The keen air reddens our cheeks and noses, and we try not to step off the hard-packed snowmachine trail into deep snow, where we'll flounder and sink.

A successful trapper not only understands wolf behavior but uses the wolf's own nature against it. Anything unnatural troubles a wolf, and trappers take advantage of this to manipulate or distract the animals. A trapper, for example, might hang a ribbon of surveyor's flagging to scare a wolf off the trail and into a trap or snare. A wolf's tendency to step over a twig planted in the trail can direct its foot into a trap.

Masek chose this place because wolves tend to relax a bit when they can see clearly around them. As he unloads his gear from his snowmachine sled, he compresses some of what he's learned in two decades of trapping into a few hours. Lesson No. 1: the slightest sign of anything unnatural can spook a wolf, especially the reek of humans. Wolves have, as one biologist describes it, "a big honking nose and they really know how to use it."

So don't spit, don't smoke, and don't pee on the trail, Masek says. Keep clothing, gear, and equipment scrupulously free of disturbing scents. Use only clean, dry, cotton work gloves. Prepare snares and traps by washing them in solvent or boiling them in water fragrant with local plants. Dye them black with logwood crystals to eliminate a distracting shine. Hang them outdoors away from human smells. Try not to contaminate them with sweat, fuel, and other scents while handling them. Make yourself null, a sensory void in the olfactory landscape.

Setting a trap in exactly the same spot where a wolf will step is a more challenging problem. Fortunately for trappers, wolves and other animals prefer trotting dead center along the trail of snowmachine tread. Human tracks, however, worry them, and snowshoe prints simply scare them off. (The trappers speculate about this more than once: Some lingering smell? An inbred association between snowshoes and traplines?) In the field, Masek works off the back of his snowmachine sled, standing on a rectangle of plywood to avoid disturbing the trail.

Masek holds up a trap, a No. 9 Manning that costs about a hundred dollars. The offset jaws spread into a nine-inch circle. When the jaws clamp shut, a three-eighths-inch gap remains between the steel arcs. The mechanism acts like a handcuff by grasping a knob above the foot rather than pinching the toes or cutting into the paw, causing less damage and pain to the wolf.

In his shop, Masek modifies his traps in various ways. He laminates an extra layer of steel along the jaws to strengthen and spread the holding surface, which is easier on the animal's leg. He also bolsters various parts so that wolves can't destroy them. "I've got traps that are almost mangled, with the pan crushed down, the trigger dog bent, toothmarks in the steel," he says. "Wolves have tremendous force in their jaws so they can crush moose bones."

Trappers are always fooling with gear, trying to build a better mousetrap, so to speak. Masek's been inventing. He holds up what he jokingly calls a "bed pan," a round section of galvanized stove pipe that has been modified into a pan that can hold a No. 9 trap. The pan works like a cookie cutter in the snow, outlining the trap bed. The trap fits inside the pan, and Masek inserts the device into a small white garbage bag to prevent snow from clogging the jaws. He settles the pan into the trail bed and lightly brushes snow over the plastic cover with a small hand broom. "Usually you want to be able to see a gray shadow," he says, straightening to study the way the trap barely darkens the snow.

The pan allows a snowmachine to drive across the trap without triggering it or pushing snow into the jaws. The trap lies concealed beneath the snowmachine track, with no visible sign to any wolf that lopes down the path. "Out on an open trail, they're bobbing around, enjoying the view, looking for a moose, and they'll step right into it and, poof, get nailed," Masek says.

Sometimes, something goes wrong. The wolf plants a foot on the trap, takes a few steps, and then the trap fires. "You've just educated one wolf," Masek says flatly.

A trap can be used as a kind of trigger for snaring a pack. The first wolf along the trail steps into a leghold trap, causing the others to explode off the trail and bolt through the trees, where a score or more of wire snares fill most of the gaps and openings. Masek shows us how to hang the handmade snares by wrapping the stiff end of the holding wire around a sturdy, small tree. Each snare falls open about knee-high above the snow, opening into a seventy-two-inch loop. From a few feet away, we can't even see the snares dangling among the branches. The idea is that as the wolf's head enters the snare, its forward motion slips the loop closed. A small locking device prevents the snare from reopening. When it works right, the wolf's struggle pulls the loop tighter, and the animal dies quickly from suffocation as its trachea collapses.

Everything doesn't always work right, though. Sometimes a snowfall will raise the snowpack so that the snares no longer hang eighteen inches above the ground. Instead of naturally thrusting their heads through the loops, the wolves charge through them or step into them and become entangled. Sometimes wolves snared by the leg chew off their own limbs.

Masek knows many other ruses. He points out a piece of driftwood that would make a natural scent post, a place where wolves might stop and mark their territory. At such a spot he would set a trap beneath a pawprint and then recreate the track. He's studied the way male dogs lift their legs—where they stand, how high they spray. He takes out a duct-tape-wrapped bottle of dog urine and splashes it like canine graffiti into the snow, where it will attract the attention of passing wolves. Friends gather chunks of frozen urine from their dog yard; Masek warms it in the field by storing the bottle next to his snowmachine manifold.

He also saves wolf urine from the trail, sometimes distracting and exciting one pack by marking their urine posts with scent from a different pack. Sometimes, if he catches an alpha female, he uses her urine to confuse her puppies; they sniff around, thinking she's nearby, and often blunder into traps.

This wrenching picture makes me imagine that when one wolf is caught, the others stick around, trying to figure out what's happening. Sometimes they do, Masek says, and sometimes they don't. "If an adult gets caught they may mill around. Half the time if it's a puppy, they might not even look back. If you get the adult, you may have caught the killer, the breeder, the smart one. Clip him and the rest have to work harder to live," he says.

Someone asks what happens when the trapper returns to his line and finds a wolf waiting in a trap. "Some adults might howl and snap and lunge at you," Masek says, his face revealing nothing. "A puppy tends to cower. It won't make eye contact with you."

I make myself think about this scene. I wonder what it's like to shoot a wolf that is looking at you with its amber eyes, rage or fear in its heart. But I don't ask. It seems too personal, something between trappers and wolves. Part of me recoils from knowing, too, as if the explicit knowledge of death will make it my fault as well.

Because I don't know wolves, I first think the black animal lying on the floor of the meeting hall that night is a sleeping dog. A large sleeping dog. I realize my mistake when I see its leaden stillness.

Fairbanks trappers Greg and Mike Chapin discovered the wolf this morning in one of their blind-set traps on the Chena River. A pair of wolves had followed the trail on and off for about four miles. They stepped over two traps before this wolf planted its foot into the third one, a No. 9 Manning leghold. For perhaps thirty-six hours, it waited in the trap before the brothers arrived. Greg Chapin killed it by shooting once with his .22 caliber rifle crosswise through its chest. "It stood about three seconds and fell over," he says.

The wolf is a young female, a yearling or a two-year-old. About the size of a German shepherd, she weighs 65 or 70 pounds. Ripples of silver highlight her black fur. She's still slightly warm. Greg, 31, holds up a broad front paw, the one caught in the leghold, and says, largely for my benefit, "Not a broken tendon. The skin's not broken, nothing."

The woodstove warms the room, and the trappers chat and joke while Greg begins skinning the wolf as it lies on a table. He's a beefy man with receding red hair that makes him look like a tonsured monk. He handles the wolf straightforwardly, not as if it were something revered or reviled but simply a dead animal. Every winter he and his brother run their eleven-mile trapline along the upper reaches of the Chena River; they've taken as few as four wolves and as many as fourteen in a season.

"I always start with the mouth," he says, picking up a small, wickedly sharp knife and making short slicing strokes around the wolf's black lips. He peels back the snout; as soon as the nose flops loose, the animal loses some part of its wolf identity. I see the trappers looking at me sideways; they're wondering if I might start crying, or run outside, or throw up. But I can be as detached as they are, and so I simply sit taking notes, and soon they forget I'm there.

Chapin slits the hide from the paws up along the wrist, then breaks the joint at all four paws. A few men step forward to help him hoist the animal by its rear leg from a gambrel so that it hangs head down, blood pooling on the floor beneath it. After awhile, Chapin stuffs a wad of newspaper in its mouth to slow the blood.

Slowly he works off the hide, exposing the blue-red flesh and sinew, the stretch and compression of muscle and tendon. A wolf's thick fur sheaths the sleek architecture of something meant to run, to kill, to survive.

The talk turns to the uncanny nature of wolf senses. Chapin recalls a wolf he caught three months ago that was moving about a hundred yards in front of the pack. From the tracks, he saw that after the lead wolf was trapped, the others stopped, left the trail, and headed into the brush. A couple of weeks later, three wolves that he believes belonged to a different pack traveled down the same trail. When they arrived at the spot where the first group departed, they also suddenly stopped and abandoned the trail, as if they knew something dangerous and disturbing awaited them. "So in their standing and dancing around, they communicated something," Chapin says of the original pack.

The trappers spend a lot of time this weekend exchanging similar wolf lore, mulling over what it all means. Ben Hopson leaves skinned wolf carcasses near his traps to attract other wolves. Mike Johnson says such carcasses spook wolves in his part of the Brooks

Range. Some believe that wolves notice stepping sticks placed in trails as clearly as if they were little signs that announce "Trap Ahead." Others are convinced they work. Different wolf packs learn different things; the experiences of their leaders shape the group intelligence. This is how the trappers learn, too, by sharing knowledge difficult to come by.

"Another thing I know is that it's a lot easier to catch wolves in a bar than it is out on a river," Chapin says, and others laugh knowingly.

Somebody asks Chapin about the fur's value. He studies the black hide, silver gleaming in it like light upon water, and says, "I wouldn't sell it for less than two hundred and probably two and a half." When Fairbanks fur buyer Dean Wilson eyeballs it the next day, he pegs it at three hundred dollars; it would be worth more if the neck pile was deeper.

Chapin takes care with skinning because the demand for taxidermy mounts creates much of the wolf market. For some, the fur is not enough to evoke the wolf; it must be draped over a form and posed realistically with cold marbles for eyes. People also covet wolves as wall hangings and especially as trim for parkas, mitts and other winter garments. Nearly three-quarters of wolf sales remain within Alaska, where it is not considered shameful but practical to wear animal fur.

Several factors determine the value of a wolf pelt, most importantly size and color. Taxidermists love an Alaska wolf that's seven feet long or more, Wilson says; it just sounds good. This particular wolf stretches to about seven feet, four inches. Color matters, too. Of all the wolf shades—gray, blue, red, white, black—white is the rarest. Also important are the fur's depth and texture, particularly to parka makers. They want a ruff thick enough to swallow a prodding finger up to the second knuckle.

Chapin shares a cleaning tip with his fellow trappers. "When you got grays with a brown cast, wash 'em. Take 'em to a laundromat. It's amazing how much of that is dirt."

"What happens if you do that and they catch you?" someone calls out.

"They ask you not to come back," Chapin answers, his grin hinting at personal experience in this breach of etiquette.

Conversations eddy as the hide slacks off the wolf. A raw, meaty smell and the hot stove make the room close and stuffy. The trappers stand around talking guy talk with their hands shoved deep in their pockets, their hats tipped back on their heads. They jaw about the merits of various snowmachines, the trapper's iron dog. They compare the amount of fur in their parts of the country.

"Here's a trivia question," Chapin announces. "How many toenails are there on an entire wolf?"

People shout out guesses. Eleven. Fourteen. Twenty. Never counted 'em.

The answer is eighteen. "Sixteen and two dewclaw nails," says Masek, who leans against the wall with arms crossed. Masek knows everything there is to know about wolves, it seems.

"How do you turn a fox into a wolf?" a trapper yells. "Marry her!" Gusts of laughter.

"Instead of a No. 9, it was a wedding ring, eh?" someone says. Guy talk.

"How many trappers does it take to make popcorn?" No answer. "Three—one to hold the pan and two to shake the stove!"

Chapin finishes unpeeling the wolf, stripping it to a lean, whippet-like shape. The hide remains intact through the belly and chest. He pushes the wolf's ears inside out with the blunt end of a broomstick, so they will dry into their alert shape. Then he pulls the hide through itself, until the meaty side faces outward. Now comes the most tedious task of all, fleshing the hide. Chapin drapes the fur over a fleshing beam, a hinged log attached to a stand. The butt of the beam rests against Chapin's leg as he scrapes away gobbets of meat with long knife strokes, trying to avoid nicking the pelt.

"You got to be really careful on the belly," he warns. "The skin is really tender on the belly."

The wolf's paws rest on the table behind him, the long, elegant bones ruddy with blood. Each foot is worth $1.50; the penis bone brings another buck and a half. Indians use them to make breast-plates that sell for ten thousand dollars. An intact wolf skull brings twenty-five dollars, more for a large one. Scent glands from the feet, ears, tail and anus, and such organs as the bladder, brains and gall-bladder are saved to age in a jar and use later as lure. Lure, I hear someone explain to the Norwegian students, is like "perfume on a woman"; the scent intrigues and draws wolves to trap sets.

The young, black she-wolf has been transformed into an assem-blage of products and possibilities: ornaments and fur, essences and emblems. She has literally been dismantled, and even examining her piece by bloody piece, I feel no closer to understanding the enigma of wolves. Something tightens in me when I think of her terrible beauty, the lovely sharpness of her teeth, the predatory brilliance of her gaze. But that is only what I see. The trappers see a pelt, a pay-check, a trickster outwitted by a human. We're the ones who write the stories, and so what else can a wolf be except a symbol for every-thing good and bad about us, everything we want, everything we've lost?

Nearly three hours after beginning, Chapin makes his last flesh-ing strokes. He slips the hide, still inside out, over a stretching plank shaped like a surfboard. The hide needs to dry for a day or so before it's ready to be tanned commercially. "Come in with three or four of these, you'll be up all night," Chapin says, wiping his forehead with the back of his gory hand. To earn his three hundred dollars, he's spent perhaps thirty hours checking the trap, killing the wolf, and skinning the hide. It's not just the money he's after, he says. But when he tries to explain, all he can do is telegraph clichés: "The challenge. Being outdoors. The wilderness."

That night, most of us sleep in the same room, spreading our sleeping bags across couches and mattresses thrown on the floor. Here's another thing about trappers: They snore. The room seems to swell and toss on the waves of their long, shuddering breaths, the snores of the innocent, of men at peace with themselves. Someone talks to himself in the urgent dialect of sleep.

In the corner, the wolf hide dries, shaped more rigidly than the wolf itself ever was. Sleep comes to me slowly in the hot, noisy room. I see the wolf running in a black ripple through the snow. I see the lustrous pelt hanging on my wall, where I can touch the shining fur every day. I could climb into it, peer through the eyeholes, wear the wolf's face like a mask. Embraced in a wolf skin, I could run for miles through the forest, searching for the smell of living blood. But I would wear death, too. I would look out into the world through the eyes of death.

In winter the flat, frozen surface of the upper Chena River becomes a boulevard for wildlife, where tracks inscribe the snow in a calligraphy of motion. Everything is going somewhere. I ride behind trapper Phil Rogers on his Tabasco-red snowmachine, clinging to his stout midriff. The long, ivory hairs of his wolf ruff tickle my nose as I press my face against his back. Rogers shouts out track identifications as we skim across the snow: Moose. Marten. Fox. Wolf.

The wolf tracks emerge from the forest and dip onto the river, gradually curving across the channel. The trail arrows toward a downed spruce tree jutting across the river. Yellow snow around the tree indicates the wolves' interest; they've made it into a scent post. Several hundred yards later, the tracks separate around an overflow spot on the river, revealing three animals, probably young ones by the print size. Fur between their foot pads dragged as they walked, grooving the snow between tracks. The tracks seem so clear that I exclaim about their freshness, but Rogers points out the hoarfrost blurring the outlines.

"The wolf makes his living with his feet," is how state biologist Mark McNay had described it the night before. Packs travel continuously as they search for game, often using the same routes year after year as they cover distances that average 600–700 square miles. "To do that they really got to pick 'em up and put 'em down," Mc-Nay told us. Jim Masek once trapped a mangy wolf on the Minto Flats that had been radio-collared on the Kenai Peninsula, a good five hundred miles by air to the south.

We follow the wolf tracks as if they were a story, and not far up the river, we come upon the climax. All that remains of the moose calf are scattered bits of fur and bone, and a jagged ridge of ribs. Ravens, foxes, and other animals trampled the snow, sharing the bounty. The experienced trappers speculate about where the cow's carcass lies—perhaps off the river, in the forest.

"You hear a lot about wolves killing the old, sick, weak, and young, and there's some truth to that," McNay explained. "A better and more accurate view is that wolves prey on vulnerable animals, old, young, middle-aged . . . Any animals can be vulnerable if the wolves catch them in the right situation. Generally wolves don't." Winter is all about vulnerability; in the deep Interior snows, moose find it difficult to move about on their willowy legs.

After hearing McNay's talk, I find it easier to imagine what happened here on the river. Killing is usually an exhausting, bloody business for the wolf and the moose. Generally, only the most experienced animals in the pack attack first, searching for a hold on the rump or nose, wearing away the moose's strength until they can force it down and feast on all the rich, nourishing blood and meat. Usually the prey of wolves do not perish from anything as merciful as a crushed trachea; most die from shock and blood loss. More than one trapper remarks on the gruesome and often lengthy death of moose and caribou, but McNay pointed out the enormous size difference between a 100-pound wolf and a one thousand-pound moose. "I don't want to give the impression that wolves are somehow ruthless, abnormally aggressive killers," he said. "That's the only way they can kill. If you had to kill a moose with your mouth, you'd do it, too."

The wolf does not automatically prevail, either. Moose can

charge, fling off a wolf that's hanging by its jaws, kick viciously. Wolf autopsies commonly show fractured ribs, cracked skulls, even broken and rehealed legs. A moose can even throw jabs like a boxer, McNay noted, adding that he once saw a moose coldcock another moose. "But that's another story," he said.

Trappers don't always find kills so well-devoured as this calf. "This is responsible in part for the idea that wolves are killing and 'wasting' meat," McNay told us. "In many cases they kill, eat, and then travel and come back." But the trappers do not seem entirely convinced that wolves subscribe to a philosophy of "waste not, want not." During the weekend, I hear these characterizations, which I suspect are really justifications:

"When you see these wolves cruising down a river running, you realize they're nothing but a stomach and a set of jaws."

"I've seen moose with their guts pulled out, and nothing eaten."

"Wolves are the biggest killers of wolves. It's not uncommon that they eat each other in traps. You can come back and find only the head."

"Last winter there was a tendency to kill for the fun of it. That's what they are—a killing machine."

Now that this moose is dead, it represents a natural bait site for wolves, which tend to return again and again to kills, even if only to chew nostalgically on a few bones. The trappers discuss where they would place their snares, the proper arrangement of traps. A raven flies overhead, and a veteran trapper from Tok turns his head to follow the black motion, his eyes as quick as a marten's. "If we could follow that raven, we'd find that cow," he says mostly to himself. There are things about this killing place that I don't see, signs I can't decipher.

We return the way we came as the milky winter sky dims and the forest darkens around us. I try to identify the tracks we cross by their gait and size. The wolf trail, I see, makes the steadiest, deepest path through the snow. Wolves don't wander like dogs. They know where they're going. Sometime soon, they'll be back; they are always circling their world with their feet.

All weekend, I puzzle over Mike Johnson, the Brooks Range trapper, who wears a T-shirt portraying an Alaska wolf, the kind of romanticized shirt a tourist might buy. At first I wonder if the shirt is some kind of joke, like the T-shirts sold by the Alaska Trappers Association that say, "PETA: People for the Eating of Tasty Animals." This is a poke at the animal rights group People for the Ethical Treatment of Animals. I wonder if Johnson is indulging in irony, wearing that shirt blazing with the silvery face of a wolf.

He answers my questions openly, with none of the shyness you might expect from a man who's just emerged from a winter in his cabin on the Arctic Circle, along the flanks of the Brooks Range. He resembles a jovial Mennonite with his moustache-less beard and his wide, toothy smile. Unlike many trappers, Johnson works alone, living on his trapline five months out of the year. To do that, a person must not mind his own company, nor the constant presence of winter. "I tell myself jokes out loud," Johnson confides.

Johnson, 54, came to Alaska in 1971 coveting the same things most Alaskans desire—wilder country, a different kind of life. Eight years ago, after his marriage dissolved, he bought his trapline and moved north to live the way he had always wanted. In the summers, he runs halibut charter boats out of Homer.

"I don't know anybody who works harder than trappers for the money," Johnson says. "Trappers are people who cannot stand idleness," he tells me, and I can see this in him. This afternoon he explained to his colleagues how he survives on the trapline alone. He showed off the come-along winch he added to his snowmachine to hitch it out of bad spots, the complicated engine modifications, the hip boots he fashioned out of giant inner tubes so he won't freeze his feet in overflow. He painted his ax and the butt of his rifle fluorescent orange so he can find them against the snow. To lose them would be disastrous.

This winter, Mike Johnson is going broke. He can't find enough marten, the trapper's bread and butter fur. He sold one snowmachine to make payments on the other. Johnson relates all this in the same cheerful tone he uses when he talks about why he loves trapping: "It's the attraction of the wild. It's the lifestyle. The challenge of doing what I'm doing." The same words we all use, but he's the one curled in the dark bosom of the Brooks Range in January. When he visits his family in Indiana, they talk mostly about the price of corn, which is a foreign tongue he used to know, and he looks out the window and thinks about coming home.

Thinking about the T-shirt, I ask him what he thinks about wolves.

"All the things you hear are probably true, good and bad," he says, and then he considers. "I love wolves. It would be a sad day if there were not wolves in this country." He lowers his voice a little, as if he's telling a secret. "I'd rather have too many than not enough, to tell you the truth. I want there always to be wolves. Always, always."

If trappers do not regard the wolf as a symbol of wilderness, perhaps it's because people who spend so much time working in the wilderness don't need symbols. Steve Potter is a large, good-natured man who can hardly find the words to describe the way he feels sometimes out there in the woods, under the innocent sky. He struggles to tell me the feeling that took him once as he watched a flock of snowy ptarmigan sweep across the black-green expanse of forest. After tangling himself in awkward words and long pauses, he finally gives up. You had to be there, is all he can say. But I know what he means. Being there means seeing all of it—what's beautiful and impossible to express, what's painful and hard to watch.

Trappers believe that if anyone understands nature, it's them, not the city folks who hang photographs of wolves on their cramped city walls and listen to recordings of wolf howls to drown out the sound of traffic and other kinds of emptiness. Greg Chapin rejects as well-meaning but misguided the notion that animals can and should die painlessly. "It would be neat if you could get the fur and let wolves go—like sheep," he says. "But we can't." If the wolf is just another animal out there trying to hustle up a living, well, then, so is the trapper. "I would never kill the last wolf. I don't hate wolves," he says. "But [trapping] is no more cruel, no less cruel than anything that happens in nature. It's no less natural than the wolf killing the moose. The wolf kills the moose to eat it, and I kill the wolf."

I envy his certainty; everything has its place in the world, including him. Anyone who hunts or traps must come to some similar reconciliation. Alaska's native cultures encompass a complicated relationship with the animals they kill, because their own survival—spiritual and physical—depends on a respectful attitude toward their fellow creatures. Most trappers employ less formal and articulate relationships, but what seems like callousness is often, I believe, something closer to affection. In the *Alaska Trapper Magazine,* a young man writes of a lonely winter working his trapline on the Black River, two hundred miles northwest of Fairbanks and as far from anywhere as you'll find. For months a lone gray wolf shadowed his cabin. "It was just he and I here on the Black, and I felt an affinity growing between us," the trapper wrote. In January, the trapper discovered his "befriended wolf" in a No. 9: "Soon he was sharing a ride in my sled with a marten. Now I was alone on the Black." As I read this account I wonder which seems worse, to kill an animal you feel a kinship with, or to kill an animal you feel nothing for?

I worry over this problem during the weekend, returning to it again and again, the way wolves return to a killing place. First I think of animals I ate during the weekend that I didn't kill: Moose. Black bear. Cow. Pig. Northern pike. I didn't even say grace beforehand. Even as a vegetarian, I could shed the conceit of guilt only if I didn't know that my mere presence in Alaska requires space, habitat, and resources that animals depend on. And if I didn't wear fur, I would wear manufactured gear: petroleum-based, nonrecyclable, nonrenewable garments. A trapper tells me, "Fur is organic. It doesn't ruin one thing in the woods to use it." Except the animal itself, of course.

Eventually I ask Steve Potter, in a circuitous and abstract way, about killing wolves. He explains without hedging, as if this is something he's thought about a lot. After all, he's been trapping since he was a kid, and now he's teaching his own eleven-year-old son to catch marten and beaver. "The way I feel is, there's no difference between a wolf and a mouse," he says. "They're each a life, and you can't take any life lightly. When you come on an animal alive, you want to dispatch it as quickly as you can."

It sounds right that a person shouldn't distinguish between the value of a mouse and the value of a wolf. Still, I can't shake the sense that killing a wolf is different somehow. Does the wolf recognize impending death, having delivered it so often?

Delicately, I ask again, this time a coworker who traps recreationally. Once, Norm says, looking away, he found a wolf alive in a trap. But he didn't have a gun to kill it. So he attached a Conibear trap used for killing wolverines to a stick and poked the contraption at the wolf. The wolf snapped at the trap and the trap snapped back, catching the wolf's jaw and immobilizing it. Then Norm smashed the wolf's skull with a stick, shattering the ridge above its eye and killing it instantly. "It was a messy death," he says, regret shading his voice. "It was beneath its dignity."

Norm's story makes me feel a little weak inside, because he's saying wolves do require a separate honor. It's true that I can also think of worse fates for an animal. Zoos, for example, and the way all wild animals go blank in cages, as if some part of them is not there. Neglected dogs chained in suburban yards. Cats abandoned to pounds. A thousand kinds of death await animals, none easy. It's the deliberateness of killing an animal, whether for food or fur, that seems like a barbaric throwback, something humans used to do until we evolved into the kind of creature that doesn't need to kill to survive. Yet, anyone who eats a Big Mac or an Easter lamb or a slab of salmon prepared by a fancy chef has simply delegated the killing to others. We want to believe a wolf has more intrinsic value than a chicken raised in an industrial coop. A wolf means more to us because we've made it something more; we believe it lives the life we want to live. But most wolves perish no more nobly than chickens. Biologist David Mech has said that a wolf usually dies in one of two ways: It starves to death, or another wolf eats it.

Still, some would argue, people have no place within these events; what happens in nature is none of our business. I used to feel this way myself, that the mere presence of a human in the wilderness was enough to taint it forever. That a wolf would kill a wolf seemed acceptable because it was "natural"; that a man would kill a wolf, unforgivable. I've used the same tone other nature lovers do as they talk about the "natural circle of life" in hushed and reverent tones, as if it were a church we could never attend but only stand outside, listening to the godly and mysterious harmonies issuing from within. The circles of life and death wheel about each other in great concentric spirals. Humans, like wolves, have never been anything else but killers.

When trapping school is over, and the trappers have all returned to town or to their traplines, I cross the frozen lake just past nightfall and wait by the narrow road for my ride home. The temperature floats into the 30s, and the air seems impossibly warm, comforting. Behind thin clouds, the moon blurs.

I think about wolves. In these two days of talking about trapping, the only thing missing was the wolf itself. I have seen the deliberate pace of its tracks, the scattered remains of its meals, the stripped cipher of its carcass. Harder to picture is the elusive, living creature, the shape of its eyes, the heat of its breath, the way its tail plumes behind as it runs.

I've seen a wolf only once, during a fall drive through Denali

National Park. The wolf was the color of a clouded sky. A radio collar ringed its neck, a constant insult to its supple motion. The wolf padded steadily down the middle of the road, as if it had a long way to walk. People yanked their cars to the roadside to let the animal pass and then hung their heads from windows, following with their eyes. A man standing outside his car closed the door against himself, like a shield.

We all looked hungrily at the wolf, because not often will a wolf pass a few feet away from you without intervening bars or fences. My first thought—what a big dog—evaporated the moment I glimpsed its eyes—not the color, which I don't remember, but the inner, private light. The wolf glanced neither right nor left, but only ahead, as if none of us was there. Down the road it walked for miles, and we all looked and looked.

Not far from where I wait this night, wolf tracks course down the frozen Chena River. Somewhere out there, wolves lope through the dark, or sleep, or kill. Somewhere out there, a wolf waits in a trap, anchored to approaching death. The wolf is a predator. The wolf is prey.

All those who care about nature fashion a private covenant with it. Some people love wilderness best from a distance; it's the easiest way, this unconditional love. Totems of wildness substitute for wildness itself. Put a poster of a wolf on the wall and admire it like a movie star, like someone you wish you were. Whatever happens in the wild happens without you, because you are not part of it.

Some people draw near to wilderness, into a harder but truer place. They kill animals to eat them or wear them or sell them, never looking away from what they are about to do. By acknowledging the death that arrives through their own hands, surely they secretly wonder if they can't somehow master the way death will come to them.

And some people, like me, want to look. We want so much to belong to nature, to be kin to every part of its difficult beauty, but in the end, we turn away. All we can do is follow the tracks, knowing that some day, the wolf will circle around to us.

joyce carol oates

This eloquent and exacting essay reminds us to beware of the easy platitudes that leap to our lips when experiencing nature—how misleading and shallow they can be, how ineffective in conveying what nature can be. Written in "resistance" to nature, this piece frames Oates's "chronic uneasiness with Nature-mysticism"— but also her grudging recognition of its embodiment of what lies beyond human imagination.

against nature

We soon get through with Nature. She excites an expectation which she cannot satisfy.

THOREAU, *Journal* (1854)

Sir, if a man has experienced the inexpressible, he is under no obligation to attempt to express it.

SAMUEL JOHNSON

The writer's resistance to Nature.

It has no sense of humor: In its beauty, as in its ugliness, or its neutrality, there is no laughter.

It lacks a moral purpose.

It lacks a satiric dimension, registers no irony.

Its pleasures lack resonance, being accidental; its horrors, even when premeditated, are equally perfunctory, "red in tooth and claw" et cetera.

It lacks a symbolic subtext—excepting that provided by man.

It has no (verbal) language.

It has no interest in ours.

It inspires a painfully limited set of responses in "nature-writers"—REVERENCE, AWE, PIETY, MYSTICAL ONENESS.

It eludes us even as it prepares to swallow us up, books and all.

. . .

I was lying on my back in the dirt-gravel of the towpath beside the Delaware-Raritan Canal, Titusville, New Jersey, staring up at the sky and trying, with no success, to overcome a sudden attack of tachycardia that had come upon me out of nowhere—such attacks are always "out of nowhere," that's their charm—and all around me Nature thrummed with life, the air smelling of moisture and sunlight, the canal reflecting the sky, red-winged blackbirds testing their spring calls—the usual. I'd become the jar in Tennessee,[1] a fictitious center, or parenthesis, aware beyond my erratic heartbeat of the numberless heartbeats of the earth, its pulsing pumping life, sheer life, incalculable. Struck down in the midst of motion—I'd been jogging a minute before—I was "out of time" like a fallen stunned boxer, privileged (in an abstract manner of speaking) to be an involuntary witness to the random, wayward, nameless motion on all sides of me.

Paroxysmal tachycardia is rarely fatal, but if the heartbeat accelerates to 250–270 beats per minute you're in trouble. The average attack is about 100–150 beats and mine seemed so far to be about average; the trick now was to prevent it from getting worse. Brainy people try brainy strategies, such as thinking calming thoughts, pseudo-mystic thoughts, *If I die now it's a good death,* that sort of thing, *if I die this is a good place and a good time,* the idea is to deceive the frenzied heartbeat that, really, you don't care: you hadn't any other plans for the afternoon. The important thing with tachycardia is to prevent panic! You must prevent panic! Otherwise you'll have to be taken by ambulance to the closest emergency room, which is not so very nice a way to spend the afternoon, really. So I contemplated the blue sky overhead. The earth beneath my head. Nature surrounding me on all sides, I couldn't quite see it but I could hear it, smell it, sense it—there is something *there,* no mistake about it.

[1] **jar in Tennessee:** A reference to Wallace Stevens's poem "Anecdote of the Jar."

Completely oblivious to the predicament of the individual but that's only "natural" after all, one hardly expects otherwise.

When you discover yourself lying on the ground, limp and un-resisting, head in the dirt, and helpless, the earth seems to shift forward as a presence; hard, emphatic, not mere surface but a genuine force—there is no other word for it but *presence*. To keep in motion is to keep in time and to be stopped, stilled, is to be abruptly out of time, in another time-dimension perhaps, an alien one, where human language has no resonance. Nothing to be said about it expresses it, nothing touches it, it's an absolute against which nothing human can be measured . . . Moving through space and time by way of your own volition you inhabit an interior consciousness, a hallucinatory consciousness, it might be said, so long as breath, heartbeat, the body's autonomy hold; when motion is stopped you are jarred out of it. The interior is invaded by the exterior. The outside wants to come in, and only the self's fragile membrane prevents it.

The fly buzzing at Emily's death.[2]

Still, the earth *is* your place. A tidy grave-site measured to your size. Or, from another angle of vision, one vast democratic grave.

Let's contemplate the sky. Forget the crazy hammering heartbeat, don't listen to it, don't start counting, remember that there is a clever way of breathing that conserves oxygen as if you're lying below the surface of a body of water breathing through a very thin straw but you can breathe through it if you're careful, if you don't panic, one breath and then another and then another, isn't that the story of all lives? careers? Just a matter of breathing. Of course it is. But contemplate the sky, it's there to be contemplated. A mild shock to see it so blank, blue, a thin, airy, ghostly blue, no clouds to disguise its emptiness. You are beginning to feel not only weightless but near-bodiless, lying on the earth like a scrap of paper about to be blown off. Two dimensions and you'd imagined you were three!

---

[2] **fly buzzing at Emily's death:** Reference to a poem by Emily Dickinson, "I heard a Fly buzz—when I died—."

And there's the sky rolling away forever, into infinity—if "infinity" can be "rolled into"—and the forlorn truth is, that's where you're going too. And the lovely blue isn't even blue, is it? Isn't even there, is it? A mere optical illusion, isn't it? No matter what art has urged you to believe.

Early Nature memories. Which it's best not to suppress.

. . . Wading, as a small child, in Tonawanda Creek near our house, and afterward trying to tear off, in a frenzy of terror and re-vulsion, the sticky, fat, black bloodsuckers that had attached them-selves to my feet, particularly between my toes.

. . . Coming upon a friend's dog in a drainage ditch, dead for several days, evidently the poor creature had been shot by a hunter and left to die, bleeding to death, and we're stupefied with grief and horror but can't resist sliding down to where he's lying on his belly, and we can't resist squatting over him, turning the body over. . . .

. . . The raccoon, mad with rabies, frothing at the mouth and tearing at his own belly with his teeth, so that his intestines spilled out onto the ground . . . a sight I seem to remember though in fact I did not see. I've been told I did not see.

Consequently, my chronic uneasiness with Nature-mysticism; Nature-adoration; Nature-as-(moral)-instruction-for-mankind. My doubt that one can, with philosophical validity, address "nature" as a single coherent noun, anything other than a Platonic, hence dis-credited, isness. My resistance to "Nature-writing" as a genre, ex-cept when it is brilliantly fictionalized in the service of a writer's individual vision—Thoreau's books and *Journal,* of course—but also, less known in this country, the miniaturist prose-proems of Co-lette (*Flowers and Fruit*) and Ponge (*Taking the Side of Things*)—in which case it becomes yet another, and ingenious, form of story-telling. The subject is there only by the grace of the author's language.

Nature has no instructions for mankind except that our poor beleaguered humanist-democratic way of life, our fantasies of the individual's high worth, our sense that the weak, no less than the strong, have a right to survive, are absurd.

In any case, where *is* Nature? one might (skeptically) inquire. Who has looked upon her/its face and survived?

But isn't this all exaggeration, in the spirit of rhetorical contentiousness? Surely Nature is, for you, as for most reasonably intelligent people, a "perennial" source of beauty, comfort, peace, escape from the delirium of civilized life; a respite from the ego's ever-frantic strategies of self-promotion, as a way of insuring (at least in fantasy) some small measure of immortality? Surely nature, as it is understood in the usual slapdash way, as human, if not dilettante, *experience* (hiking in a national park, jogging on the beach at dawn, even tending, with the usual comical frustrations, a suburban garden), is wonderfully consoling; a place where, when you go there, it has to take you in?—a palimpsest of sorts you choose to read, layer by layer, always with care, always cautiously, in proportion to your psychological strength?

Nature: as in Thoreau's upbeat transcendentalist mode ("The indescribable innocence and beneficence of Nature—such health, such cheer, they afford forever! And such sympathy have they ever with our race, that all Nature would be affected . . . if any man should ever for a just cause grieve"), and not in Thoreau's grim mode ("Nature is hard to be overcome but she must be overcome").

Another way of saying, not *Nature-in-itself* but *Nature-as-experience*. The former, Nature-in-itself, is, to allude slantwise to Melville, a blankness ten times blank; the latter is what we commonly, or perhaps always, mean when we speak of Nature as a noun, a single entity—something of ours. Most of the time it's just an activity, a sort of hobby, a weekend, a few days, perhaps a few hours, staring out of the window at the mind-dazzling autumn foliage of, say, Northern Michigan, being rendered speechless—temporarily—at the sight of Mt. Shasta, the Grand Canyon, Ansel Adams's West. Or Nature writ small, contained in the backyard. Nature filtered through our optical nerves, our "senses," our fiercely romantic expectations. Nature that pleases us because it mirrors our souls, or gives the comforting illusion of doing so. As in our first mother's awakening to the self's fatal beauty—

>   I thither went
> With unexperienc't thought, and laid me down
> On the green bank, to look into the clear
> Smooth Lake, that to me seem'd another Sky.
> As I bent down to look, just opposite
> A Shape within the watr'y gleam appear'd
> Bending to look on me, I started back,
> It started back, but pleas'd I soon return'd,
> Pleas'd it return'd as soon with answering looks
> Of sympathy and love; there I had fixt
> Mine eyes till now, and pin'd with vain desire.

—in these surpassingly beautiful lines from Book IV of Milton's *Paradise Lost.*

Nature as the self's (flattering) mirror, but not ever, no never, Nature-in-itself.

Nature is mouths, or maybe a single mouth. Why glamorize it, romanticize it, well yes but we must, we're writers, poets, mystics (of a sort) aren't we, precisely what else are we to do but glamorize and romanticize and generally exaggerate the significance of anything we focus the white heat of our "creativity" upon . . . ? And why not Nature, since it's there, common property, mute, can't talk back, allows us the possibility of transcending the human condition for a while, writing prettily of mountain ranges, white-tailed deer, the purple crocuses outside this very window, the thrumming dazzling "life-force" we imagine we all support. Why not?

Nature *is* more than a mouth—it's a dazzling variety of mouths. And it pleases the senses, in any case, as the physicists' chill universe of numbers certainly does not.

Oscar Wilde, on our subject: "Nature is no great mother who has borne us. She is our creation. It is in our brain that she quickens to life. Things are because we see them, and what we see, and how we see it, depends on the Arts that have influenced us. To look at a thing is very different from seeing a thing. . . . At present, people see fogs, not because there are fogs, but because poets and painters have taught them the mysterious loveliness of such effects. There may have been fogs for centuries in London. I dare say there were. But no one saw them. They did not exist until Art had invented them. . . . Yesterday evening Mrs. Arundel insisted on my going to the window and looking at the glorious sky, as she called it. And so I had to look at it . . . And what was it? It was simply a very second-rate Turner, a Turner of a bad period, with all the painter's worst faults exaggerated and over-emphasized."

(If we were to put it to Oscar Wilde that he exaggerates, his reply might well be: "Exaggeration? I don't know the meaning of the word.")

. . .

Walden, that most artfully composed of prose fictions, concludes, in the rhapsodic chapter "Spring," with Henry David Thoreau's contemplation of death, decay, and regeneration as it is suggested to him, or to his protagonist, by the spectacle of vultures feeding off carrion. There is a dead horse close by his cabin and the stench of its decomposition, in certain winds, is daunting. Yet: ". . . the assurance it gave me of the strong appetite and inviolable health of Nature was my compensation. I love to see that Nature is so rife with life that myriads can be afforded to be sacrificed and suffered to prey upon one another; that tender organizations can be so serenely squashed out of existence like pulp—tadpoles which herons gobble up, and tortoises and toads run over in the road; and that sometimes it has rained flesh and blood! . . . The impression made on a wise man is that of universal innocence."

Come off it, Henry David. You've grieved these many years for your elder brother John, who died a ghastly death of lockjaw, you've never wholly recovered from the experience of watching him die. And you know, or must know, that you're fated too to die young of consumption . . . But this doctrinaire transcendentalist passage ends *Walden* on just the right note. It's as impersonal, as coolly detached, as the Oversoul itself: a "wise man" filters his emotions through his brain.

Or through his prose.

Nietzsche: "We all pretend to ourselves that we are more simpleminded than we are: that is how we get a rest from our fellow men."

> Once out of nature I shall never take
> My bodily form from any natural thing
> But such a form as Grecian goldsmiths make
> Of hammered gold and gold enamelling

To keep a drowsy Emperor awake;
Or set upon a golden bough to sing
To lords and ladies of Byzantium
Of what is past, or passing, or to come.

WILLIAM BUTLER YEATS, "Sailing to Byzantium"

Yet even the golden bird is a "bodily form taken from (a) natural thing." No, it's impossible to escape!

The writer's resistance to Nature.

Wallace Stevens: "In the presence of extraordinary actuality, consciousness takes the place of imagination."

Once, years ago, in 1972 to be precise, when I seemed to have been another person, related to the person I am now as one is related, tangentially, sometimes embarrassingly, to cousins not seen for decades,—once, when we were living in London, and I was very sick, I had a mystical vision. That is, I "had" a "mystical vision"— the heart sinks: such pretension—or something resembling one. A fever-dream, let's call it. It impressed me enormously and impresses me still, though I've long since lost the capacity to see it with my mind's eye, or even, I suppose, to believe in it. There is a statute of limitations on "mystical visions" as on romantic love.

I was very sick, and I imagined my life as a thread, a thread of breath, or heartbeat, or pulse, or light, yes it was light, radiant light, I was burning with fever and I ascended to that plane of serenity that might be mistaken for (or *is*, in fact) Nirvana, where I had a waking dream of uncanny lucidity—

My body is a tall column of light and heat.

My body is not "I" but "it."

My body is not one but many.

My body, which "I" inhabit, is inhabited as well by other creatures, unknown to me, imperceptible—the smallest of them mere sparks of light.

My body, which I perceive as substance, is in fact an organization of infinitely complex, overlapping, imbricated structures, radiant light their manifestation, the "body" a tall column of light and blood-heat, a temporary agreement between atoms, like a high-rise building with numberless rooms, corridors, corners, elevator shafts, windows. . . . In this fantastical structure the "I" is deluded as to its sovereignty, let alone its autonomy in the (outside) world; the most astonishing secret is that the "I" doesn't exist!—but it behaves as if it does, as if it were one and not many.

In any case, without the "I" the tall column of light and heat would die, and the microscopic life-particles would die with it . . . will die with it. The "I," which doesn't exist, is everything.

But Dr. Johnson is right, the inexpressible need not be expressed. And what resistance, finally? There is none.

This morning, an invasion of tiny black ants. One by one they appear out of nowhere—that's their charm too!—moving single file across the white Parsons table where I am sitting, trying without much success to write a poem. A poem of only three or four lines is what I want, something short, tight, mean. I want it to hurt like a white hot wire up the nostrils, small and compact and turned in upon itself with the density of a hunk of rock from the planet Jupiter. . . .

But here come the black ants: harbingers, you might say, of spring. One by one by one they appear on the dazzling white table and one by one I kill them with a forefinger, my deft right forefinger, mashing each against the surface of the table and then dropping it into a wastebasket at my side. Idle labor, mesmerizing, effortless, and I'm curious as to how long I can do it, sit here in the brilliant March sunshine killing ants with my right forefinger, how long I, and the ants, can keep it up.

After a while I realize that I can do it a long time. And that I've written my poem.

sandi wisenberg

It's common to read about the feelings of awe or reverence that nature can inspire. Wisenberg's essay, however, focuses on an entirely different reaction— the kind of outdoor agoraphobia it can inspire in city dwellers. Nature, she argues, can be seen as the ulti- mate nothingness—or the part of ourselves we are afraid to get lost in.

plain scared or "there is no such thing as negative space," the art teacher said

In a college art class I learned that negative space was the nothing behind the figure you were looking at. But years later another teacher told me that this was not so. There is always something there, he said. If you look, you will see it.

Kenophobia is the fear of empty rooms. Fear of empty places. Agoraphobia is the fear of open places. But it is not the agora, the marketplace, that frightens me. I am not afraid to leave the house. I am afraid to leave the city. To be more precise—to venture from the SMSA.

I live on the North Side of Chicago. I find the word "kenophobia" in a book in the main library of Evanston. About twenty years ago, I lived in a dorm room in Evanston. The room was empty when I arrived and empty when I left. I remember one June I kept a university library book almost until the minute the taxi came to take me to the airport. I wanted to keep, as long as possible, some connection with the place I was leaving empty.

. . .

I am afraid of being erased. One night in a lover's apartment, after he told me he didn't want to see me anymore, I left this note in his desk: I was here. I was once a part of your life. He has since moved to San Francisco. I do not know what became of the desk.

We are all afraid of being erased. Our names in water writ. Of the earth disappearing. We are small and the night looms.

The night ends. The prairie goes on forever. A sameness, for the uninitiated, the way all the seasons in Miami seem alike to newcomers. I am uninitiated.

We all fear the blank page, the blank mind dry of thought.

In and around Chicago, experts are replanting the prairie. I think this involves both public and private funds. I like reading about such things. I don't mind walking through these prairies if they are small and surrounded by city. It's the big areas I don't like; I don't like to hike. I like to walk through cities, looking in store windows.

I grew up in Texas, came to the Midwest at eighteen. I grew up with ranch houses and sidewalks. I loved taking the bus downtown and walking among abandoned railroad cars, buying old records in a shabby pawnshop. I'd eat lunch at Woolworth's and buy makeup at Neiman-Marcus.

In my twenties I moved from Illinois to Iowa to Florida back to Illinois. In Iowa I liked the pale green bowls of hills along the highway. I admired them from behind the windows of cars. The hills looked like paintings. In Miami in the newspaper office where I worked, we worshipped the sun from afar. During particularly dramatic sunsets, we reporters would stand near our desks, looking through the windows closest to us, facing west, waiting, watching.

. . .

My only forays into nature are very tame—residencies at artists' colonies. I have to pack along piles of little white tablets made of cortisone. When my asthma's bad I take the pills for eight or nine days in a row. I'm allergic to nature. Ragweed, grasses, mold, spores, hay, milkweed—things I can name and things I can't name.

The first artists' colony I went to had once been Edna St. Vincent Millay's retreat a few hours from Manhattan—strawberry farm, hills, pond, trees. At Millay, I learned what foxglove was, and phlox, learned how to spot jack-in-the-pulpit and lady-slipper, all veins and sex. The colony's assistant director told me about a New York artist who had come to the colony and had walked around the grounds a while. Then he'd fled inside and reported that he'd seen an animal. What was it? she'd asked. He didn't know. He couldn't tell whether it was a squirrel or a deer.

During my residency, there were two painters who gushed over the landscape. They tried to match the colors of nature with the colors of paint. Cerulean Blue? they would ask each other, pointing at the sky. Havannah Lake?

It is land. It is only land.

The assistant told me that the pioneers from the East feared the flat open land of the West. For some of them, the horizon was too large. They couldn't see themselves in it. They were diminished. Some Easterners returned. Some carved themselves into the Western landscape.

I am not from the East but I understand those Easterners. I don't like limitless horizons. I don't embrace endless fields. I like nature with borders.

The plains scare me.

I am plain scared.

I am terrified of the universe that has no end. I am afraid to step behind the curtain, ask, What is the system behind this solar system? And behind that.

There is no negative space, only positive space having a bad day.

Franz Kafka was born in a city and was buried there. In 1912 he wrote: Ever since childhood, there have been times when I was almost unhappy about my inability to appreciate flowers. This seems to be related in some way to my inability to appreciate music.

I like flowers. A flowerbed is not the same as a field. Which life depends on. Wildlands are beautiful, they say. They must be saved. There is music in the prairie, they say.

Kafka is less foreign to me than Wendell Berry. I feel closer to Mikhail Zoshchenko's Moscow of the bureaucratic 1920s, than Larry McMurtry's Texas.

I find myself inside books by writers who write in fast, urgent sentences with no time for landscape. Writers of closeup conversations—internal and external—writers of the life of streets, cafes, stores, restaurants. Writers who rent. But there are others, so many others; I am not always curled up with my own kind. But I skip the parts, all the parts, about nature.

When I was younger, my friends and I would find books with sex in them. We would read those parts aloud, skip everything else.

Therefore, nature is the opposite of sex.

I know two women in Western Michigan who like to read farm novels. One of them has tiny plastic cows and horses super-glued to her dashboard. I don't think I've ever read a farm novel, though I imagine myself finding pleasure in following the slow quiet rhythms of crops pushing their way skyward, in descriptions of the dirt and sweat and dampness of stables, the lowing and groaning. Pure, sweet tiredness after you latch the door, blow out the lantern.

I was at the late Kroch's and Brentano's bookstore on South Wabash Avenue in Chicago. A street with the same name as a river, believed to be taken from the Miami Indian word for "gleaming white." At the bookstore I picked up a book, *A River Runs Through It*. Originally a sleeper of a book reissued, glamorized by Hollywood. It is my friend K.'s favorite book. I never talk to K. anymore because he met his ex-girlfriend through me. Somehow that is a problem though we were never lovers. These are the sorts of things I write about—things that happen indoors. I like K.'s writing, respect his judgment. But I didn't buy the book. I was afraid I would not enter it, afraid of some flatness of surface, nothing to hold onto. Like being afraid to enter into a conversation with a person who has a difficult accent or an unfathomable expression; scratch and scratch and still there may be nothing there.

(But so many other people liked the book. K. loved it, and he's from Manhattan. He likes to fish.)

Or like being afraid of sex, afraid to enter its raw territory, afraid I will find myself in the middle of it, not want to be there, and feel alone, terribly alone, too aware of my surroundings.

Many years ago I had an internship in Downstate Illinois at the *Quincy Herald-Whig*. I made friends with a young reporter there from a smaller town. She told me, All cities are alike. She didn't see the point in going to more than one of them.

. . .

I use free address labels from the Sierra Club and Nature Conservancy. I am not a member. Over the years I've joined the National Trust for Historic Preservation and the Chicago Architecture Foundation. I used to love the before and after spreads in magazines on restored opera houses, movie theaters saved from the wrecking ball and transformed into quaint shopping malls. I loved reading about the resurrection of inner cities, led by young urban pioneers, before "yuppie" was a bad word, or maybe even a word at all.

In Chicago once I met a lawyer who worked for the National Trust. *Soul mate,* I thought. She said, "I'm really an environmentalist, I don't really have a feeling for architecture." I was appalled. This was hard for me to understand. I told her over and over, "You must see the Victorian Gothic apartments at Chicago and Wabash. The building is in danger. It is beautiful. It must be saved."

They say you'll see everybody you know if you stand long enough at the corner of State and Madison. I see Louis, that is all that matters. I am talking about a building. I am talking about Carson Pirie Scott designed by Louis Sullivan. The green and rust filigree ironwork. The design is inspired by organic shapes, the same energy of nature that animated Whitman. This ersatz vegetation fills my heart, the way that Sullivan's first view of a suspension bridge shook him up as a boy. An exhilaration. The same feeling I get from walking down a certain street in my neighborhood, Roscoe—the pedestrian scale of the two-flats and three-flats, the undulation of the brick fronts, the Italianate eyebrows on windows, decorative carvings on graystones—the way *someone* must react to the undulations of corn, clouds, furrows.

Or the straight vastness of the Great Plains with their wheat, earth, sand, clay—whatever is on them, in them.

. . .

I liked *Charlotte's Web*—and it appears to have been a farm novel.

I fear the Other.

I am afraid nothing is out there but God and landscape, and he doesn't exist and land can't talk. I don't know the language of it.

I like crowded civic and political events during which everyone believes something important is happening.

We city folks go to therapy.

We fantasize about strangers on the El.

We fool ourselves into thinking we have a shared destination.

We fool ourselves into thinking we don't.

This is the secret, the secret I have always known: that the bare open plain is my heart itself, my heart without connection; that the bare cinder block room is my soul, my soul without connection—the place I fear I will end up when the fear of loss of connection overrides everything else.

I long to receive this benediction: May you see that something is always there, have hope for the heart to rise up for, come to a feeling of settlement, find a light way of walking on the earth.

hal herring

In this complex reflection on his "lifelong reverence" for living things, Herring asks a question that has surely occurred to many young hunters, "How is it that blood-lust and the love of nature could be so inextricably wound?" In considering possible answers, Herring invokes the Alabama waterways and fields of his youth—and his continuing fascination with catching the fish he calls redhorse.

silver redhorse

Moulder Branch connected to Hurricane Creek, which fed into the Flint River much farther away than a person could hope to reach without a driver's license. The Flint, in turn, made its loops away from the mountains through flat cotton and soybean country to pour into the Tennessee. This connection was immensely important, because it meant that big-water fish—river drum, carp, even striped bass and sauger, which we called jack salmon—could find their way during high water upstream into the hinterlands, where the water was born of limestone caverns and dark seeps in the low, flat-topped foothills of Alabama's Cumberlands. I liked old ponds, their quiet waters weedy and concealing, trembling with the movements of bass and shellcrackers. But no mystery on earth meant as much to me when I was fourteen as that system of creeks and small rivers braiding toward the Tennessee.

Moulder Branch began as Sneed Spring, a crystal-clear stream that emerged from a shadowed, fern-hung hole in a small cliff, one visible vein of a thousand that coursed unseen through the heart of the mountains. The rocks on its bed were covered with a black-green moss that shivered in the current, and small clouds of bright-colored dace and sculpin swept up into the darkness of the cave and back out into the sunlight, joined at times by other minnows who followed an opposite life and had no color at all, were clear as glass. If you could catch them, you could watch their organs working through their skin—yellow stomach, blue heart, blue brain.

During the third week of March, schools of spawning silver redhorse appeared on the gravel beds and shoals of Moulder Branch, about four miles below the cave. The creek at this point had been joined by the waters of two more large wet-weather springs and several washes and was about twenty feet wide, although it shrank to a trickle in the late summer. The redhorse were members of the lowly sucker family that spent most of their lives in the deep holes of the Flint River or in the giant Tennessee. Their traveling habits lent them a profound air of mystery, the attraction of the wanderer from far away who appears suddenly and gives beauty and energy to a creek that was, in its middle reaches, pretty ordinary. They were a striking red color in the clear water and ranged in size from a foot or so to about twenty inches. They traveled in schools of dozens, and in such a small and seasonal creek, they presented an amazing sight. To a boy who longed for trout and salmon, for wild Alaskan rivers, they were a priceless gift. I began to watch for them the first week of March, just after the close of rabbit season, when the trees were just beginning to bud. The pounding of rain on the roof above my bed would awaken me late at night, and I would imagine them, lifting up from the dark gravel beds and mussel piles deep in the muddy Tennessee, catching the taste of the rising waters there in Moulder Branch, a taste of rich loam washed down through sinkholes in the mountains, bloodroot, ginseng, polished limestone, the scent of subterranean creatures.

As I watched for them, I dreamed of the wonders that they must be passing in their journey: sunken barges, alligator turtles, catfish as big as a man, lost relics of war and human endeavor. From the muddy channel of the Tennessee they moved up into the Flint, where the water was stained red from the clay of the cotton fields, and the thick primeval salamanders called hellbenders drifted above a rocky bed strewn with potsherds and stone arrowheads. The Flint suffered from the runoff of a mixture of chemicals that we called simply "cotton poison," and I don't think the redhorse lingered there. It was another twenty river miles to the mouth of Hurricane Creek and at least fifteen more to the mouth of Moulder. I don't know when they started this journey each year, or how long it took them, but what they accomplished each spring was nothing less than a passage between worlds.

At that time in my life, I was intensely solitary, by choice and design. I have since struggled in fiction to capture the feeling that pervades my memories of those creeks and that landscape and that age. I felt then that I also passed between worlds that had distinct boundaries. I had good friends at school, but I hated the confinement of school to the point that I was often physically ill. I never considered playing any sports that would require me to spend even one extra minute on the grounds of the school, and I rushed home to go immediately out walking or hunting or fishing. My real life, the one in which I felt at ease, was on the creeks and in the woods and along the edges of the fields, and I didn't feel any need to share it. After the exhausting raucousness of a day of junior high, the silence of that world was like falling into a feather bed. Because even then landowners were jealous of their hunting rights and property lines, I was often trespassing, and my wanderings were best kept to the thickets and the woods. I traveled a lot during hunting season in the low beds of washes, following the tracks of coon and fox and coyote. Like them, I didn't much care for open ground.

The place where Moulder Branch pours into Hurricane is narrow enough to leap across, and when I knew it best, it was partially blocked by a gradually tilting sycamore three feet through. The water had gouged a deep hole beneath the roots of the tree, and during floods it poured over the pistol-butted trunk, and the whole tree vibrated out to the tips of its branches. When the water dropped and changed from brown to translucent green, I could straddle the sycamore and watch for the flash of redhorse feeding in the hole. Until they reached the shallow spawning grounds, they would take a night crawler or red worm fished directly on the bottom, and I usually caught quite a few from the side of the creek opposite the sycamore, where the bank was low enough to land them. These fish I always released, because the hook in the mouth did not mortally injure them, and I didn't really like to eat them. They were bony in the extreme, although between the bones, the flesh was white and firm. I eventually learned to pressure-cook them, a process that melts the smaller bones, but by then it seemed like too much trouble.

Later in the month, when the redhorse moved farther up the creek, the only way to take them was by "snatching"—that is, snagging them with a treble hook. I also hunted them with a light bow and old aluminum arrows, with frog gigs, homemade spears, and a pistol loaded with .22 shots. With these methods, catch-and-release was not an option.

The spawning grounds were along a section of creek lined with big red oaks and hackberries, with a thicket of sumac and locust saplings taking over a cow pasture on one bank and a cornfield on the other. It was one of the best places in the valley to hunt fox squirrels, which didn't leave their nests until midmorning and foraged in the corn rather than frantically gathering nuts in the woods like their gray cousins. The redhorse gathered on a long, dangerously shallow gravel bed, with shoal water below, where the riffles would hide them if need be until they could reach a deeper section below a cut bank. No ospreys or eagles lived in that part of Alabama, and the trees on both banks met high above the water, shielding them from hawks. In days past, a lot of people, tenant farmers and sharecroppers who did not ignore free fish, came to take them with seines and treble hooks, but the land around there had actually lost population since the '50s, and those who remained were bent on other tasks. Although I never saw anyone other than myself fishing there, all the local old timers who saw me knew exactly what I was doing.

The trick was to thread the brush and flood trash to the edge of the creek without spooking the whole school, cast the single treble across almost to the other side and let it roll slightly downstream. Then you twitched it, reeling in about six inches of line, almost exactly like working a plastic worm for bass. The redhorse varied widely in size, and you tried to pick an individual fish to snag. The hookup was usually not a great surprise, but because they were often hooked in the tail, and the right fish could weigh up to four pounds, the fight was dramatic and worthwhile. The struggle would put the whole school immediately to flight. Usually I would make several probing casts into the hole under the cut bank and take a couple more that way. After that, it would be time to walk, seek another gravel bed where another group was holding, or try whatever holes could be found along the way. A lot of times I would leave my rod and reel stashed along the creek somewhere and go off looking for snakes or studying the plants that came up specifically at that time. The fields and hedgerows that would be a jungle by mid-May were still bare or just beginning to green, but the delicate plants of the woods' floor were already at the height of their flowering. The muted power of the March sun, falling unhindered through the leafless trees, was perfect for hepatica, trillium, troutlily, and bloodroot. Later, when the trees had leafed and the tough plants of the fields were in full riot, these plants would have passed their prime and be barely noticeable beneath the deep shade of the oaks.

One afternoon, waiting for the redhorse to come back up onto the gravel, I heard a tremendous splash, and an eight-point whitetail buck came galloping down the creek, ran off the shoal into the deep, and swam below me, not a yard from my feet. Nothing was chasing him that I could see, and when he left the creek, he walked away slowly into the thicket.

Bow fishing for redhorse was not too different from snatching with a treble hook if you shot from the bank. Except for the fact that at fourteen it was still wonderful to be out in the world with a powerful weapon rather than a fishing rod. The height of sport with the bow was to wade up behind the fish, which was almost impossible and which I accomplished only twice that I remember. Shooting into deep water was difficult because of the refraction problem, and when you did manage to hit one, you usually were in for a soaking when you went in after it. I had a bow-fishing rig, a coffee can wound with braided line and held to the bow with a long bolt and a piece of flatiron. You could buy a special fishing arrow with a hole in front of the nock where you tied on the line. The first time I ever used this rig, I shot at a very large and very expensive grass carp that a neighbor had bought to control algae in his catfish pond. I saw the enormous fish, went home, got the rig and came back, obsessed. The first shot launched the heavy arrow about ten feet before the braided line wrapped around my forearm, peeled off the skin all the way to my wrist, and then brought the arrow winging back at my face. The grass carp lived through this attempt.

So I hunted redhorse with regular aluminum arrows, the older the better, because they could survive only so many strikes into the rocks of the bottom. Broadheads hit the water and veered off to either side, so I used target points or the special flats I made up for hunting rabbits, with a .38 brass fitted over the tip. A strike anywhere in front of the dorsal fin killed the fish outright, and they could be retrieved easily as they drifted along, slowed by the dragging of the arrow.

Why, when I so loved to see the living redhorse on the shoal, did I need to kill them? Why would I wait for them, dream of their passage, depend on them as the true harbingers of beloved spring, and still creep up to the cut bank, point my cheap pistol down at the shallow water, and shoot the biggest one I saw?

The question certainly never occurred to me then. (It might help to know that during those years I often lost the first fish of every trip simply because I was so anxious to begin fishing that I could not finish my knots correctly.) Only in recent years, after an intense and continuing apprenticeship in the art of finding game and taking fish, have I begun to wonder how it is that bloodlust and the love of nature could be so inextricably wound for me. During most of that apprenticeship, the desire to touch whatever was my quarry was foremost and assumed. Stints on commercial fishing boats (jobs I gleefully took on because they offered the chance to fish for fun during breaks and while traveling to and from the fishing grounds), working in seafood packing houses, and a very brief time hunting coyotes for hides, caused me to realize early that my very soul was imperiled by viewing living creatures as potential cash money. This view requires that the seeker abandon any concepts of the sacred nature of the creature sought and ignore its attendant mysteries in an attempt to bring it to hand in a practical and efficient manner. A swordfish, which is one of the greatest predators ever to swim the waters of creation, brings $4.75 a pound. A coyote, which you have followed and watched as it hunts mice, does inexplicable dances in morning sunlight and calls out in bizarre cadences to its fellows, brings $55–$60, which beats wages working for someone else and allows you to wander around on the grasslands all during the late winter without looking like the slacker you probably are. Your .22 bullet takes the coyote in the brain while he is thinking . . . *What?* You have no time to ponder; you must immediately go looking for the next one. Rent is due; the clutch is going out in the truck. Reverence falls by the wayside. You cannot serve two gods at once. Sadly enough for me, since I live in good country and am usually unemployed, I believe that paid guiding for fish and game falls under the same cloud.

But what about killing for free? What about snatching spawning redhorse with a treble hook? I can only say that I had not evolved past the point where I wished mightily to hold in my hands the mystery that fascinated me. I still haven't. I most appreciate the journey of the redhorse, the clear cave waters of the spawning grounds, the distant, muddy, secret world of its home, when I snag it, fight it, and hold it in my hands. Maybe it is the substance of creation that I want to touch. Trying to find a way to catch them, I studied them more closely than I ever would, had my interest been only in seeing them. This has proven true with every fish and animal I have ever sought to kill. The mystery expands as one enters it, like opening a door into a castle or entering a cave. Snatching red-horse, I was out on the creek almost every day for the three weeks the fish were there. I knew every hole, gravel bar, cut bank. I saw the same copperhead three times, the same crows, deer, skunks, the same trees until I knew each one individually, and I can see them all in my mind right now. It is in this study, this knowing, that rever-ence for the whole of the world that sustains us is born. This rever-ence can make us stronger, less careless, less destructive. It is a clear, good thing. I am grateful that I do not have to try to live without it.

Anyone may by now be justified in asking what I did with the redhorse that I snagged, shot, speared and so on. I strung them through the gills on a forked green ash or willow stick and dragged them up to the paved road that ran along the foot of the mountains at the far side of the cove where we lived. A mile or so back, there was a deep hollow, with another small spring creek, where an old man named Fred Johnson and his wife, Sary, held out in a partially collapsed log cabin. No one used the scrubby pasture of the hollow, and the cabin had been abandoned for twenty years. They owned no land, did no work that I knew of, paid no rent. A much larger clap-board house had stood at one time at the mouth of the hollow, closer to the road, and the old couple had lived in it for a while with an assortment of other relatives, but someone had burned it to the ground, and everyone had scattered except for them.

Fred and Sary Johnson lived without electricity or plumbing in the one, tight room of the cabin, growing turnips in the yard, forag-ing, killing coons and possums. They kept an assortment of "catch dogs," small, often mangy feists that attacked whatever wildlife pre-sented itself and relieved Mr. Johnson of the need to kill game with .22 cartridges, which cost money. These dogs were locally famous for disappearing and giving Mr. Johnson an excuse to travel far and wide in search of them across private lands otherwise off limits to his hunting. That was how I met him, far off in a place called Duskins Hollow, where we both were trespassing, looking for ginseng. When I arrived with the redhorse, Sary was usually sitting quietly on the porch in an old reclining lawn chair, wrapped in blankets against the chill of the March afternoon, the front door open, and a hot fire barely lighting the dark room behind her. She greeted me but did not usually rise from her cocoon. Mr. Johnson was usually there with her or within shouting distance in the woods. He was jovial, with a little bit of the friendliness of the con man in him. Sometimes he was reeling and red-faced with drink. He was seriously happy to get the fish. Once, he went back with me to the shoals where I had caught them and snatched some from under the cut bank with a willow pole, ten feet of string and a treble hook that he borrowed from me and later returned.

Mr. Johnson had rebuilt an old flume that carried water from a seep spring by the cabin into a concrete cattle trough, and he cleaned the redhorse on a plank set over the outflow from the trough. If he was sober, he took a shovel and buried the offal carefully at the edge of the woods; otherwise, he flung it far and wide as he talked. I never hung around long, and I don't remember how they cooked the fish, though I guess it must have been on a rack over the fireplace. Once the next fall when I met him on the road, he gave me two enormous ginseng roots, bigger than any I had ever seen, and I wore one of them on a string around my neck for a while, until too many people at school asked what it was. A year later, the Johnsons were gone, and a year after that, some deer hunters took over the cabin, used it for a few weekends, and burned it down.

It would be easy to close this story, or essay, or whatever it is, with a litany of destruction: cabins burned, creeks channelized, housing developments planned, the redhorse gone as surely as are Fred and Sary Johnson. And I could, in truth, write it that way. The fields on either side of Moulder Branch were sold to a farmer who was a devotee of clean farming, and he did channelize all the washes and scraped them clear of the hedgerows that had been the nesting place of quail and bluebirds and just about everything else. I met him once, and he looked out over the scarified land and said to me,

"I've put a lot into this place, but I've just about got it looking like I want it to." His efforts inspired the county to go on a campaign of its own, spraying herbicide on the hedgerows along the roads, laying in culverts, straightening side creeks. The runoff moved too fast down into Moulder Branch, and the bed of the creek no longer held enough water in the spring for the redhorse to spawn. Although Sneed Spring produces as much water as ever, during the summer the middle reaches of the creek are entirely dry. The lands all along the creek are leased for big money to urban deer hunters who brook no trespass on their investment. It is a stricter, balder, less sheltering world.

But, true to its ability to inspire my lifelong reverence, it is by no means a delicate world. The redhorse are there still, though they are limited now to the main branch of Hurricane Creek. March a year ago I was thirty-two years old, and home for a visit. My nephew, who was eight, was there with my sister. It was a close, warm day, building overcast, and I could feel the fall of the barometer in my sinuses. We rummaged through the equipment shed and turned up an old spiderweb-encrusted Fenwick spinning rod and a green and white ceramic Zebco Cardinal, the finest spinning reel available in 1976. We stripped a Jitterbug of its two big trebles, swapped the line on the Cardinal for fresh ten-pound test, and set off for the creek.

Moulder Branch was too low, even in the hole beneath the bridge, to hold fish of any size. We set off downstream to a place where another big spring comes in and builds the volume of the creek. Nothing there. I was worried that my nephew would tire before we found anything worth catching, but he was excited and up for the walk. I had forgotten how fraught with fantastic possibility a fishing trip can be when you are eight. A long walk down Moulder Branch searching for redhorse can be on a par with any trip to Alaska or the Congo. I wanted to feel the same way, and I did. At the mouth of the creek, where it pours into the main Hurricane, a wide fan of gravel had built up and created a shallows and shoal system that pushed the main channel of Hurricane far over. That main channel was deep, and dark green. The big sycamore at the mouth of Moulder Branch was long washed away, and the hole beneath it was filled with clean gravel. A group of big redhorse came up over the lip of the gravel from the main channel and milled just below us. Smaller fish followed, swept in an entire school over the gravel and back into the channel. "There they are!" I said, thrilled. My nephew was solemn, staring at the fish. He grabbed for the fishing rod in a near frenzy and bungled the first cast, almost landing our only two treble hooks against a logjam. He reeled fast and tried again, this time arcing the hooks over the gravel bed, over the redhorse. "Now," I said, "jerk and reel, not too hard, not too fast. Look, you can see the hooks there, just on the other side of that fish!" He jerked once, exactly right, and the rod bowed. The sound of the creek was the sound of beauty itself. The new leaves on the big hardwoods all around us glowed a dusty green. The light coming down into the water was a pure butter yellow. Off to the south was the thunder of a storm.

leslie roberts

Roberts's piece is not only about death, it is suffused with it—as well as with the fierce desire to live, even in a cruel world. As part of the crew of a ship exploring the coast of Antarctica, Roberts is witness to both violent and peaceful death, as well as to the vivid specter of her own. As she says, in this place, "if you forget something or you get lost, you die."

the entire earth and sky

This is the period between life and death. This is the way the world
will look to the last man when he dies.

RICHARD BYRD, Alone (1938)

On this cold April morning, I am about to set myself free. I am
bound for the Antarctic shore in a small inflatable boat, leaving behind the rotund black, white, and ochre research ship where I have
lived for the past three and a half months, now swaying in the
waves, in front of cliffs appearing hewn from slub steel. So we are at
anchor, stopped, south of Argentina, south of Drake's Passage, en
route to a small research station that is further south still, in order to
get a look at this part of the Antarctic peninsula. But we are in no
particular hurry today, it's clear and reasonably warm for the early
austral autumn, about forty degrees Fahrenheit. We want to walk
on land.

There are four of us headed to the island: Maggie—Mags for
short—an able-bodied seaman who drives the inflatable, two scien-
tists, Ingrid and Pablo, and Werner, who works in the engine room
and doubles as a "survival expert" for shore parties.

Werner, an Austrian who pronounces his name with a V sound
(Verner), begins the same lecture I have heard on each of these
shore-bound cruises. He's thin, maybe six feet tall, and has deeply
wrinkled skin, a gray afterthought of beard. He wears a bright or-

ange survival suit, one that will float and keep the wearer alive for a few minutes if one were to hit the liquid-ice water. Mags gets one as well. Me, the reporter, and the two environmental scientists wear only our Gore-Tex parkas, fleece jackets, standard camping-store attire. No one talks about how the life-extending gear is divvied up, why there isn't enough for everyone. It's just how it is.

Werner is OK unless something goes wrong. Then, as I have witnessed, hang on to your hat. Werner screams, he waves his arms around wildly, he becomes a sort of Teutonic cartoon character speaking a mixed language, Germanglish. I first saw this side two weeks into the cruise, when he was teaching me how to steer the ship. Why a guy from the engine room was given the honor only occurred to me later. I had wanted to learn to steer; it looked fun and interesting and reminded me of all my favorite ahoy-matey novels, the stuff that satisfied my wanderlust when I was too young to act on it. I wanted to know what it felt like to steer a ship across the open ocean, to move past tabular icebergs alone in the sea. Who knows when I would get such an opportunity again?

Of course, no one needed to know that I lay in my bunk each morning and discussed with God sinking ships, floating hopelessly alone on the sea, a watery death. God and I had cut a deal. This ship would not sink, but if it did, I would be one of the people who was rescued. Sure, I told God, it would be harrowing if this had to happen, but when they shot off the pressurized containers, releasing the soft, lozenge-shaped lifeboats, I would climb the ladder down the side of the ship, get in one, and then a helicopter would come and fish us out. I had to keep this mantra to myself, of course, because the idea that someone at the helm is considering her abandon-ship routine at any given moment, while trying to ease the vessel through floating ice or across dark and wind-blown seas, may be grounds to lose the privilege.

Four hours on the bridge, "watch," meant steering for one hourlong shift, shifting to the bridge deck and scanning the sea with glasses, coming inside and doing a fire watch below decks, closing doors knocked open by the pounding sea, making tea and Milo, an Ovaltine-like malt drink, for the entire watch complement: in our case, four. I would begin my four-hour shift by conversing with God, not being in the moment, moving in the wheelhouse almost as if in a dream. I would look around and think, *Wow! This is great! Well, how did I get here!* Then feeling us rolling, each one of us four or six on the bridge moving the same way to the same swells, moving across the water, going somewhere all the time, hearing the mates, Bernadette or Ken or Bob, call out in British-accented curling words, from the chart room, "Steer one eight zero, please." There was nowhere else for my mind to turn. Be here now. Not the detail-collecting, wide-net casting mind that had seemed me for almost ten years.

When it is time, I pull open the heavy door that leads to the outdoor bridge deck, slamming it shut, cut off from the wheelhouse. There's been no threat of being washed overboard, but I am careful to make detailed assessment of the motion of waves. Is the main deck awash? How spiked do the sea waves appear? What else is out here with us, how much ice, how many yards, miles of tabular bergs, calved from an ice tongue further south still, now roaming the frigid water, islands unto themselves. I am alive, I shout into the cold wind that blasts my white cheeks while I stand on an anchor chain, looking through green field binoculars for ice in a sea of dark water, white foam and yes! Ice! I see it! I wave to the watch on the bridge, call out the size, ice coming, four points off the starboard bow, each piece a bit bigger than a rabbit. A herd of ice rabbits dancing across the water, dancing right along with me.

When I am to learn to steer, some time after I learn how to look for ice (look for the white that doesn't disappear, raising a new set of questions regarding absolute present tense. Disappear, to pass from view, to cease to be.) The ship, about the same age as me, twenty-seven, refitted with more modern satellite navigation devices, still sports an old-timey wheelhouse. The wheelhouse is forward on the ship, sitting about a third of the length of the ship from the prow.

The wheel is varnished, grainy hardwood, maybe four feet across. People have been holding it like this for almost thirty years. It is not unlike driving an old standard-shift car, one where muscle matters. The wheel makes itself known in a gentle, insistent tension, a weight, across the palms of my hands. I realize it is not the ship communicating with me on these hands, but the sea. I hold the wooden wheel, which has singular, carved handles. It is harder to turn than I expected, a sort of pushing back almost, the kind of tension you get when you lean into someone unexpectedly on a bouncing train. "Pardon me," the ship seems to say, "you're stepping on my foot." I watch the compass spin, encased in glass, like a snow-shake for a child only this one spins and when the snow settles it tells you where in the hell you are going because out here, yes out in the middle of this biggest, darkest, roughest sink on the planet, there are no road signs, just this and the faith that Ken and Bernadette and Bob really do know how to do the math that allows a ship to travel in a straight line using a compass, which appears in the Bible, in II Kings, meaning a curved or roundabout course, but for us meaning destiny, hope, the thirty-two points of a 360-degree circle. I watch it spin around, far from the heading called out to me by the mate Bob, who has offered to let me learn to steer on his watch.

"So Werner," I say, "how do you know how much to turn it if you are aiming for a five degree course correction?"

Werner begins to tell me about this, but the mate interrupts. It is Bob's watch, Black Bob he's called, and the night before he grabbed the cook out of her bunk by her hair because she had served rice three nights in a row. Me and the mates want potatoes, he told her.

Now Bob is in the chart room and wants me to head one seven eight. I turn the wheel what feels like an appropriate amount, wait for the compass to stop spinning, call out in a hearty voice, "One seven eight, sir."

But as I say this, the compass continues to move, one eight zero, one eight five, one nine zero. The ship, this fat tug, is suddenly threading the needle in the cresting seas of the Southern Ocean, and now we're taking the wave abeam, or at a perpendicular angle, which is uncool because it causes the ship to ricochet and things begin falling off shelves and people become nauseous and worst of all there is an endless, distinct smacking sound, reminding us all where we are and what is out there, on the other side of the ship's metal shell.

Bob is standing behind me, pulling his navy watch cap further down on his purple-red face. "What in the bloody hell are you doing?"

I see the compass one nine five, two zero zero, the numbers climb. The ship is pounded by the sea.

"I can't steer!" I scream out, almost beginning to cry. "Someone else grab the wheel!"

I let go. But Bob grabs my hands, places them back on the handles. "You stay on your wheelwatch until you are relieved."

I glance at the clock, another forty-five minutes to go, and I think of hair being grabbed, being dragged out of bed, you won't steer like a drunken sailor on my bloody watch, ya' shite for brains! I stay put.

Werner is standing to my right, talking fast. "Ease her back to the starboard. I mean move her to your port. Or your left. Whatever seems easier for you to remember. Too far! Ease it back, the other way! Too far! You're overcorrecting! We'll be feeling the waves again from the other side."

Minutes creep by, we're still not on course. We're still pounded by the sea. Boom! The stairway door opens and the first mate, Ken, appears. He shakes a big head of gray curls. "Oh," he says looking at me and smiling, "it's you. I was wondering who was making the ship do a 180. I thought Bob was enjoying too many sneaky coffees."

He nods and rolls a cigarette. "Skipper wants me to stay up here for awhile," he says. I glance at Bob, whose face is now as blue as his cap. What an insult! Sending another mate up to check on your watch. I feel the sweat on my hands, wipe them one at a time on my Gore-Tex jacket, wonder why in the world no one will step in.

Werner begins to shout at me. Jumps. Waves his arms. The others stare out the bridge windows, smoke, watch the horizon. I live. Time stops. Time stops until the watch is over. No one mentions the bad steering. My name will appear on the next day's roster of wheel-men. I am on from midnight to one A.M., noon to one P.M.

Now, as we head toward, shore, Werner begins the list. "Do not wander off. Do not interfere with the environment. Do not take anything, leave anything behind. If you must smoke," he adds, look-ing at me with narrowed eyes, "you must take all of the paper and tobacco back to the ship." I smile at him, my winsome American smile that says, yes, I know about this rule now, after three months of it. But I know Werner is not mean, he is Austrian and cannot help himself. Rules matter.

Maggie, the American driver, noses the boat in toward the rocky edge that will serve as our landing spot. We have a joke, she and I. No matter how many survival expert-hippie-environmental scien-tists there are in a boat, they all sit there trying not to be the first one out. They don't want to get wet. So they wait to see if someone, any-one else, will get out, grab the painter and pull, heave ho!, the small craft toward the beach. Maggie and I no longer stand for the sus-pense. When we come ashore, I always ride in her boat, sit in front, resting my knees against the inflated section that forms the prow. She stands in the back, eyes to the shore, no-nonsense and all con-centration. The boats don't flip easily, but you come in on a bad beach where there's a sharp drop-off and suddenly you have people hopping out into ten feet of frigid water.

As we edge toward the rocky shore, I look back, she nods, look-ing very Steve McQueen. At her signal, I haul my backpack on and perch myself, poised to push off and away from the boat, snag the painter and then heave-ho while she yanks up the prop and wades up to help. The scientists, a chubby Argentine and a game-legged Belgian, are out and pulling bits and pieces of things out of Ziploc plastic bags. When we have the boat secured, she radios in to the ship. They can see us from the bridge. It's perfectly bright and still and wildly monochromatic, except for the water, which defiantly refuses to go to black. It says, hey, I'm azure, I'm cobalt. Come on over and stare down to the bottom. I am air. See through me.

Werner tells us routinely not to go out alone, to always take a survival pack and a buddy. But after months of warnings and knowing that people are no more than one hundred yards behind the next hill, I need to break out. "This is the Antarctic," the survival guy likes to murmur, half smiling, "check your packs, and re-check your packs and never let the shore or the ship out of your sight. In the Antarctic, if you forget something or you get lost, you die." *Right,* I think. *Save the drama for the ladies back on the home shore.*

When the boat is secure, I light a cigarette with Mags in the protective shadow of a rock. The worst thing that has happened so far was running out of beer and potatoes for awhile. Then it was port of call Ushuaia, Patagonia. But those last few days counted as distress on board, after almost three weeks steaming from New Zealand, no land and finally, not a beer in sight. Now those were emergencies, squads of long-haired, forty- and fifty-year-old men, wearing tie-dyed T-shirts that say Water for Life! and ripping into supply closets, swearing and shouting that there must be some overlooked cases of Double Brown and Steinlager. Real emergencies of the gut.

Mags heads off to look at an iceberg grounded, rotting, a hundred yards up the coast. I turn and walk in the opposite direction. Werner is perched on a nearby hill, surveying the water with binoculars.

I walk for ten, twenty, thirty minutes. I am wearing old Timberland boots, a light yellow-beige suede, boots I bought at L.L. Bean in Freeport, Maine, on a weekend road trip with my Uncle Peter. These boots have seen wide stretches of the Appalachian Trail in Virginia and in Maine they have hiked the snow of Mt. Katahdin, the steep brush-covered treks over Arthur's Pass in New Zealand, through the Nullarbor Plain of Australia, into the foothills of the southernmost tip of the Andes. Boots mean business. They keep my feet warm and dry and are also aesthetically pleasing to me. I hate the rubber and Vibram-soled superboots worn by the crew. They look like they are about to walk on Mars, dressed as some 1950s kid would imagine a spaceship crew to look. No, these boots are leather and worn and have covered ground on every continent in the world. They offer me the promise of experience and the hold of an old friend's hand.

I look about but the rest of the shore party is nowhere in sight. We have a couple hours alone, then more boats will come, with more people from the crew. My window for solo exploration is narrow and I walk carefully but quickly over the rocky beach strewn with chunks of ice. I round the corner and stop.

Before me they rise. Bones. An immense skeleton, stretching along the shore in front of me. The individual vertebrae begin the size of softballs, grow to the size of coffee tables. I step into the tail. I pick my way through the vertebrae, touch enormous ribs that stretch toward the sky. They are wearing in the cold, salty air and their surface is gray, rough, pocked with caverns, holes where black grit has taken residence. It is big, crazy, a Georgia O'Keeffe meets Robert Motherwell moment, curvilinear forms twisting over black rock, fist-sized chunks of ice and all pinned down by a nickel-plated sky.

I step back outside the enormous ribs. I touch one arch, feel deep dives, resonating with power, and wit, and gentle understanding, all the things I've been told whales possess. While whales do not hold me in thrall, I have discovered kinship with them during these months at sea. You might even say I get what it's like to live like they do, owning the ocean in their hey, I'm as big as a football field way. Part of me lingers over the rude end so many have met: oil, bone, sushi.

I wonder how this particular whale met its fate, and how long it has taken for all not bone to dissolve away. Whales. Perfect for ocean, big, immensities that dive and move and sing across water that conducts sound farther than air.

But there's nothing but bone here. Things in the Antarctic don't decay the way they do in more temperate climes; they sort of freeze dry and tighten. Dead animals end up looking like the mother stored in the fruit cellar in *Psycho,* the work of an amateur taxidermist who was not entirely sure how to make a lifelike rendition. But this skeleton is picked clean.

It's cold on this beach, colder than I thought and the ends of my fingers are getting the familiar sensation of sorry, blood is now being diverted to essential organs, brain, liver, heart. It's the wind really, the air is almost balmy when it stops, but the wind wants to blow in a non-pattern of strong gusts and still. I take a few more notes then head out further, toward the point. The shore is not sandy, it is a narrow steep hill of black volcanic rocks and a rough, soil-like material. It's hard to walk along, not strolling, more picking your way along the fringe, eyes focused on the chunks, which in the glowing pale of this overcast day look entirely unremarkable.

Across this narrow finger of sea are enormous cliffs that rise and are lost in a thick foglike cloud belt. When we arrived here yesterday in the early dawn, it was a brilliantly sunny late afternoon, the light was purple and maroon and tangerine and the clouds were so much tulle thrown down over this quilt of rock and light and texture.

Light does strange things at sixty-five degrees south. Now, whatever impressionist canvas I saw in the morning light is gone. In its place is a different story, a landscape that reminds me that people do come here and get lost and freeze to death, looking up at those same black and white and indifferent cliffs.

I want to walk all the way to the point, to see how the land curls back on both sides, to see if any icebergs are floating on the horizon. As I get into rhythm on the sloping shore, I cast my eyes forward and see, perhaps not twenty yards away, a long black seal, head resting on the ground.

Dead? It is curled in a most unnatural way, head extended forward onto the rocks, hindquarters hiked in the air. It must smell me, Gore-Tex and Velcro and Capilene and polar fleece and mint-flavored lip balm. It lifts its head in panic, throwing its narrow, pointed snout around, fixing black eyes on me, opening its mouth and making a sound so unlike anything I have ever heard, a moaning, screaming fury. I stop when I am within ten yards because the seal has started to move. Once I watched a leopard seal, one of the carnivorous varieties, chase and attack like a dog when one of my shipmates threatened to come too close. It was the strangest animal attack I had witnessed, how amazingly swift the seal moved across the ice, how wide its mouth opened, how firmly it bit this young Swede's leg. Who would have thought that seals were fast on the attack when they were out of water?

But this is a Weddell seal, or a Crabeater, not the sort that has large, fang-like teeth and a desperate thirst for blood. I squat down, watching it try to move. There is a deep indentation in its back; it looks like someone has taken a two-by-four and struck it solidly across the spine, leaving behind a deep furrow.

Most likely, it was attacked by an orca or a large leopard seal and somehow managed to escape an immediate death. But it is clear she is on her way out, she knows it, I know it, and now it is here on this steep and unforgiving shore waiting to die, alone.

For reasons that remain unclear, this makes me both angry and sad. I begin to cry, wiping my nose on my blue Gore-Tex sleeve, listening to the poor miserable bitch's lonely baying. I wonder if I should kill it. Find a rock, pound its head in? What then?

I think about the doctor on the ship. Maybe she can put the seal to sleep, inject it with a dose of morphine and bring this all to a close. But I know no one will go for that. We're not supposed to take rocks, let alone wheel ourselves into assisted suicides for doomed marine mammals.

No, I am alone and powerless in this company. It rests its head against its front flippers, not closing its eyes, instead watching me and offering no sign of its thoughts.

So. I see how the beach will change, adding something new, something old to its collection. And the newest piece will rest there, another hundred or more years as the salt air gradually grinds bones to powder.

But first there will be the moment when time stops for those eyes, when they no longer register the color and smell of the world and then all the cells of that form will join the cascade of mortality. Oily skin collapsing into a hollow, fleshy flippers evaporating into stiff side boards, all the promise of the ocean and the hunt and the rolling, tumbling ecstatic engagement with sea and air washing away in the end.

I pull out my Olympus OM-1, a fully manual camera that gets the job done on the days when fancy electronic machines seize up in the cold. I am shooting black and white with a variety of colored filters. The filters add a depth and richness and will, I hope, give the newspaper readers some sense of what this place is. I know words already escape me. I screw on my 28mm lens and squat on my haunches, taking several wide-angle shots of the seal in her final resting spot. Then I change to the 70mm and come in close on her face. She is tired, annoyed, enraged that I have added a further dimension of menace to her deathbed.

I stop shooting, finish making notes about the frames and the time and place and the camera lens and film used. I scratch out some words, I write: *I came upon a seal with a broken back. Maybe some other meaning? Weave into longer narrative about the unforgiving nature of the Antarctic?* The seal is watching me from the corner of her eyes, head resting on front flippers. She looks like a big, fat, hairless dog. "There is nothing I can do for you, my friend," I say aloud. As I begin picking my way back toward the skeleton, I hear her expel a loud breath, turn and see a cloud of wet white vapor float from her nostrils, head resting on flippers.

I return to the whale, stand again in the rib cage. I cannot touch the sides or top when I am at the largest vertebrae. I am Jonah. I bend my head back, arching, and lift my hands toward the sky, bright pink-gloved hands meeting, hanging on to one another. The bones reach up with me, extending and curling and enclosing me in its hand. Whales sing different songs depending on where they live, songs changing continuously and individual singers adopting new material, singing in units, for hours, sometimes for days. I balance on a chunky piece of vertebrae, an ottoman of bone, part of the triptych, me all the way in, the seal stepping out, whale long since vanished. I continue to stretch, hold my hands over my head and arch back until the horizon seems to reorient itself, the entire earth and sky.

bill bryson

This excerpt from Bryson's best-selling book illustrates that humanity's primordial fear of wild beasts has survived the twenty-first century intact—and that the more you know about bear attacks, the less prepared you may be.

a walk in the woods

On the afternoon of July 5, 1983, three adult supervisors and a group of youngsters set up camp at a popular spot beside Lake Canimina in the fragrant pine forests of western Quebec, about eighty miles north of Ottawa, in a park called La Vérendrye Provincial Reserve. They cooked dinner and, afterward, in the correct fashion, secured their food in a bag and carried it a hundred or so feet into the woods, where they suspended it above the ground between two trees, out of the reach of bears.

About midnight, a black bear came prowling around the margins of the camp, spied the bag, and brought it down by climbing one of the trees and breaking a branch. He plundered the food and departed, but an hour later he was back, this time entering the camp itself, drawn by the lingering smell of cooked meat in the campers' clothes and hair, in their sleeping bags and tent fabric. It was to be a long night for the Canimina party. Three times between midnight and 3:30 A.M. the bear came to the camp.

Imagine, if you will, lying in the dark, alone in a little tent, nothing but a few microns of trembling nylon between you and the chill night air, listening to a four-hundred-pound bear moving around your campsite. Imagine its quiet grunts and mysterious snufflings, the clatter of upended cookware and sounds of moist gnawings, the pad of its feet and heaviness of its breath, the singing brush of its haunch along your tent side. Imagine the hot flood of adrenaline, that unwelcome tingling in the back of your arms, at the sudden rough bump of its snout against the foot of your tent, the alarming wild wobble of your frail shell as it roots through the backpack that you left casually propped by the entrance—with, you suddenly recall, a Snickers in the pouch. Bears adore Snickers, you've heard.

And then the dull thought—*Oh, God*—that perhaps you brought the Snickers in here with you, that it's somewhere in here, down by your feet or underneath you or—*Oh, shit, here it is.* Another bump of grunting head against the tent, this time near your shoulders. More crazy wobble. Then silence, a very long silence, and—wait, *shh-hhh* . . . yes!—the unutterable relief of realizing that the bear has withdrawn to the other side of the camp or shambled back into the woods. I tell you right now, I couldn't stand it.

So imagine then what it must have been like for poor little David Anderson, aged twelve, when at 3:30 A.M., on the third foray, his tent was abruptly rent with a swipe of claw and the bear, driven to distraction by the rich, unfixable, everywhere aroma of hamburger, bit hard into a flinching limb and dragged him shouting and flailing through the camp and into the woods. In the few moments it took the boy's fellow campers to unzip themselves from their accoutrements—and imagine, if you will, trying to swim out of suddenly voluminous sleeping bags, take up flashlights and makeshift cudgels, undo tent zips with helplessly fumbling fingers, and give chase—in those few moments, poor little David Anderson was dead.

Now imagine reading a nonfiction book packed with stories such as this—true tales soberly related—just before setting off alone on a camping trip of your own into the North American wilderness. The book to which I refer is *Bear Attacks: Their Causes and Avoidance,* by a Canadian academic named Stephen Herrero. If it is not the last word on the subject, then I really, really, really do not wish to hear the last word. Through long winter nights in New Hampshire, while snow piled up outdoors and my wife slumbered peacefully beside me, I lay saucer-eyed in bed reading clinically precise accounts of people gnawed pulpy in their sleeping bags, plucked whimpering from trees, even noiselessly stalked (I didn't know this happened!) as they sauntered unawares down leafy paths or cooled their feet in mountain streams. People whose one fatal mistake was to smooth their hair with a dab of aromatic gel, or eat juicy meat, or tuck a Snickers in their shirt pocket for later, or have sex, or even, possibly, menstruate, or in some small, inadvertent way pique the olfactory properties of the hungry bear. Or, come to that, whose fatal failing was simply to very, very unfortunate—to round a bend and find a moody male blocking the path, head rocking appraisingly, or wander unwittingly into the territory of a bear too slowed by age or idleness to chase down fleeter prey.

Now it is important to establish right away that the possibility of a serious bear attack on the Appalachian Trail is remote. To begin with, the really terrifying American bear, the grizzly—*Ursus horribilis,* as it is so vividly and correctly labeled—doesn't range east of the Mississippi, which is good news because grizzlies are large, powerful, and ferociously bad tempered. When Lewis and Clark went into the wilderness, they found that nothing unnerved the Native Indians more than the grizzly, and not surprisingly since you could riddle grizzly with arrows—positively porcupine it—and it would still keep coming. Even Lewis and Clark with their big guns were astounded and unsettled by the ability of the grizzly to absorb volleys of lead with barely a wobble.

Herrero recounts an incident that nicely conveys the near indestructibility of the grizzly. It concerns a professional hunter in Alaska named Alexei Pitka, who stalked a large male through snow and finally felled it with a well-aimed shot to the heart from a large-bore rifle. Pitka should probably have carried a card with him that said: "First make sure the bear is dead. Then put gun down." He advanced cautiously and spent a minute or two watching the bear for movement, but when there was none he set the gun against a tree (big mistake!) and strode forward to claim his prize. Just as he reached it, the bear sprang up, clapped its expansive jaws around the front of Pitka's head, as if giving him a big kiss, and with a single jerk tore off his face.

Miraculously, Pitka survived. "I don't know why I set that darn gun against the tree," he said later. (Actually, what he said was, "Mrffff mmmpg nnnmmm mffffffn," on account of having no lips, teeth, nose, tongue, or other vocal apparatus.)

If I were to be pawed and chewed—and this seemed to me entirely possible, the more I read—it would be by a black bear, *Ursus americanus*. There are at least five hundred thousand black bears in North America, possibly as many as seven hundred thousand. They are notably common in the hills along the Appalachian Trail (indeed, they often *use* the trail, for convenience), and their numbers are growing. Grizzlies, by contrast, number no more than thirty-five thousand in the whole of North America, and just 1,000 in the mainland United States, principally in and around Yellowstone National Park. Of the two species, black bears are generally smaller (though this is a decidedly relative condition; a male black bear can still weigh up to 650 pounds) and unquestionably more retiring.

Black bears rarely attack. But there's the thing. Sometimes they do. All bears are agile, cunning, and immensely strong, and they are always hungry. If they want to kill you and eat you, they can, and pretty much whenever they want. That doesn't happen often, but—and here is the absolutely salient point—once would be enough. Herrero is at pains to stress that black bear attacks are infrequent, relative to their numbers. For 1900 to 1980, he found just twenty-three confirmed black bear killings of humans (about half the number of killings by grizzlies), and most of these were out West or in Canada. In New Hampshire there has not been an unprovoked fatal attack on a human by a bear since 1784. In Vermont, there has never been one.

I wanted very much to be calmed by these assurances but could never quite manage the necessary leap of faith. After noting that just five hundred people were attacked and hurt by black bears between 1960 and 1980—twenty-five attacks a year from a resident population of at least half a million bears—Hererro adds that most of these injuries were not severe. "The typical black bear–inflicted injury," he writes blandly, "is minor and usually involves only a few scratches or light bites." Pardon me, but what exactly is a light bite? Are we talking a playful wrestle and gummy nips? I think not. And is five hundred certified attacks really such a modest number, considering how few people go into the North American woods? And how foolish must one be to be reassured by the information that no bear has killed a human in Vermont or New Hampshire in two hundred years? That's not because the bears have signed a treaty, you know. There's nothing to say that they won't start a modest rampage tomorrow.

So let us imagine that a bear does go for us out in the wilds. What are we to do? Interestingly, the advised strategems are exactly opposite for grizzly and black bear. With a grizzly, you should make for a tall tree, since grizzlies aren't much for climbing. If a tree is not available, then you should back off slowly, avoiding direct eye contact. All the books tell you that if the grizzly comes for you, on no account should you run. This is the sort of advice you get from someone who is sitting at a keyboard when he gives it. Take it from me, if you are in an open space with no weapons and a grizzly comes for you, run. You may as well. If nothing else, it will give you something to do with the last seven seconds of your life. However, when the grizzly overtakes you, as it most assuredly will, you should fall to the ground and play dead. A grizzly may chew on a limp form for a minute or two but generally will lose interest and shuffle off. With black bears, however, playing dead is futile, since they will continue chewing on you until you are considerably past caring. It is foolish to climb a tree because black bears are adroit climbers and, as Herrero dryly notes, you will simply end up fighting the bear in a tree.

To ward off an aggressive black bear, Herrero suggests making a lot of noise, banging pots and pans together, throwing sticks and rocks, and "running at the bear." (Yeah, right. You first, Professor.) On the other hand, he then adds judiciously, these tactics could "merely provoke the bear." Well, thanks. Elsewhere he suggests that hikers should consider making noises from time to time—singing a song, say—to alert bears of their presence, since a startled bear is more likely to be an angry bear, but then a few pages later he cautions that "there may be danger in making noise," since that can attract a hungry bear that might otherwise overlook you.

The fact is, no one can tell you what to do. Bears are unpredictable, and what works in one circumstance may not work in another. In 1973, two teenagers, Mark Seeley and Michael Whitten, were out for a hike in Yellowstone when they inadvertently crossed between a female black bear and her cubs. Nothing worries and antagonizes a female bear more than to have people between her and her brood. Furious, she turned and gave chase—despite the bear's lolloping gait, it can move at up to thirty-five miles an hour—and the two boys scrambled up trees. The bear followed Whitten up his tree, clamped her mouth around his right foot, and slowly and patiently tugged him from his perch. (Is it me, or can you feel your fingernails scraping through the bark?) On the ground, she began mauling him extensively. In an attempt to distract the bear from his friend, Seeley shouted at it, whereupon the bear came and pulled him out of his tree, too. Both young men played dead—precisely the wrong thing to do, according to all the instruction manuals—and the bear left.

I won't say I became obsessed with all this, but it did occupy my thoughts a great deal in the months while I waited for spring to come. My particular dread—the vivid possibility that left me staring at tree shadows on the bedroom ceiling night after night—was having to lie in a small tent, alone in an inky wilderness, listening to a foraging bear outside and wondering what its intentions were. I was especially riveted by an amateur photograph in Herrero's book, taken late at night by a camper with a flash at a campground out West. The photograph caught four black bears as they puzzled over a suspended food bag. The bears were clearly startled but not remotely alarmed by the flash. It was not the size or demeanor of the bears that troubled me—they looked almost comically unaggressive, like four guys who had gotten a Frisbee caught up a tree—but their numbers. Up to that moment it had not occurred to me that bears might prowl in parties. What on earth would I do if *four* bears came into my camp? Why, I would die, of course. Literally shit myself lifeless. I would blow my sphincter out my backside like one of those unrolling paper streamers you get at children's parties—I daresay it would even give a merry toot—and bleed to a messy death in my sleeping bag.

Herrero's book was written in 1985. Since that time, according to an article in *The New York Times,* bear attacks in North America have increased by 25 percent. The *Times* article also noted that bears are far more likely to attack humans in the spring following a bad berry year. The previous year had been a very bad berry year. I didn't like the feel of any of this.

Then there were all the problems and particular dangers of solitude. I still have my appendix, and any number of other organs that might burst or sputter in the empty wilds. What would I do then? What if I fell from a ledge and broke my back? What if I lost the trail in blizzard or fog, or was nipped by a venomous snake, or lost my footing on moss-slickened rocks crossing a stream and cracked my head a concussive blow? You could drown in three inches of water on your own. You could die from a twisted ankle. No, I didn't like the feel of this at all.

deborah archer

Archer's tale is one of love and regret, in which the un-earthing of the hidden functions as both metaphor and setting. While sketching the beauty of discovering bits of the unknown, Archer also notes that if you "bring something to the surface . . . you become responsible for it." Throughout, this intensely personal piece accu-rately describes our tendency to allow our past to arouse in us a desire we can never fill: to fix a moment that has already been lost.

finding fossils

Take me to the river. Dip me in the water, wash me down.

DAVID BYRNE

A danger comes with digging into the earth, never knowing what you might excavate. As well as a temptation, to be sure; to push in, fingers flexed, feeling your way by inches; to touch what has been so carefully arranged not to be touched.

I sit here, now, at my desk, palming the crinoids, brachiopods, and corals, marveling at them. They seem my possessions, yet so emphatically are not mine, I must smile as I write this. Here lies part of the danger: bring something to the surface and you become responsible for it, marked by it, attached to it. You can't put it back because it will never fit how and where it once did. You've changed the landscape. And at times I feel the burden of my excavations like the weight of a lover I wronged very long ago. But then I'm speaking of more than fossils.

I want to trace a fire: define the spark and delineate the slow smolder to combustion. When did I recognize this acquaintance as my friend? What secret did we first share? Was it hers or mine, to begin with? At what moment did I see her and feel love? And when did I know it as such?

It's important that I follow it back, chart it, fix it, put it on a nice, linear timeline. Manageable, I want to make it manageable and able to be dealt with rationally. If I can commit it to language I'll have a tidy bundle of occurrences, bridled by syntax and bound by convention. That's what I need; it's what we all need, right? We can't think otherwise. And yet I know already, before the beginning, that the following will be nothing more than an exercise, a little workout. For how can I say the space that is us?

Perhaps the first question I should answer is why I feel compelled to try. I'll tell you: because part of my life depends upon it. In another time and place I might be writing love poetry instead, or maybe some lusty little limerick personally experienced. Or she and I might even be writing together, a new language, upon each other's bodies. But this time and place calls for sublimation: I feel connected to her, yes, but a connection that must be explained some other way.

So let me talk about chemistry, the sharing of atoms at the base molecular level, the mingling of auras, the compatibility of Cancer and Pisces. Chance: a particular angle of light caught and reflected. I nearly recall an instant when our pulse-beats vibrated into mid-air and merged momentarily in almost-silent thunder. But what, finally, does any of this explain? Does it move me any closer, or farther? It moves me, most definitely, but in-place. I need more language. Slather these pages wild and dripping with words in hope that I will find it, make it mine, and be done with it.

I opened my eyes, and she was there. That is all. Or at least that is all I honestly remember of it.

It was spring—March—and the sounds of ice cracking on the creek behind us lulled and reassured me. Such a tender breaking; rhythmic, patient. The creek takes it so slowly, the ice seems to be willing, anticipating its return to fluid. So all one hears is a soft "crack," but one must hear that because no matter how willing, the heartbeat moment of separation which precedes any union deserves its sound to be heard and appreciated.

Gold chains dribbled from her neck, and they were coming down to meet me. Hands full, cupping her newly-found ancient treasures, arms outstretched, moving toward me.

"Look what I've got!"

She offers me her hands. I try to concentrate, to look at what she wants me to see.

"Check out this speckled crinoid."

A dot of creek mud is drying on the outside of her right index finger, just above the first crease.

"Yeah, that's cool; I've never seen one like that."

"And this piece of bone . . . what do you think this is?"

The dark bone lies in easy contrast to the flesh of her palm. I focus, attempting to decode a history. So smooth here; the lines deep, but polished by time and friction. And yet so rough there, dry, jagged even; the part that has not touched, or been touched, enough. Her fingers curl slightly, upward and inward, ready to close in a split second, withdrawing bone, palm, lines, history. I wait. Steady. No sign of closure. I reach out, right thumb and index finger gingerly grasping the bone, tips brushing her palm, knuckles kissing the curl of her fingers. For one breath, my hand is almost in hers.

Just a few months before, the fossils themselves had been everything. A small group of us began exploring the banks and beds of the Little Nemaha River, near Unadilla, about thirty minutes southeast of Lincoln, Nebraska. I don't really know how it started: Ward was already an amateur fossiler; Renay and Stacey had found some "stuff" while fishing and they showed it to Ward; Mikki got interested; eventually one of them asked if I'd like to join them. I don't remember if it was Mikki who asked.

I was hooked within the first ten minutes. My first time out I found a large, fully intact *Spirifer* brachiopod. I had no idea what it was but sensed that it was something "good," so I toted it upstream to where Ward was digging.

"Is this anything?"

"Goddamn! That's a brachiopod! Where the fuck did you find that?!"

And so it began. For Renay, it was a kind of competition; she always located the "best" spot, found the "biggest" crinoid, collected the "most" bones. For Ward it seemed a more serious fun. For me, it was pure sensual pleasure. Fingers sifting sand; mud squishing between toes; eyes slow-dancing across zillions of rocks, pebbles, sticks, and tufts of weeds for one glimpse of a discrete shape or a subtle texture—that one glimpse which is the difference between finding fossils and looking for them. The sweat, the burrs, the rolling lap of the musky Little Nemaha. I held in my hands the remains of creatures who were alive three hundred million years ago. Alive here, where I crouched, underneath a vast ocean. The connection was unfathomable.

I don't know when I began to recognize that it seemed to be the same for Mikki. None of us really talked while fossiling, save the occasional hoots of discovery followed by lively but succinct affirmations. A quiet, solitary pursuit—each to her or his own space and concentration—one does not fossil *with* someone. But there were the drives to and from, and for some reason, I always rode with Mikki.

That smell inside her truck . . . what is it? Clean, deep, slightly spicy, laced with cedar or sandalwood, maybe? I thought it her scent, until I finally asked what shampoo, soap, laundry detergent she used; the source, please, of this delectable air. She said it was the stuff she used to clean the upholstery. I'm still not sure if I believe her. I mean how embarrassing, aroused to the verge of wetness by two-dollar leather cleaner from Target. Not that Mikki knew that I was aroused . . . well, maybe she did . . . I don't know. She knew I liked the smell, and that became a sort of joke for her to tease me with.

"Hey, Deb, you wanna go fossiling? I've just cleaned the upholstery in my truck," she would taunt me over the phone, her voice rising just-so on the words "upholstery" and "truck" so that it wasn't a statement but rather unfinished, expectant, as if she might say something more, as if she were waiting for me to say something.

Was that how it started—the innuendo, the playful bantering— did it start with the damn smell inside her truck? No, that can't be right because either the smell wasn't there or I didn't notice it for months. No, it started before that. Again, I am stuck: *when* doesn't really matter; I want to understand *why*. And yet it appears I am capable only of telling a story: this is what seems to have happened, as far as I am able to grasp it. It's a fine enough story and ought to do, finding fossils and friendship; once upon a time, two people simply spoke to each other. Except that I find myself, increasingly, in a near-unbearable ache of wanting to kiss her mouth.

So here I sit, tugging at loose threads, hoping to snag the one that will suddenly make clear the entire pattern or, at the very least, will undo it.

I was approaching something about talking, about speaking to one another—the quiet that attends fossiling, the sketchy absent-mindedness of our early conversations, the gradual unfolding of past lives and contemporary longings. The first secret shared was Mikki's, and I suppose that marks the initiation of friendship, that first little foray into the realm of trust. And, yes, I still hold it. The second was mine. Then eventually came those secrets born mutually, simultaneously; those secrets breathed into being through the existence of *us,* that strange and ethereal entity *we,* not her not me, somehow both and yet neither. Conceived through communion, it is the evidence, the confirmation of our connection, this entity, and she cannot even think of it, remember or imagine any of it without me. Nor can I without her. But what neither of us knew at its inception, yet would come to be intractably unmistakable, is that this *we* is other to both of us.

Talking—yes, we sometimes talked, but mostly I watched her. She handled each fossil, rock, and bone fragment tenderly, deliberately. She turned each find over and over, noting each nuance, brushing away the camouflaging dirt with her fingertips and her breath. She wetted them in the creek then began again, turning, examining—as if what she sought from/with them could never be sated. And yet the touching, washing, exploring satisfied her completely.

Mikki was gentle; that's what I saw. And I remembered what gentleness is and that I, too, once was gentle. Her hands and fingers graceful; tentative but precise. I imagined the delicacy and delight with which those hands must partake of living creatures, the polymorphous appreciation of flesh, muscle, bone; breast, brow, instep, the crook of the elbow, the quirk of a toenail. I wanted to be gentle again, to relish all that enchanted me. I watched Mikki, felt the hotspot of the sun on the nape of my neck, the polish and scrape of the rocks against my bare soles, and wondered, just briefly, what synesthetic word might capture the texture, scent, heat, and meaning of this space.

At some point, Mikki and I began fossiling alone, just the two of us. I'm not sure how that happened either; it seems to me now as if suddenly it was just us—no discussion, no explanation. Perhaps Mikki and I went one time when no one else could go, and it simply stayed that way. Clearly we enjoyed it since either one of us might have picked up the phone to invite the others. Neither of us did. Fossiling became Mikki's and mine.

December 2: one of those magical Midwest winter warmfronts. In the midst of gray snowy days, brittle windchills, and barren landscapes—surprise—the sun shimmies forth in a sweltering sixty-five degrees. People smile, venture about in shirt sleeves anxious to make the most of the moment. Mikki and I headed for Unadilla. With the prickly weed growth of spring and summer a flattened yellow-brown, the hike was easy, and we chased our little creekbed further than we'd gone before. We discovered a sandy white beach with a seductive rock bed just a few yards further up. The problem was that our great discovery lay on the other side of the creek. We stood for a moment, gazing at the coveted spot. When Mikki turned to me, beaming, reaching for her boot laces, I would have sworn she was ten years old.

"You've got to be kidding me! That water's gonna be freezing fucking cold!"

But I was already untying my own boots. Before I could get my first one off, Mikki had doffed boots and socks, rolled up her jeans, and slipped into that damn water. She moved swiftly, smoothly through the knee-deep current, as if it were a summer wading pool. The shocking frigidity proved too much for me, however, so that only one foot and leg could bear it at a time. Each step forward with one foot sent the other flying up and back with all the force of the swear words I hurled. Mikki stood poised, thawing her toes in the sun-hot sand, engulfed in full-body laughter.

"You're splashing the water ON TO YOURSELF!"

"I (splash) can't (splash) HELP IT!"

She doubled over, laughing so hard that no sound came out. She was right, of course; as I splash-cursed my way across, I drenched my entire backside. It didn't matter. I would have dropped to my knees and plunged my face into that water to make her laugh like that.

Something happened that day, turned and surfaced, something more than earth and fossils. Perhaps it was the serendipity of it all— the unexpected warmth, the inviting landscape, the exciting discovery—catching us unguarded. We stuck close together. We talked; I know we talked, although I can't recall the specific content or words. What comes to me now is the feeling, as sharp and tender and rife with tacit possibility as sudden heat in December. We were becoming joined in something beyond fossiling. I know we both felt it, although neither acknowledged it. Acknowledge what? Say what? I enjoy your company? I'm having a really good time? Not enough, not even close. Where are the words for those feelings, those sensations that emanate from a place where language does not even exist? What does one do with *that*?

Nothing. We did nothing with it for a long time. Although we occasionally went fossiling bundled in heavy coats and gloves just to be out there, to be in that place. Not the geographic location, exactly. I mean, we would say we were going to Unadilla, and that was in fact where we would drive to. But the place we sought was *us,* the inarticuable connection that effervesced whenever *we* became present. And here it becomes almost impossible to talk about it.

The location, the drive away—these things are important. The drive to some *other* area, not where Mikki and I lived, worked, and carried each of our daily lives. The location itself—a slit in the earth, inviting us to go down, to press our bones to hers, inhale her, finger her treasures, linger in her wetness. She received us, simply, allowing us to unfold her: she beckoned *us* into being.

We did, at last, acknowledge it—or at least we tried to. The only words we could think of to say, "I love you"; true, but still insufficient. We would try again, each of us stumbling, groping through stilted telephone conversations and brief moments of soliloquy, about to arrive at something, cut short by "I don't know" or "that's not it" or "I don't know how to say it." But of course we did not know how to say it; there is no way to say it. *We* came into being out there, some place *other,* and every time the *we* spilled over into each of our daily lives, it became more and more other to each of us.

We had uncovered more than we'd bargained for, been offered a gift we were ill-equipped to receive. Having come so close, we seemed compelled to recreate distance, to reestablish boundaries. "I need to figure out what this means to me," "I must focus on myself," each of us said, in so many words, more than slightly shaken and certainly confused.

It seems to me now, sometimes, that there must have been other options, other possibilities available to us. We might have responded beyond our well-learned fear of change, of all that is unknown, different, our fear of revelation itself, which is nothing more—nor less—than fear of ourselves. Instead, giddiness gave way to guilt, recognition to responsibility. Each word we uttered became suspect, an ulterior accomplice to some indefinite transgression.

Mikki and I ceased fossiling together for some time. We began again, slowly, back in a group. Then about a year-and-a-half after our first trip to Unadilla, Mikki and I returned on a remarkably warm New Year's Day. The landscape, of course, had changed: the mutations and evolutions of creekbeds, stories all in themselves.

We couldn't go far, the creek being large, unstable sheets of ice. I stood alone out on the farthest point I could safely reach, stretching my eyes toward the bend in the bank that obscured the beach, the site of our coming together, and of our pulling apart. I squinted until she blurred—the womb of the earth who had given birth to *us*. This day, as before, she held the weight of us, drifted with our breathing, shifted with our toes and fingers. She harbored us, celebrated the energy of *us* permeating her 300 million years back.

"Hey, Deb, you've gotta see this!" floated out to me, summoning me back through time and space.

Mikki had found something.

I bowed my head and smiled into the earth.

john mcphee

John McPhee's work represents the very best of nature writing, and this excerpt from his award-winning book shows the way McPhee can weave personal and scientific observation together into a narrative as powerful as any novel. During a visit to Scotland, McPhee and his family go in search of the Loch Ness monster—and find that the image of this beast is everywhere.

pieces of the frame

On the edge of Invermoriston forest, I was trying to explain raised beaches, the fifty-foot beaches of Scotland, so called because they are about that far above the sea. Waves never touch them. Tides don't come near reaching them. Shell and shingle, whitened like bones, they are aftereffects of the ice, two miles thick, that once rested on Scotland and actually shoved Scotland down into the earth. When the ice melted, the sea slowly came up, but so did the land, sluggishly recovering its buoyancy over the molten center of things. After the sea had increased as much as it was going to, the land kept rising, and beaches were lifted into the air, some as much as fifty feet.

That was how I understood the story, and I was doing what I could to say it in a way that would make it intelligible to an audience of four children (mine—all girls, and all quite young), but the distractions were so numerous that I never really had a chance. My family and I were having a lakeside lunch—milk, potato sticks, lambs' tongues, shortbread, white chocolate, Mini-Dunlop cheese— beside a stream in a grove of birches that was backed by dense reforested pines. The pines covered steep slopes toward summits two thousand feet above us. It was late spring, but there were snowfields up there nonetheless, and the water we drank had been snow in the mountains that morning.

Near us, another family, also with small children, was having what was evidently a birthday picnic. They had arrived after we were already settled, and they had chosen—I don't know why, with acre upon acre of unpeopled and essentially similar terrain to move about in—to unpack all their special effects (a glistening white cake, noisemakers, conical cardboard orange hats) only forty or fifty yards away. I tried to ignore them and go on with my ruminations on the raised beaches. There were no raised beaches in that place, at least not in the usual form, but the children had seen them and had played on them elsewhere in the Highlands, and I thought that if they could understand how such phenomena had come to be, they might in turn be able to imagine the great, long lake now before them—Loch Ness—as the sea loch, the arm of the Atlantic, that it once was, and how marine creatures in exceptional variety had once freely moved in and out of it, some inevitably remaining.

Losing interest in the birthday party, my youngest daughter said, "I want to see the monster."

This had already become another distraction. In much the way that, in the United States, NO HUNTING signs are posted on every other tree along blacktop country roads, cardboard signs of about the same size had been tacked to trees and poles along the lake. There were several in the birch grove. Printed in royal blue on a white background, they said, "Any members of the general public who genuinely believe they have seen an unusual creature or object in or on the shores of Loch Ness are requested to report the occurrence to Expedition Headquarters at Achnahannet, two miles south of Urquhart Castle. If unable to report in person, they may telephone the Expedition (No. Drumnadrochit 358). Reports will only be of interest from people willing to give their full name and address and fill in a Sighting Report Form, which will be sent on request. Thank you for your cooperation. Published by the Loch Ness Phenomena Investigation Bureau, 23 Ashley Place, London, S.W. 1, and printed at the Courier Office, Inverness."

"What makes you think the monster wants to see you?" I said to my youngest one. "There won't be any sightings today, anyway. There's too much wind out there."

The wind on the lake was quite strong. It was blowing from the north. There were whitecaps, and the ranks of the waves were uniform in our perspective, which was high. Watching the waves, I remembered canoe trips when I was ten or eleven years old, trying to achieve some sort of momentum against white-capping headwinds between Rogers Rock and Sabbath Day Point on Lake George. Lake George was for beginners, who could learn in its unwild basin the essentials they would need to know on longer trips in later years in wildernesses they would seek out. But now, watching the north wind go down the lake in Scotland, I could not remember headwinds anywhere as powerful and savage as they had been in that so-styled lake for beginners, and I could feel again the skin rubbed off my hands. The likeness was in more than the wind, however. It was in the appearance, the shape, and the scale—about a mile from side to side—of Loch Ness, which, like the American lake, is at least twenty times longer than it is wide, a long deep cleft, positioned like some great geophysical ax-cut between its lateral hills. I remember being told, around the fire at night, stories of the first white man who saw Lake George. He was a traveling French priest, intent on converting the Mohawks and other nations of the Iroquois. He had come from Orléans. He said that the lake was the most beautiful he had ever seen, and he named it the Lake of the Blessed Sacrament. The Indians, observing that the priest blessed them with his right hand, held him down and chewed away his fingers until the fingers were stumps and the hand was pulp. Later, when the priest did not stop his work, the Indians axed the top of his skull, and then cut off his head.

Lake George is so clear that objects far below its surface, such as white stones or hovering bass, can be seen in total definition. The water of Loch Ness is so dark with the tints of peat that on a flat-calm day it looks like black glass. Three or four feet below the surface is an obscurity so complete that experienced divers have retreated from it in frustration, and in some cases in fear. A swimmer looking up toward a bright sky from a distance of inches beneath the surface has the impression that he is afloat in very dark tea. Lake George is nearly two hundred feet deep in places, has numerous islands, and with its bays and points, is prototypal of beautiful mountain lakes of grand dimension in every part of the world. Loch Ness is like almost no other lake anywhere. Its shores are formidably and somewhat unnaturally parallel. It has no islands. Its riparian walls go straight down. Its bottom is flat, and in most places is seven hundred feet deep, a mean depth far greater than the mean depth of the North Sea. Loch Ness holds a fantastic volume of water, the entire runoff of any number of northern glens—Glen Affric, Glen Cannich, Glen Moriston, Glen Farar, Glen Urquhart. All of these valleys, impressive in themselves, are petals to Glen More, the Great Glen. Loch Ness is the principal basin of the Great Glen, and the Great Glen is the epicenter of the Highlands. A few miles of silt, carried into the lake by the rivers, long ago dammed the seaward end, changing the original sea loch into a fresh-water lake, but so slowly that marine creatures trapped within it had a chance to adapt themselves. Meanwhile the land kept rising, and with it the new lake. The surface of Loch Ness is fifty-two feet above sea level.

My wife listened with some interest when, repeating all this, I made an expanded attempt to enrich everyone's experience, but nothing was going through to the children. "I want to see the monster," the youngest one said again, speaking for all. They didn't want to know how or why the so-called monster might have come into that particular lake. They just wanted to see it. But the wind was not slowing up out there on the lake.

All of us looked now at the family that was having the birthday picnic, for the father had stood up shouting and had flung a large piece of the birthday cake at his wife. It missed her and spattered in bits in the branches of a tree. She shouted back at him something to the effect that he was depraved and cruel, and he in turn bellowed that she was a carbon of their bloody mother and that he was fed up. She said she had had all she could ever take, and was going home— to England, apparently. With that, she ran up the hillside and soon was out of sight in the pines. At first, he did not follow, but he suddenly was on his feet and shouting serial threats as he too went out of range in the pines. Meanwhile, their children, all but one, were crying. The one that wasn't crying was the girl whose birthday it was, and she just sat without moving, under a conical orange hat, staring emptily in the direction of the lake.

We went to our car and sat in it for some time, trying not to be keeping too obvious an eye on the children in the birch grove, who eventually began to play at being the bailiffs of the birthday picnic and made such a mess that finally the girl whose birthday it was began to cry, and she was still crying when her father came out of the pines. I then drove north.

The road—the A-82—stayed close to the lake, often on ledges that had been blasted into the mountainsides. The steep forests continued, broken now and again, on one shore or the other, by fields of fern, clumps of bright-yellow whin, and isolated stands of cedar. Along the far shore were widely separated houses and farms, which to the eyes of a traveler appeared almost unbelievably luxuriant after the spare desolation of some of the higher glens. We came to the top of the rise and suddenly saw, on the right-hand side of the road, on the edge of a high meadow that sloped sharply a considerable distance to the lake, a cluster of caravans and other vehicles, arranged in the shape of a C, with an opening toward the road—much like a circle of prairie schooners, formed for protection against savage attack. All but one or two of the vehicles were painted bright lily-pad green. The compound, in its compact half-acre, was surrounded by a fence, to keep out, among other things, sheep, which were grazing all over the slope in deep green turn among buttercups, daisies, and thistles. Gulls above beat hard into the wind, then turned and planed toward the south. Gulls are inland birds in Scotland, there being so little distance from anywhere to the sea. A big fireplace had been made from rocks of the sort that were scattered all over the meadow. And on the lakeward side a platform had been built, its level eminence emphasizing the declivity of the hill, which dropped away below it. Mounted on the platform was a 35mm motion picture camera with an enormous telephoto lens. From its point of view, two hundred feet above the lake and protruding like a gargoyle, the camera could take in a bedazzling panorama that covered thousands of acres of water.

This was Expedition Headquarters, the principal field station of the Loch Ness Phenomena Investigation Bureau—dues five pounds per annum, life membership one hundred pounds, tax on donations recoverable under covenant. Those who join the bureau receive newsletters and annual reports, and are eligible to participate in the fieldwork if they so desire. I turned into the compound and parked between two bright green, reconditioned, old London taxis. The central area had long since been worn grassless, and was covered at this moment with fine-grain dust. People were coming and going. The place seemed rather public, as if it were a depot. No one even halfway interested in the natural history of the Great Glen would think of driving up the A-82 without stopping in there. Since the A-82 is the principal route between Glasgow and Inverness, it is not surprising that the apparently amphibious creature as yet unnamed, the so-called Loch Ness Monster, has been seen not only from the highway but on it.

The atmosphere around the headquarters suggested a scientific frontier and also a boom town, much as Cape Canaveral and Cocoa Beach do. There were, as well, cirrus wisps of show business and fine arts. Probably the one word that might have been applied to everyone present was adventurer. There was, at any rate, nothing emphatically laboratorial about the place, although the prevailing mood seemed to be one not of holiday but of matter-of-fact application, and patient dedication. A telephone call came in that day, to the caravan that served as an office, from a woman who owned an inn south of Inverfarigaig, on the other side of the lake. She said that she had seen the creature that morning just forty yards offshore—three humps, nothing else to report, and being very busy just now, thank you very much, good day. This was recorded, with no particular display of excitement, by an extremely attractive young woman who appeared to be in her late twenties, an artist from London who had missed but one summer at Loch Ness in seven years. She wore sandals, dungarees, a firmly stretched black pullover, and gold earrings. Her name was Mary Piercy, and her toes were painted pink. The bulletin board where she recorded the sighting resembled the kind used in railway stations for the listing of incoming trains.

The office walls were decorated with photographs of the monster in various postures—basking, cruising, diving, splashing, looking up inquisitively. A counter was covered with some of the essential bibliography: the bureau's annual report (twenty-nine sightings in the previous year), J.A. Carruth's *Loch Ness and Its Monster* (The Abbey Press, Fort Augustus), Tim Dinsdale's *Loch Ness Monster* (Routledge and Kegan Paul, London), and a report by the Joint Air Reconnaissance Center of the Royal Air Force on a motion picture of the monster swimming about half a mile on the lake's surface. These books and documents could, in turn, lead the interested reader to less available but nonetheless highly relevant works such as R.T. Gould's *The Loch Ness Monster and Others* and Constance Whyte's *More Than a Legend*.

My children looked over the photographs with absorption but not a great deal of awe, and they bought about a dozen postcards with glossy prints of a picture of the monster—three humps showing, much the same sight that the innkeeper had described—that had been taken by a man named Stuart, directly across the lake from Urquhart Castle. The three younger girls then ran out into the meadow and began to pick daisies and buttercups. Their mother and sister sat down in the sun to read about the creature in the lake, and to write postcards. We were on our way to Inverness, but with no need to hurry. "Dear Grammy, we came to see the monster today."

. . .

From the office to the camera observation platform to the caravan that served as a pocket mess hall, I wandered around among the crew, was offered and accepted tea, and squinted with imaginary experience up and down the lake, where the whitecaps had, if anything, increased. Among the crew at the time were two Canadians, a Swede, an Australian, three Americans, two Englishmen, a Welshman, and one Scot. Two were women. When I asked one of the crew members if he knew what some of the others did, vocationally, when they were not at Loch Ness, he said, "I'm not sure what they are. We don't go into that." This was obviously a place where now was all that mattered, and in such a milieu it is distinctly pleasant to accept that approach to things. Nonetheless, I found that I couldn't adhere completely to this principle, and I did find out that one man was a medical doctor, another a farmer, another a retired naval officer, and that several, inevitably, were students. The daily watch begins at four in the morning and goes on, as one fellow put it, "as long as we can stand up." It has been the pattern among the hundreds of sightings reported that the early morning hours are the most promising ones. Camera stations are manned until ten at night, dawn and sunset being so close to midnight at that latitude in summer, but the sentries tend to thin out with the lengthening of the day. During the autumn, the size of the crew reduces precipitously toward one.

One man lives at the headquarters all year long. His name is Clem Lister Skelton. "I've been staring at that bloody piece of water since five o'clock," he said, while he drank tea in the mess caravan.

"Is there a technique?" I asked him.

"Just look," he said. "Look. Run your eye over the water in one quick skim. What we're looking for is not hard to see. You just sit and sort of gaze at the loch, that's all. Mutter a few incantations. That's all there is to do. In wintertime, very often, it's just myself.

And of course one keeps a very much more perfunctory watch in the winter. I saw it once in a snowstorm, though, and that was the only time I've had a clear view of the head and neck. The neck is obviously very mobile. The creature was quite big, but it wasn't as big as a seventy-foot MFV. Motor fishing vessel. I'd been closer to it, but I hadn't seen as much of it before. I've seen it eight times. The last time was in September. Only the back. Just the sort of upturned boat, which is the classic view of it."

Skelton drank some more tea, and refilled a cup he had given me. "I must know what it is," he went on. "I shall never rest peacefully until I know what it is. Some of the largest creatures in the world are out there, and we can't name them. It may take ten years, but we're going to identify the genus. Most people are not as fanatical as I, but I would like to see this through to the end, if I don't get too broke first."

Skelton is a tall, offhand man, English, with reddish hair that is disheveled in long strings from the thinning crown of his head. In outline, Skelton's life there in the caravan on the edge of the high meadow over the lake, in a place that must be uncorrectably gloomy during the wet rains of winter, seemed cagelike and hopeless to me—unacceptably lonely. The impression he gave was of a man who had drawn a circle around himself many hundreds of miles from the rest of his life. But how could I know? He was saying that he had flown Supermarine Spitfires for the R.A.F. during the Second World War. His father had been a soldier, and when Skelton was a boy, he lived, as he put it, "all over the place." As an adult, he became first an actor, later a writer and director of films. He acted in London in plays like *March Hare* and *Saraband for Dead Lovers*. One film he directed was, in his words, "a dreadful thing called *Saul and David*." These appearances on the surface apparently did not occur so frequently that he needed to do nothing else for his livelihood. He also directed, in the course of many years, several hundred educational films. The publisher who distributed some of these films was David James, a friend of Skelton's, and at that time a member of

Parliament. James happened to be, as well, the founder of the Loch Ness Phenomena Investigation Bureau—phenomena, because, for breeding purposes, there would have to be at least two monsters living in the lake at any one time, probably more, and in fact two had on occasion been sighted simultaneously. James asked Skelton if he would go up to the lake and give the bureau the benefit of his technical knowledge of movie cameras. "Anything for a laugh," Skelton had said to James. This was in the early 1960s. "I came for a fortnight," Skelton said now, in the caravan. "And I saw it. I wanted to know what it was, and I've wanted to know what it was ever since. I thought I'd have time to write up here, but I haven't. I don't do anything now except hunt this beast."

Skelton talked on about what the monster might be—a magnified newt, a long-necked variety of giant seal, an unextinct *Elasmosaurus*. Visitors wandered by in groups outside the caravan, and unexplained strangers kept coming in for tea. In the air was a feeling, utterly belied by the relative permanence of the place, of a country carnival on a two-night stand. The caravans themselves, in their alignment, suggested a section of a midway. I remembered a woman shouting to attract people to a big caravan on a carnival midway one night in May in New Jersey. That was some time ago. I must have been nineteen. The woman, who was standing on a small platform, was fifty or sixty, and she was trying to get people to go into the caravan to see big jungle cats, I suppose, and brown bears—"Ferocious Beasts," at any rate, according to block lettering on the side of the caravan. A steel cage containing a small black bear had been set up on two sawhorses outside the caravan—a fragment to imply what might be found on a larger scale inside.

So young that it was no more than two feet from nose to tail, the bear was engaged in desperate motion, racing along one side of the cage from corner to corner, striking the steel bars bluntly with its nose. Whirling then, tossing its head over its shoulder like a racing swimmer, it turned and bolted crazily for the opposite end. Its eyes were deep red, and shining in a kind of full-sighted blindness. It had gone mad there in the cage, and its motion, rhythmic and tortured, never ceased, back and forth, back and forth, the head tossing with each jarring turn. The animal abraded its flanks on the steel bars as it ran. Hair and skin had scraped from its sides so that pink flesh showed in the downpour of the carnival arc lights. Blood drained freely through the thinned hair of its belly and dropped onto the floor of the cage. What had a paralyzing effect on me was the animal's almost perfect and now involuntary rhythm—the wild toss of the head after the crash into the corner, the turn, the scraping run, the crash again at the other end, never stopping, metronomic—the exposed interior of some brutal and organic timepiece.

Beside the cage, the plump, impervious woman, red-faced, red-nosed, kept shouting to the crowds, but she said to me, leaning down, her own eyes bloodshot, "Why don't you move on, sonny, if you ain't going to buy a ticket? Beat it. Come on, now. Move on."

"We argue about what it is," Skelton said. "I'm inclined to think it's a giant slug, but there is an amazingly impressive theory for its being a worm. You can't rule out that it's one of the big dinosaurs, but I think this is more wishful thinking than anything else." In the late 1930s, a large and exotic footprint was found along the shore of Loch Ness. It was meticulously studied by various people and was assumed, for a time, to be an impression from a foot or flipper of the monster. Eventually, the print was identified. Someone who owned the preserved foot of a hippopotamus had successfully brought off a hoax that put layers of mockery and incredibility over the creature in the lake for many years. The Second World War further diverted any serious interest that amateurs or naturalists might have taken. Sightings continued, however, in a consistent pattern, and finally, in the early 1960s, the Loch Ness Phenomena Investigation Bureau was established. "I have no plans whatever for leaving," Skelton said. "I am prepared to stay here ad infinitum. All my worldly goods are here."

A dark-haired young woman had stepped into the caravan and poured herself a cup of tea. Skelton, introducing her to me, said, "If the beast has done nothing else, it has brought me a wife. She was studying Gaelic and Scottish history at Edinburgh University, and she walked into the glen one day, and I said, 'That is the girl I am going to marry.'" He gestured toward a window of the caravan, which framed a view of the hills and the lake. "The Great Glen is one of the most beautiful places in the world," he continued. "It is peaceful here. I'd be happy here all my life, even if there were nothing in the loch. I've even committed the unforgivable sin of going to sleep in the sun during a flat calm. With enough time, we could shoot the beast with a crossbow and line, and get a bit of skin. We could also shoot a small transmitter into its hide and learn more than we know now about its habits and characteristics."

The creature swims with remarkable speed, as much as ten or fifteen knots when it is really moving. It makes no noise other than seismic splashes, but it is apparently responsive in a highly sensitive way to sound. A shout, an approaching engine, any loud report, will send it into an immediate dive, and this shyness is in large part the cause of its inaccessibility, and therefore of its mystery. Curiously, though, reverberate sound was what apparently brought the creature widespread attention, for the first sequence of frequent sightings occurred in 1933, when the A-82 was blasted into the cliffsides of the western shore of the lake. Immense boulders kept falling into the depths, and shock waves from dynamite repeatedly ran through the water, causing the creature to lose confidence in its environment and to alter, at least temporarily, its shy and preferentially nocturnal life. In that year it was first observed on land, perhaps attempting to seek a way out forever from the detonations that had alarmed it. A couple named Spicer saw it, near Inverfarigaig, and later described its long, serpentine neck, followed by an ungainly hulk of body, lurching toward the lake and disappearing into high undergrowth as they approached.

With the exception of one report recorded in the sixth century, which said that a monster (fitting the description of the contemporary creatures in the lake) had killed a man with a single bite, there have been no other examples of savagery on its part. To the contrary, its sensitivity to people seems to be acute, and it keeps a wide margin between itself and mankind. In all likelihood, it feeds on fish and particularly on eels, of which there are millions in the lake. Loch Ness is unparalleled in eel fishing circles, and has drawn commercial eel fishermen from all over the United Kingdom. The monster has been observed with its neck bent down in the water, like a swan feeding. When the creatures die, they apparently settle into the seven-hundred-foot floor of the lake, where the temperature is always forty-two degrees Fahrenheit—so cold that the lake is known for never giving up its dead. Loch Ness never freezes, despite its high latitude, so if the creature breathes air, as has seemed apparent from the reports of observers who have watched its mouth rhythmically opening and closing, it does not lose access to the surface in winter. It clearly prefers the smooth, sunbaked waterscapes of summer, however, for it seems to love to bask in the sun, like an upturned boat, slowly rolling, plunging, squirming around with what can only be taken as pleasure. By observers' reports, the creature has two pairs of lateral flippers, and when it swims off, tail thrashing, it leaves behind a wake as impressive as the wake of a small warship. When it dives from a still position, it inexplicably goes down without leaving a bubble. When it dives as it swims, it leaves on the surface a churning signature of foam.

Skelton leaned back against the wall of the caravan in a slouched and nonchalant posture. He was wearing a dark blue tie that was monogrammed in small block letters sewn with white thread—L.N.I (Loch Ness Investigation). Above the monogram and embroidered also in white thread was a small depiction of the monster— humps undulant, head high, tail extending astern. Skelton gave the tie a flick with one hand. "You get this with a five-pound membership," he said.

The sea-serpent effect given by the white thread on the tie was less a stylization than an attempt toward a naturalistic sketch. As I studied it there, framed on Skelton's chest, the thought occurred to me that there was something inconvenient about the monster's actual appearance. In every sense except possibly the sense that involves cruelty, the creature in Loch Ness is indeed a monster. An average taken from many films and sightings gives its mature length at about forty feet. Its general appearance is repulsive, in the instant and radical sense in which reptiles are repulsive to many human beings, and any number of people might find difficulty in accepting a creature that looks like the one that was slain by St. George. Its neck, about six feet long, columnar, powerfully muscled, is the neck of a serpent. Its head, scarcely broader than the neck, is a serpent's head, with uncompromising, lenticular eyes. Sometimes as it swims it holds its head and neck erect. The creature's mouth is at least a foot wide. Its body undulates. Its skin glistens when wet and appears coarse, mottled, gray, and elephantine when exposed to the air long enough to become dry. The tail, long and columnar, stretches back to something of a point. It seemed to me, sitting there at Headquarters, that the classical, mythical, dragon likeness of this animate thing—the modified dinosaur, the fantastically exaggerated newt—was an impediment to the work of the investigation bureau, which has no pertinent interest in what the monster resembles or calls to mind but a great deal in what it actually is, the goal being a final and positive identification of the genus.

"What we need is a good, lengthy, basking sighting," Skelton said. "We've one long surfacing—twenty-five minutes. I saw it. Opposite Urquhart Castle. We only had a twelve-inch lens then, at four-and-a-half miles. We have thirty-six inch lenses now. We need a long, clear, close-up—in color."

My children had watched, some months earlier, the killing of a small snake on a lawn in Maryland. About eighteen inches long, it came out from a basement window well, through a covering lattice of redwood, and was noticed with shouts and shrieks by the children and a young retriever that barked at the snake and leaped about it in a circle. We were the weekend guests of another family, and eight children in all crowded around the snake, which had been gliding slowly across the lawn during the moments after it had been seen, but had now stopped and was turning its head from side to side in apparent indecision. Our host hurried into his garage and came running back to the lawn with a long shovel. Before he killed the snake, his wife urged him not to. She said the snake could not possibly be poisonous. He said, "How do you know?" The children, mine and theirs, looked back and forth from him to her. The dog began to bark more rapidly and at a higher pitch.

"It has none of the markings. There is nothing triangular about its head," she told him.

"That may very well be," he said. "But you can't be sure."

"It is *not* poisonous. Leave it alone. Look at all these children."

"I can't help that."

"It is *not* poisonous."

"How do you know?"

"I know."

He hit the snake with the flat of the shovel, and it writhed. He hit it again. It kept moving. He hit it a third time, and it stopped. Its underside, whitish green, segmental, turned up. The children moved in for a closer look.

leslie leyland fields

As Leyland's story shows, humans can live almost
everywhere—even on tiny Harvester Island, in the Gulf
of Alaska—but in these places the line between life and
death can be extremely thin. Leyland demonstrates
this by sketching Harvester Island's one beach—her
and her family's "highway and bridge" to the outside
world—and another, even more important. Caught by
an early storm in a small boat, Leyland describes what
it is like to know that your survival depends on a
stretch of friendly shoreline.

beaches, found and nearly lost

Last month, on the minus tides, I had my first breakfast of kelp. I hadn't thought of eating out on the beach, but there it was, a shock of sea lettuce, lime green, wigging a rock at my feet. It was much greener than the long-distance produce in my refrigerator, and I hadn't eaten yet. I nibbled. It was salty, of course, and a bit more slick than I was used to, the leaves sliding between jaws that now moved sideways. This was grazing indeed. The taste was pleasant though; the mild crunch felt fresh. Next I tried bull kelp, the long tubular plant with a bulb and ribbon-like strands sprouting from the "head." I have long known they are edible, had even tried pickling them years before, but after the third failed batch, I had decided that "edible" was a highly imprecise term. But here, now . . . I took a reckless bite of the ribbony hair. Slick again, not slimy—an important distinction—and salty, slightly crisp with the raw flavor of ocean. An obvious choice, that kelp should be so seasoned, but it pleased me that it should taste so exactly like the smell of this beach.

I treasure this beach, because I must, because without it I could not live on Harvester Island. It's a small island, three hundred fifty acres, on the west side of Kodiak Island, the third largest island in the United States. Despite its size, there are only fifteen thousand residents, twelve thousand of whom live in the town of Kodiak. The road system around this island the size of Connecticut officially boasts a mere ninety-four miles. From our side of this huge wilderness island, the closest road is eighty miles away, across ocean and bays, ragged mountains, glaciers. The water, then, is our highway, open skiffs our only transport, the beach, our on-ramp to the wide blue road. This one expanse of sand links me to the world more vitally than my VHF radio, or even my new radio-telephone: it is the bridge to my local world, the one my body breathes and moves in. Because of this one beach, I can live here.

I would not have thought it, twenty years ago when I first came, that an island, sunk to its teeth in water, could have only one small beach, or none. As a childhood peruser of *National Geographic,* I expected long expanses where the land in all its dress and flora crumbles slowly to sand, then leans down into the continent of water. It seems the proper way for land to meet ocean. There must be a playing field upon which sea and land agree to meet, to mingle, exchanging air, water, soil, inhabitants. Let there be commerce between the two, as it is in the Carribean, in Indonesia, the South Pacific, the many islands whose beaches I have walked where sands halo each island. I am still muffling those expectations.

There are other beaches on our island, but of the worst kind. They lie on the backside where the land pitches from a nine-hundred-foot peak nearly straight down to water. These beaches collect driftwood, not sticks, but logs: cottonwood, cedar, fir, spruce, substantial forests. Our buildings out here are strapped onto pilings dragged from these beaches. The logs not used for building are firewood. We are always on the lookout for good wood, and these beaches are some of the best. But they are deceptive. Come high tide, even a few hours short of highwater, they are gone, swallowed by the flood. They invite picnics, exploration, beachcombing, but should you trust your eyes only and be left without a craft, you would find yourself back against the cliff as the advancing waters consume you foot by foot. There is no succor there to the traveler or the fisherman whose machinery lets go.

Despite my dependence upon this one beach, you will not hear me call it beautiful. Most of the shoreline of Kodiak Island, as elsewhere in southcentral and southeastern Alaska, is serious, solemn, even. In most places the sand is not white or any shade of light but volcanic black. On gray days the beach is gray; on sunny days, black; when wet, ebony. For sand we count grades of gravel, from fine to coarse to fields of boulders. The beaches are treeless, offering no shelter from squalls of mosquitos, rain, the relentless day and night sun during an August heat wave. On these beaches, swimming is a test of courage. Though the water warms from a winter chill of thirty-eight degrees up to a summer warm of fifty-five degrees, we dare only brief immersions. Hypothermia sets in in fifteen minutes. On this beach we hand-over-hand pull our nets, from skiffs to shore, from shore to skiffs. On net-mending days we stretch the ocean-green webbing from one end of the beach to the other, and stand, days, until they are done. This is not a vacation beach; this is a working beach.

I look at beaches all the time when traveling in the skiff. It's not just visual beachcombing for driftwood or pilings; it's much more serious. When I was twenty-three and traveling alone in the skiff, I needed a beach desperately. It began here, probably, the habitual and almost subconscious categorizing of every shoreline into "good beach, no—cliffs, useless beach."

Duncan and I were spending the winter at the island. We had been married three years by then, had just graduated from college. Though his family had lived there for seventeen summers and falls, no one had ever spent the winter. We were warned against it. There was plenty of substance to the warnings. The island dots the edge of the Shelikof Strait, a body of water two hundred miles by forty, sandwiched between Kodiak Island and the Alaskan Peninsula. Mountains rise up on both sides. On the Peninsula side, two- to three-thousand-foot mountains soar straight up from water, and behind these, another range that escalates to 12,000 feet. On the Kodiak side, mountains from 1,000 to 4,000 feet line the Strait. The result, a forty-mile tunnel that corrals winds, chutes them into velocities that spin our wind gauge to the hurricane mark at least several times a year. What it does to the water is worse. The Straits are relatively shallow, as saltwater goes, much of it less than one hundred twenty fathoms. At these depths, and with the wind tunnel, calm can erupt into gale, flat water into twenty-foot boils in minutes. Many vessels, from skiffs to multi-million-dollar crab boats over one hundred feet have sunk within minutes in the Shelikof. No one likes these waters.

But the sun was shining that morning. It was April, almost warm. After a long winter on the island, spring seemed possible, and I wanted out on the water, alone. There was even a reason to go, an errand that seemed important at the time. I persisted in my persuasion, finally succeeding in breaking the rule we made and had kept unfailingly until then—that neither of us would travel alone in the skiff. Duncan was not happy; I was exuberant.

I was off. It was my exuberance alone that seemed to speed my wooden skiff over the miles of smooth water. To be alone, really alone after a close winter in the company of one was glorious and giddy. And the sun on my face, a landscape that moved and changed, the whirr of making my own wind . . . It lasted twenty minutes. Then, as suddenly as the pulling of a shade, a snow squall hit. The mountains navigating my passage, guiding me clear from the Shelikof Strait, disappeared. In the blinding snow and fog, all that was left was my sixteen-foot skiff, my hand shielding my eyes, and the same circle of turbulent water I couldn't seem to break out of.

I don't know how long I wandered in the fog before I found land again. It was as good as home for a few minutes, until I realized, as I followed the line of cliffs, that I was somewhere I had never been. I clung as close to the shore as I dared, watching for rocks, tracing its outline with my wake. I could not let go of this one anchor—the solidity of land in a world blurred into degrees of nebulous.

I needed one of two things: something I recognized—a promontory, a hill, anything I could name and follow back to my own bay; and if not that, at least a beach. A voice in my head, it was Duncan's voice, said, *Find a beach, build a fire and wait.* Those were his departing words to me, said with a melodrama and foreshadowing I scoff at in inept novels and that I scoffed at then. And now I was living what I was too affected to read. But I could find neither of these, not one familiar rock, not one spread of sand beyond the tide's reach to beach the skiff, to rest. Just cliff and cliff, rocks jutting black rising into fog, the suck and rain of surf as it battered the shale . . . Time was irrelevant, except as it related to the expenditure of gas. That I was conscious of. It was a constant worry. I was almost to the end of the six-gallon tank, and I had another, but how long would that last and what then? If only I could find a beach.

I did, but not until the gas ran out, not until the engine died, not until I was nearly against the cliffs with nothing but oars, not until I was at the end of all I knew to do. Then I stood, helpless, hands at my sides, and shouted a prayer through the clouds, a prayer for mercy, a prayer for a beach. This is part of why I know about mercy: immediately the snow stopped, the fog lifted, and for the first time in hours I could see. There across the water was an island, and on that island was a beach. It was small, just a hand's breadth from half a mile away, but I could get there with my oars.

When you're on the water, any beach is home. The slide of the skiff bottom onto sand, that sound, is like the crunch of gravel under your tires as you pull into your driveway. I claimed that beach as home. My first task—to build a fire. We kept a survival kit in the skiff stocked with strips of inner tubes and matches, flares, a polyurethane tarp. For the rest of the day, I paced the fifty-foot width of gravel, gathering wet driftwood to feed the fire I had finally gotten started with a thorough dousing of gasoline. Through those hours, several search planes flew directly overhead, but they never saw me, despite the flares, the fire, the desperate arm-waving. The beach was too small, tucked between cliffs and overhanging trees. I was invisible even to the Coast Guard helicopter that hovered nearby, and passed on. Then, dark. The boats running rescue grids out in the Shelikof Strait gave up. Planes flew home. It was quiet.

I settled down for a night on this beach I now knew so well, every foot of it. I knew I would not sleep for fear of bears, whose trails all seemed to converge on this one beach. Two skulls kept their presence actual, not merely hypothetical. While readying for a long night's waking, I heard an engine—a last plane. Someone was flying in the dark—for me. I felt hope, and I felt shame, too, unworthy of all that was risked on my behalf. When I could see its lights, I threw my last bit of gasoline on the fire, as I had done before, each time a plane had passed overhead. The flames flared up, and it was that movement and light that caught the pilot's eye.

I've been past that beach a number of times since. Each time I measure my sense of it then to what I see now from the safety of a skiff whizzing past. Was the beach really that small? Was it really the only one along that shoreline? Was it really hidden by cliff and trees? Yes, yes, yes. The only one, just fifty feet across, barely visible. The alternatives, what might have happened without that beach and that sudden cloud break, are not vague suppositions. Enough people have died in enough different ways out on the water around Kodiak to know what could have, might have . . .

And so we tend our beach and watch it, we build our lives around it. Our house faces the beach, its glassed prow peering out over the bay and its mountains. The "V" of our shoreline is always in view from the front of the house. We stand guard over it because it is in perpetual motion. Just as my three-year-old commented with surprise one day while looking at the water, "Look, the rocks are floating!" so it is with the tides. And with that same science of the eye and the license of simile, I tell you it is the land that shifts and tilts and moves the tides; it is the ocean that is constant.

And what movement there is! On the east side of Kodiak Island, the tides are modest, a mere ten-foot range. Its coastline faces the Gulf of Alaska, where the pull and suck of tide is absorbed and leveled by those vast waters. But for us, just eighty miles across the mountains, the tides swell and fall twenty-eight feet. It is the Shelikof Strait, again working its muscles. The rising tide surges through its comparatively narrow passage, just forty miles wide. A seven-foot high tide on the east side of Kodiak inflates to a twenty-two-foot high tide for us. With all of that happening within six hours, the beach is in a continual state of tilting and spilling, veiling and revealing. Reefs, one-hundred-year-old boilers from extinct canneries, pilings from the same, old anchors embedded in the muck, are all in a state of appearing and disappearing through every six-hour cycle.

Best of all is the emergence of the spit. Like many spits it is deceptive, and lurks unseen until a low tide of no more than one or two drains the water away, and there it sits, an arm of sand and gravel stretching a quarter of a mile out to the middle of the channel. The spit drops off then, suddenly, at the feet of an enormous three-legged navigational marker with a bright orange triangle mounted on top. It is a most gracious curve, smoother than the bend of an arm, and made for walking. The sand is smoother than elsewhere; there are few rocks; it is the finer gravel that is swept to rest there. And these last few weeks, the crest that is our path has been densely cobbled with bright clamshells. When the low tides and the white-brick road calls, and I can ignore it no longer, I put down my broom, knife, or shovel, solicit fellow travelers, and go. I know that as I walk, from the vantage of arriving boats, it looks as though I am walking on water, crossing the channel in knee boots. From my eyes, I feel like Moses with water stacking on both sides, but my feet still on dry ground, the boots worn for emergency leakages of faith.

Others, too, apparently feel like Moses and attempt to resist mortal forces. One winter while living in a shed on the dock, just a rock's throw from the sandbar, we heard then watched in disbelief as a largish scow either refused or was ignorant of the message of the marker, which was—stay to the right, change course, low water. It bore straight on for the spit, even seeming to get a running start before charging this obstacle. We cringed waiting for the thud and groan of steel on rock and sand. The boat thudded, hit, the bow bumping up then slapping down while the stern scraped through, buoyed by the general confusion of the waters, and off it merrily went, the skipper feeling either triumphant or sheepish.

The visual variety and the expanding and contracting shorelines costs us something, though. It makes it more difficult to keep our transportation system running. We need immediate and constant access to our skiff; we can't wait for tides to float it if it has gone dry. Docks are too expensive to build and maintain and would have to extend a very long way to be useful. So we use what we call a "running line" system. Basically we form a triangle with three pulleys. The apex is out in the water. That pulley is tied to a buoy that is then anchored beyond the lowest low tide. The line is pulled through two more blocks on shore. From the shore pulley out to the buoy is about forty fathoms, two hundred fifty feet. We land our skiff on the beach, then unload, tie the skiff onto the line with a knot called a running line knot—three circlings and two tiebacks that took me all of one summer to learn because it was counter-intuitive—then pull it out safely to deep water, beyond the next low tide. We then secure the running line on shore to keep it stationary, so the wind and waves won't lure the skiff back in. The knots must be secure. You need to have a basic idea of what the tides are doing. Other than that, it's a simple system, but it pulls hard. Even with a single skiff on the line, you are pulling two thousand pounds through three pulleys with more than five hundred feet of line. When two or three skiffs are on the running line, or when the rope is clogged with kelp and seaweed, or when the wind is against you, it may take ten long minutes of gruntwork to get the skiff to deep water. Or, if you are leaving, to get the skiff to shore. By the time the skiff hits the sand, you may be winded and sweating in your layers of raingear and warm on-the-water wear before you even begin your day's work. Leavings, then, are not impulsive. Every movement, every arrival and departure is deliberate, rehearsed.

Through this process, we brought to shore and unloaded everything that is here on this island. Eight years ago when we built our house, every sheet of plywood, every beam, bed, light bulb, wringer washing machine, every bolt and wingnut slid onto the beach by skiff, was lifted over to waiting arms and backs, and packed from beach to hill, from hill to building site. Every box of cereal and diapers and everything else needed since all comes by water and beach. It is the first step of our threshold.

Beyond the course of our own comings and goings, wondrous things happen here on our waterfront. The day we arrived on the island last summer, two land otters scampered and slithered down the beach from under our warehouse, their winter home, an obvious bailout. A beaver swam over one winter, landing on our beach. Foxes prowl for clams and other edibles. A minke whale washed up one summer. A sea lion another. And always, because of the abundance, various kinds of fish find their way to the beach, in various states of disembowelment, always setting the stage for mini-epics of greed and takeovers among the shorebirds. This last summer, I watched a particularly exciting domestic drama between a pair of eagles and a pair of gulls.

The plot centered around a torn-up pink salmon, a humpy, that had floated to the high tide mark. The eagles and gulls spotted it the instant it landed, and began a furious dogfight, wheeling, dipping, shrieking their way to rights to the carcass. The gulls gave the eagles a good run, being more facile, their turns quicker, but the eagles, out of sheer intimidation, won. The two, both white-headed, signaling their adult, full grown status, landed and stood proprietarily over the fish. One eagle got to work immediately, planting both sets of talons into the flesh, then ripping and tearing the meat with its beak. His appetite was raw, the bloody and pink strings of flesh ripping from the white skin, visible even to me in the house, through the binoculars. Strangely, the other eagle did not contest the first eagle's feast, who was eating seemingly without any regard for its partner. The other eagle seemed intent on something else—the same two gulls who now stood some thirty feet away, drooling, but convinced of the wisdom of their distance. They stood locked in position, not moving, not even cocking their heads, just eyes on the eagle and the dinner they had lost. It suddenly occurred to me what was happening. The second eagle that stood there, so unconcerned over the portion being consumed by the other, was acting as guard. His belligerent stare alone held the gulls at bay. He stared not only at them, but his head made routine turns around both ways to assure a clear coast and an unthreatened plate. Eagle number two, whose patience I admired, and who I decided was the wife, held no accounting of how much was being taken by the other. What kind of agreement did these two have? Or was I simply fabricating this whole scenario? In a moment, my answer came. The eagles, in the blink of an eye, switched positions precisely. The second eagle now tore into what remained, ripping chunks of salmon meat, chugging them whole, while the first stood guard. The first, the one now with a full belly, was not quite as concerned with his guard duty, however. After a few minutes, apparently bored with watching the two gulls, he began to amble away, despite the fact that the gulls were gaining courage from his inattention and inching forward. I imagined the delinquent husband eagle whistling as he went, trying to look as nonchalant as any eagle strolling on any beach. In fact, he did stroll, down to the water's edge, where he began, strangely, to wade in the incoming surges, looking like some old bowlegged beachcomber. Periodically, he would dip his head down, and skim his beak sideways in the gravel. All of it not according to agreement, I am sure. Soon even his wanderings began to bore him, and without ado, he lifted off, leaving the other eagle still feeding, the two gulls still in rapt attendance, and decidedly closer. A few minutes later, the second eagle finished all that was good of the fish and flew off as well.

Since eagles pair for life, they were undoubtedly a husband and wife team, and clearly not newlyweds. They had been together long enough to establish a system, and then long enough for one to know just how much to stretch it, nibble at it, yaw it his way without directly breaking the rules: "But honey, I was right there if you needed me. All you had to do was screech. I know I left a few minutes early, but you obviously had those gulls under control. I could see you didn't really need my help. And besides, I just went off to look for more food—for you!"

There is no less drama in the winter. Then the deer, Sitka black-tailed, come down to the beach when the snow buries the grass. With great enthusiasm, they dine on kelp, the fettuccine noodles of bull kelp dangling from their jaws. One fall morning I woke to see eight deer frantically pacing the beach, their usually graceful stride now jerky and uncertain. They would take turns stepping into the water, then retreating, then in again, their distress apparent. Was there a bear on the island? I couldn't know. I watched that entire hour of agonizing attempts until finally, upon some signal I could not detect, they stepped in to their knees, then their bellies, and they were launched, all eight, into the forty-five-degree October water. They were amazingly buoyant, and seemed to know just what to do, how to move, how to navigate, for they arrived at what I assumed was their destination, the beach half a mile across, fifteen minutes later. Since that first sighting, I have seen bands of sometimes more than fifty bucks roving the beaches and swimming the open bays during rutting season.

There is food here on the beach: sea lettuce, bull kelp, rock weed, also known as old man's firecrackers and popping weed. Inside its bubbly green tips is a clear mucilaginous gel that reminds me of aloe. I have read it is a natural thickener, like the agar-agar of Malaysia and the East. I boiled some up one morning after a fresh harvest from the beach, and filled the house with the raw salty perfume of Ocean, thickened and pureed. In such dosages, it became a stench, and thereafter, I left the pockets of gel raw upon the rocks, splitting them for a cool soothing salve on chapped hands, but nothing more. Five years ago, I would have added clams and mussels to a list of harvestables, but we cannot eat them here, nor anywhere on Kodiak Island. Paralytic shellfish poisoning, PSP, hospitalized more than twenty people, killing three in Kodiak in 1993, and '94, and this summer, it killed another, a native man from the village of Karluk, fifteen miles from our own beach These are the highest levels of

PSP in the state. It's the same cautionary tale told to anyone who eats from the plate of nature. Creation is fractured, bent; there is poison here at the feast. Sup well but warily.

Over the years, I learned much about my beach, but it wasn't until 1989 that I came to know its every detail. It was the year I nearly lost it, the year of the oil spill, "when the *Exxon Valdez* spewed eleven million gallons of crude oil into pristine Alaskan waters." I can say all of that as if it were a single word or if it were all one hyphenated phrase, as can most Alaskans who live in the *Valdez*'s wake.

When the oil spill occurred, I felt as though I knew the beach intimately already, or rather it knew me, because for that year we didn't have an outhouse. We were building a new house. By the time we got our foundation in that fall, the ground was too frozen to dig an outhouse, so we simply hiked out to the beach. It was a perfectly agreeable system, until the winter storms and blizzards moved in. Without trees or any kind of shelter to break the wind, we found our trips pared down to the quick and purely essential.

Perhaps it was on one of those outings that I first noticed the regularity of the black oystercatchers. There was a pair of them, their shrill single-note cry somehow a perfect match to their midnight-black bodies and their startlingly red bills and feet. They were always together, these two oystercatchers, in a picture of conjugal bliss. If one was spotted standing alert on the black cliff, a moment more of peering would inexorably bring the other to view, just a few feet away. They flew like a squadron. Though they had the whole expanse of sky, they chose always to bomb the beach as a unit, just bare inches apart. I saw them every day, heard their calls as they worked the beach through the day hours in the constant search for food. I viewed them as a faithful couple—faithful to each other, faithful to this beach, which somehow seemed to need them.

When the oil oozed from Prince William Sound down the Shelikof Strait, I was still in town and could only rely on rumors and reports of the extent of the impact on Kodiak's west side. I couldn't climb onto the plane fast enough. I hit my beach and ran its shoreline, expecting to see the solid coating that Prince William Sound received. Initially I heaved relief, calmed the mounting panic I had felt as we flew. The fouling was more subtle here. By the time the oil reached Kodiak Island, it had traveled some two hundred miles and had broken up into globules, islands that hit the beaches quietly, often unseen until something living touched it. Often it arrived already thickened with bits of feathers, bones, each clump keeping its own grisly record of its victims. Some places it pooled conspicuously in dark puddles, like black blood, but in others it melted into the sand and gravel, so the visible spot fanned out much wider beneath. My relief was premature. It didn't take much oil to kill, I learned. The media posted tragic photos of birds and otters who looked as though they had been hand dipped in the sludge, but just a single drop of oil could kill waterbirds as efficiently. One drop could violate the integrity of their natural oil-coated feathers. One drop and cold ocean water bleeds into the skin, and the bird dies of hypothermia and cold. Thousands of murres died like this. My oystercatchers were at grave risk.

I spent much time that summer, then, on the beach armed with shovels, plastic bags, rakes. And to thoroughly mix my motives, I was paid for it as well. Kodiak Island's salmon fishery was completely shut down for the duration of the season. Exxon needed workers to clean the beaches, and many of the island's fishermen were already in place. Though stunned from the loss of our season and livelihood, from the insidious spread of oil, we would not give up our summer on the island. If we could not fish, we would stay and clean and protect our beaches, paid or not. I had no problem with this arrangement. Exxon negligently made the mess; how fitting that they should pay to keep the oystercatchers alive and the bald eagles and gulls, terns, murres, puffins, whatever else was at risk on this beach.

One morning, the stakes rose yet higher. Early in the season, while tending the shores, I discovered in the gravel a softly rounded hollow, and in it, three perfectly shaped rocks, speckled gray, black, and white. They were eggs, of course, and I thrilled to know my couple was going to be a family, and wondered too, at the vulnerability of their nest. The eggs were superbly camouflaged, but they lay in the open on a stretch of gravel as inviting to the foot or hoof as any other. It was pure brazenness or utter foolishness. I couldn't honestly attribute either one, though, to my birds, as much as I wanted to anthropomorphize them. They built their nest there because something unnamed, something innate to black oystercatchers, moves them and all others of their breed to build their nests on the beach. There was neither fault nor credit on their part, but on mine there came an enormous sense of responsibility. It was now my job to protect an entire family. As the mother of a new baby myself that summer, I was learning about the fierce devotion of that tie.

The parents-to-be were not happy with my appointment as godmother, though. They were furious with me and every morning greeted me and all my extra appendages—rakes, shovel, pitchfork—with shrieks and dive attacks, beating me away from their nest. I could not reassure them except to widen my berth around their eggs as I worked. I sifted and sorted, shoveled, marched and tended that ground with the aggression and persistence of a home defense league. Just one drop, just one drop was all it took. I could not forget.

A few weeks later, while maintaining my regimen, something moved at my feet. I froze, and there by my toes, equally rigid and startled, crouched a chick, gary and white, as speckled and camouflaged as its egg had been. It was paralyzed, as was I, and I knew that with all of its beating heart it was trusting in the force that pinned it to the ground, the same force that speckled it like a rocky beach to blind the predator's watch. I would not worry about eagles—that was not my domain—but Exxon's oil, yes, that invasion was mine to fight. And now the chicks, three of them. Just one drop.

Since then, I walk the tidelines almost habitually, picking up plastic that floats in with the tide, observing the puffins and eagles, smelling and sometimes tasting the kelp at low water, checking for any residual oil, all with the shrill and comforting accompaniment of midnight wings and scarlet bills. Eight years since, the beach has never been without the presence of a happily joined couple who ply the shore tirelessly. This is our garden, theirs and mine. Like Eve, I believe it is given to me to dress and keep, the most ancient and sacred of tasks. And these two oystercatchers, ever tenacious and faithful, seem to be called to the same.

sueellen campbell

As her title implies, Campbell's essay invokes a part of
experiencing nature that few writers like to dwell on—
the sheer painful slog of a serious camping trip. With
equal parts humor and honesty, Campbell reflects on
the reasons why people seek the physical challenge of
the outdoors—and why she may not be "a true pilgrim" of the miserable experience.

misery

Beyond trudging lies misery.

I can't see a thing. Only my feet, about a yard of trail, and the backs of John's legs. My glasses are foggy, my cap pulled low. It's raining. I'm sopped and chilled, sweating and shivering. Several inches of mud and standing water cover flat pieces of trail; steep pieces have turned into streams. Rocks lie everywhere, sharp ankle-ambushing rocks, rounded ones so thick with moss that ferns, even trees, sprout from them. All of it is crisscrossed with six-inch roots and hip-high fallen trees. Mushrooms smother every surface. Everything is wet, everything is slick.

Over my head is the back half of an eighty-pound canoe. Forty pounds of it rest on the top bone in my spine, the unpadded one that sticks out just enough to make a shelf. I've added cushioning—a balled-up fleece jacket—which helps when it isn't sliding sideways or down. My arms are angled sharply up, elbow joints pinched and awkward, and I'm grabbing on to the thwart, but I haven't got the arm muscle to hold any of the weight, only enough to balance it. The muscle behind my right shoulder that cramps up all the time at home is one spasm of pain. My left arm tingles as though it has fallen asleep. Sometimes I try to hunch my shoulders enough to take the weight off my spine, but then the cramp sharpens. When John takes a long step, the thwart hits the back of my neck and yanks me forward. When he swings to the left, I'm swung to the right. When he stops, the thwart slides off its cushion and down my spine, and I feel the weight in the small of my back. If I don't take steps exactly the same length as his, I lose my balance. It's a nightmare of dancing, a nasty parody of a romantic vision of marriage. I walk as straight a line as I can, right through mud and water, up the sides of cracked boulders, down root ladders. I look only at our feet.

I'm covered with bruises and sore spots. Shoulders, upper arms, elbows, forearms. Wrists, palms, fingers. Hip joints. The tops of my calves and the outsides of my legs just below my knees. My toes, my soles. The wind kicks up and John says, "Better put your jacket on. Don't want those shoulders to tighten up."

The routine is relentless: Put the canoe in the water. Sling in two heavy backpacks and arrange them on the bottom under the thwarts, straps and frames down to keep the contents dry. Push off. Paddle five or ten minutes into the wind. Glance at the view: trees and rocks, all grayed with mist. (The sun hasn't appeared once in the three chilly late-September days we've been here. This is the best time of year to come, everyone says. In the summer it's hot and muggy and the bugs are awful.) Land. Haul out the backpacks and canoe, sometimes up steep boulders or over piles of sharp rocks. Hike fifteen minutes with backpacks, waterproof ammo box, paddles, pads. Hike back, sucking on peppermints, enjoying the temporary respite, trying to be cheerful. John jokes about when I'm going to burst into tears (I won't—I never cry when those natural tranquilizers might actually help) and wonders what we would do if our limited view from under the canoe suddenly included four tall, knobby moose legs. Arrange fleece jacket into neck cushion. Heave canoe over head. Trudge. Put canoe in water, load, paddle with cramped muscles, land. And we're doing this the easy way, not the purist's way. We have real backpacks with hip straps instead of shapeless canvas and leather sacks hanging off our shoulders. We're making two trips per portage instead of one.

We're in a hurry, too, trying, though it's clearly hopeless, to keep up with our friends Lisa and Larry, who have brought us here to the Boundary Waters between Minnesota and Canada. When we arrive at a portage, they're starting their second, canoe-bearing, trip. (They're carrying the heavier rented boat, leaving their own lighter one for us. We feel a little guilty about this, but mostly grateful.) When we reach a lake with our backpacks, they're disappearing into the mist, paddles rising and dipping in perfect unison. If they get too far ahead, they wait just until they see us coming, then take off. On one long portage, they come back to help us with our canoe, explaining that this will make us all equally tired. They're trying to be tactful. "We don't know many couples who like to do this kind of thing," Lisa says, sounding perplexed and bit forlorn. "We don't mind slowing down a little for you guys." I set my jaw, shake out my right elbow, adjust the canoe on the top of my spine, and tell John I can go a little faster.

I hate this, I think. *This is awful. This is torture. How could anyone like this? Why would anybody want to come here? Why did I want to come here?* Everything hurts. I don't like the cold rain and thick mist and dark clouds. I don't like the tangled trees or piles of mushrooms or the monotony of small lakes, small hills, endless forests. I feel claustrophobic. I don't like to hurry, and I don't like not being able to see. Misery is blinding me, cutting me off. My own body is taking all my attention. The land is a blur. I feel profoundly off balance and out of place. I have no idea where I am.

Three days of this and finally I'm familiar enough with the routine to start thinking. I'll analyze how I feel, I say to myself. I'll isolate the ingredients and pin them down in my head. Maybe it will help.

The weather. Western sunshine addict returns to hated Midwest, disappears into monster rain cloud. It's not casual, my preference for sagebrush over ferns, sand over mud. John and I have avoided hiking and camping in soggy weather for years, but this time we're trapped by airplane tickets and complicated schedules. When the sun breaks through on our fourth day, my mood shoots up.

Then there are expectations. Mine had been high but ludicrously inaccurate. Slow drifting over calm sunny lakes, loons and moose, maybe wolves and northern lights. The intrigue of a new landscape, the familiar comfort of a canoe. A little bit of portaging each day, just enough work to earn my supper, plenty of stops if it turned out to be hard. I'd asked John and Lisa how much carrying to expect, but their answers had been vague enough to leave this daydream intact. And I'd thought I'd be resting the canoe on my shoulders, not my backbone.

Ah, yes, shoulders and spines. Clearly I'm not in adequate condition for this kind of travel. After a summer in the Rockies, my legs and lungs are strong, but what I need here is arm and shoulder muscles. I should have spent weeks doing pushups and moving boxes of books. My bone structure isn't helping. When I get home after the trip, I'll try to show family and friends which vertebra the canoe sat on. Nobody else has one like mine—one that sticks out without natural padding.

The company's clearly a factor, too. I feel forty years older than Lisa and Larry, not twelve. One morning we watch them paddle crisply away from us and John says, "You know, Larry was captain of the triathlon team at the University of Michigan." Lisa was a top-level triathlete, too, it turns out. When the trip is over and we're all down to T-shirts, I'll suddenly see what triangular backs they have, what rounded muscular shoulders. This information makes me feel much better—in retrospect.

And then there's pace—maybe the main ingredient. I'm realizing just how important it is to me to set my own. All those years as a camp counselor trained me to move at a speed sustainable by a twelve-year-old girl. In town I'm a fast walker, but in wild places I'm just about the slowest traveler I know. I like to mosey and dawdle. I like to drift, take silly exploratory detours, look for birds and wild animals, stop to study pieces of bark and seedpods. In a canoe I like to be pushed and spun by wind and water. Everything that lures me outdoors disappears when I have to rush.

Finally we start traveling separately between meal rendezvous and then take different routes for the last day and night. As soon as John and I slow down, my trip changes. A moose appears for a split second, huge dark antlers and massive body, then crashes away.

Pairs of loons float close to our canoe, call softly to each other. Beavers swim across our path. Through the early morning mist we hear what must be wolves. Though by now we're retracing our route, heading out, to me everything looks absolutely different. It's not just the new sunshine. It's the quality of my attention.

Now when my shoulder cramps hard and the boat slams into my spine and shoves me off a wet root into a frigid puddle, I distract myself by thinking of the stories I can tell. Misery always makes good stories. I should get a lot of mileage out of this trip.

And I do. My family and friends laugh when John and I act out the canoe routine. They exclaim and cringe and groan when I describe the varieties of pain and discomfort. "I don't think I'd like that," says my athletic, mountain-climbing niece Léa, sounding thoughtful. "Oh, SueEllen, that sounds *awful!* I'd have cried the whole time," my friend Nina commiserates. "You mean you slept *outside?* On the *ground?*" asks John's mother, a city person. They're happy that they didn't go with us, and we're heady with relief that the trip is finished. We're all reveling in what amounts to a benign, reassuring tale of survival. We were never in any particular danger and we've done no lasting damage to ourselves; in fact, by the time we get home, we're barely even stiff. Misery fades and the fun of stories takes over.

But I start to notice something else, too. Not everyone has the same reaction: a few listeners look slightly startled, then slightly amused, then tactfully entertained. Clearly the trip doesn't sound all that miserable to them. I remember once hearing a friends describe in outraged hyperbole his horror at discovering that when you backpack in the mountains you sometimes have to cross fast, icy streams on elevated logs. I'd done this maneuver often enough to react less with empathy than with a kind of Olympian amusement. When I see this same response in a few of my friends, I check their shoulders: sure enough, rounded and muscular.

One of them, Don, is a western mountain climber who recently moved to Minnesota and started canoeing in the Boundary Waters. His canoe, I learn, only weighs forty pounds—but then he carries it alone, and he uses one of those big shapeless bags instead of a backpack: a purist. I figure maybe he can explain to me—in terms I can understand—the appeal of this kind of travel in this kind of landscape. "So what's there to *like?*" I ask. "It all seemed so monotonous, so claustrophobic." "One thing I like," he says, "is how hard it is. It's shown me that mountains aren't really all that difficult. Also I like the challenge of the monotony. It's harder to read the landscape, harder to find your way. You have to look really carefully for details and differences. It teaches you how to see subtleties." This makes sense to me: when I stopped being too miserable to look around, I'd started to notice the same effect.

Another one, Mark, I meet for dinner before he's to give a talk and slide show on his recent expedition deep into an unmapped part of the Tibetan Himalayas. I know better than to tell this major-league adventurer my mild canoeing story; I only mention that I found the trip really hard, even miserable. He laughs and says, "But misery is the reason to go! It raises your consciousness." "Not mine," I blurt. "I was too uncomfortable to be conscious of anything." He laughs again and pats my back: "You're sweet."

Misery, we decide, covers a broad scale. I remember how an old boyfriend used to say that suffering is worship. That never made sense to me; it still doesn't. I guess I don't have the temperament to be a serious worshipper, a true pilgrim. (I want to add: a martyr, a masochist.) Mark and I talk about the Tibetan pilgrims we've seen approaching monasteries. That old woman I watched in western China: How many days had she spent prostrate on the frozen earth, inching her way toward this holy place? How far had she come, through what late-winter storms? Was her journey one of thanks, supplication, penance, praise? She must have been cold and exhausted, hungry and sore. Was she really full of joy? Was she miserable? What did she say?

paul lindholdt

In nature writing, people are often cast as reverent observers—but such observation presupposes a certain
distance from nature's power, "red in tooth and claw."
In an intensely personal piece, Lindholdt considers nature from the perspective of a father who has lost his
son to the sea, and for whom "every glimpse of seawater" awakens a new awareness of the beauty and the
terrible power that water embodies.

the spray and the slamming sea

For five days a choppy bay has hidden the body of my son. The newspapers say he is presumed drowned. My reverence for water deepens every hour. Now the blood is sounding in my ears like waves on the Washington shore—salt for salt, thud for thud.

Braden was kayaking with his best friend in Puget Sound at Larrabee Beach, a spot unique for its sandstone cliffs, abrasive and baroque, whose wave-etched scarps remind my eye of veins and ribs. It was March 11, 2001, still early in the year for paddling, the weather unsteady. The guys promised their moms they'd stay close to shore, off Chuckanut Drive near Bellingham, to make up for the life vest neither wore. That was the last anyone saw of them. The next day their boats washed up across the bay.

Six feet and four inches tall, buzz-cut and bullet-headed, he plays basketball with skill and flair. *Played!* Before he vanished, he was excelling in college. A paper lay on his desk, ready to hand in. An artist of the pen, he taught himself to sketch. At the age of three he sketched me—the whiskered neck unfazed by razor, the wire-rim glasses askew, the bed-head hair. Savagely we cared for each other, father and son. Now every glimpse of seawater rocks me, menaces me, unlike any other vision ever did.

When I was a child my father saved me from death by water. Fishing on a river beside him, I remember slipping and plunging into the drink. Minnows regarded me, a clumsy creature flung into their nimble midst. Those seconds spent estranged in water did not terrorize me, though. The swim was liberating, almost sensual, though I was scarcely four. Before the water could carry me away, sweep me out to sea, my daddy's strong arm straightened, collared, and hauled me back to wholesome light and air.

Two decades later I asked him for details about that close call, for the name of the river. Surprised, he told me it never happened, I did not slip, the ordeal took place only in my mind. How could that be? My memory of my swim was much too vivid to discredit.

Perhaps I died in a previous life—if I choose to open the door to reincarnation. Or maybe it was all a dream, a precaution, a harbinger of some sudden plunge to come.

Nearly one hundred searchers, all volunteers, tramp the beaches, knock on doors, and ply the waters of Puget Sound in the days after Jim and Braden disappear. Helicopter pilots scan the San Juan archipelago, giving their time freely, taking more than twenty flights. *Disappeared. Presumed drowned. Missing.* Lacking any certainty or evidence, his mother and I can plan no funeral, no burial. We wait in mystery and limbo, no closure in view.

Braden's favorite watch cap is found upon a beach. Vicki, my ex-wife, clings to me, drops rapid tears, and wrings the damp cap dry. Her sorrow has no bottom. I have come across the Cascades from Spokane, the first I have seen her in two years. Her face is swollen, barely recognizable, a product of prescription drugs and grief. She stoops.

Overwhelmed with longing and nostalgia, she won't switch off his computer. She grates at anyone who tries his bedroom door. She guards his urine crystallizing on the bathroom floor. Baseboard heat makes her home close, so I go for a walk above Larrabee.

Hikers hike at different rates. Some hikers like to hustle from start to stop, vying for new elapsed times, covering ground. Not me, I go slowly, snuffing the air, regarding birdcalls, even out the window of my moving car. I poke along, scrutinizing insects, inviting the lay of the land to invest itself in me. I can stare at a tuft of lupines a long time, charged by the way each leaf cup cradles rain, idly guessing when the tip-top of the flower head might grow ponderous enough to nod.

A trail shaded by maples and firs terraces a hill above Larrabee. Through the Earth's thin crust, tough mushrooms shove, splintering fallen tree trunks, crumbling concrete where need be. In my fragile state, fungi wield tremendous power. I pluck one, a prince mushroom, *Agaricus augustus,* its broad cap curving to upturned gills. It smells like trees. How fully mushrooms, those torpid flesh-flowers, flourish on death and decay.

The Kiowa writer N. Scott Momaday encourages "reciprocal appropriation" of the land, whereby a being respectfully surrenders to the landscape and takes it into his experience. Maybe that's what Braden did—too enthusiastically. If scape is scope, and scope suggests knowledge, then Braden knows the watery landscape at Larrabee Beach well. Knows it organically not consciously. Knows it like a fallen leaf knows rain.

During Braden's time in the womb, Mount St. Helens blew. We were camping near the town of Oroville, far north of the exploded mountain, but we heard the blast as though it were a mining charge a mile away. A radio report confirmed what happened. Vicki insisted that we flee home, first south and then west, across Stevens Pass to get to Puget Sound. The sheltering Cascades rose in advance of the mile-high curtain of ash.

In those days we camped and hiked a lot. In bear country, she had been afraid. And so I packed a handgun with us on some jaunts. One night in eastern Montana, in tornado season and terrain, a thunderstorm passed very close. The lightning's flash and thunder's crack were simultaneous events. The tent poles shone like ribs, the nylon sheath like a thin red skin. That pistol beneath the pack, that tool I toted for safety's sake, afforded her no comfort in the storm. She yodeled fear in dreams or could not sleep.

Vicki and I grieve at different rates. Hers is swift and physical, groaning, low, a blow as though from a kayak paddle jabbed to the solar plexus. My own pace on the path toward calm is a fumbling and tunneled vision, numb and vulnerable in open space.

Ten days have passed. Water haunts my rest each night. Allured by it, repulsed too, I hear its call—Triton, Shiva, an Old Testament lord all anger and caprice. From my waking dream I watch its fluid moods. To escape it I cower, but the water is booming, flashing, a tsunami poised to slam above my puny spit of sand. A dream-steed rides me, a nag whose hoofs keep relaxation distant, who rejoices that rivers do not sleep, waves never relent, the moon pulls irrepressibly, rain falls and evaporates, with or without me.

Many times I have cheated water's partner, death. The closest escape came in 1979, the year before Braden was born, while salmon fishing off the Strait of Juan de Fuca. It was May. The kings were running. Black mouths, silver sides, full of hunger and fight. They schooled beyond the mouth of Puget Sound, where the warlike Pacific throws its weight around. We nosed toward naked ocean aboard an eighteen-foot inboard.

The boat's owner, Fred, had some knowledge of ocean waves. To earn his aqua-lungs, Fred had worked as a skipper for dudes out of Westport, before he sold his soul to Boeing. But Fred liked to get too stoned for most comfort zones. With frantic care he guided his boat one-handed, smoking a reefer with the other, often tilting a beer.

The waves loomed large once we departed the harbor at Neah Bay, the same harbor famed today as a put-in point for whalers in the Makah tribe. We headed out that day in May, plunging along the whale-road, the sky clear, Vancouver Island at our backs, no wind to worry us, balancing on swells already human-high. Tatoosh Island passed to starboard and we entered open sea—*la mere,* wine-dark, prehistoric mother of us all.

Fred set aside his drink and smoke to thread a cut-plug herring on his line. One hook passed through the hollow gut of the bait-fish, emerging near its anal vent, the other bristling where the head should be. A five-ounce lead weight plummeted the line and the bait through the chop, which was already towering taller than our staggered craft.

"Put your lines in!" Fred hissed, his words an audible function of the spray and slamming sea. The skipper knew fish were there. He had seen a rip tide. The phantoms of king salmon agitated him. Presently his pole bent, and he handed the steering wheel to me. "Keep it facing the waves," he commanded, legs spread, horsing in the slug Chinook.

Cresting and lunging with random shifts in pitch, the boat mounted the wall of each successive swell, then plunged back to wallow in the trough before the next wave came. Seasick weather, our faces paled. A kind of claustrophobia ensues in heavy seas. Walls of water rise on every side, the skies shut down, and the light grows emerald and probes. One source of motion sickness in the human body is the ear, its salty water there.

The rollers came sloping, now eighteen and twenty feet in height. Backlit walls of green foam filtered light from the hidden sky, silhouetting fish like bugs in amber. Our stomachs clenched. Schools of herring swam above us, bent on spawning in the calm of Puget Sound. As if jeering, silhouettes of king salmon overtopped the deck, wave-tossed, heedless of the threat of getting caught broadside. Half the time our lines were slanting up above us. Weary and scared, my mates and I feared another boat might hit us, a wind might rise and slash the wave crests, and whitecaps might fling water to the deck. We threatened to mutiny. Capitulating with a sorry snarl, Fred wheeled the boat around.

Thoughts of Braden's final moments taunt me. My stomach cracks and growls like far-off thunder, gnawing at itself, fraying the sleeves of sleep. I have been trying to read philosophy, just turned off the lamp, and a tide of advice from the *Enchiridion* rises.

Epictetus, the Roman slave who wrote that book of consolation, spoke in loaded language of the transience of life. "On a voyage," he noted, "when the ship is at anchor, if you disembark to get water, you may amuse yourself by picking up a stone or a shell on the beach. But your thoughts ought to be on the ship every minute, to be always attentive, for fear the captain should call, and then you must leave all your things behind."

Unlike the Greek and Roman Stoics, I rely on spoken words to get me through. If the Ancient Mariner told his story to absolve himself, I lean on speech to air my grief. My mouth a vent, a compression release, eases the tension in my head. The mariner in the poem by Coleridge kills an albatross and pays hard penance by wearing its corpse around his neck, wandering the high seas, and telling his pain to anyone who'll heed him.

"The Ancient Mariner" is a sonorous swatch of sorrow about the sea. So is much of America's literature—from Poe's Pym, to Melville's Ishmael, to Whitman's "cradle, endlessly rocking." The heedless sea, creator and destroyer, redeemer and swift doom.

Two weeks after Braden's cap turns up on the sand, I am buckling on a life jacket. Alex, Derrick, and Neil tote their canoes and kayaks to the bank of tiny, swift Rock Creek. My hands are trembling at the jacket clasps. These young men, students and friends, have scanned the maps and hiked the cliffs above the Eastern Washington stream. Alex and Derrick are thrilled to be here. For seven hours we will dodge rocks, portage past falls and logs, and clamber slopes to pictographs scrawled on basalt walls.

No one knows for sure where we're going, only where we parked the shuttle car. No one in our party has paddled this stream before. At the shuttle drop-off spot a farmer, a red-faced Marlboro smoker with swollen ankles and scared hair, calls us crazy for tackling this stretch of water, this stony plunge through canyons fed by Rock Lake.

I push the bow of my boat out. Flycatchers and magpies flit and gather sticks for nests. It is still the month of March. Storm clouds threaten rain, although Rock Creek in this drought year is barely navigable—narrow, twisting, boulder-strewn. Fences cross it; fallen trees, called strainers or sweepers, can stop and swamp unwatchful boaters with the current's force. Herds of mule deer file the hillsides, ears twitching, gazing over shoulders as they go. Someplace in some sudden canyon, none of us is sure exactly where, a fifty-foot waterfall will obstruct our way.

My kayak knifes its way downstream. Nearly at the water level, I sit so low as to be part of the flow, an integer in nature's equation. I stroke right, gouge left, and lean the molded plastic craft before each turn. We're in class-one whitewater, non-technical, a piece of cake. Waves spray over the gunwale, wetting faces and arms and legs. Besides our life jackets, known among river rats as PFDs for personal flotation devices, we are wearing no special helmets, dry suits, or other gear. Hanging branches bruise us. Our muscles strain. Exhilaration and anxiety mix freely, compounding the fatigue and chill.

On one sudden right-hand hairpin, in a pool scooped at the base of steepling basalt columns, Alex and Neil capsize. Almost instantly they bob to the surface, holding paddles in one hand and the canoe in the other. They ride out the turn, before pulling up on a grassy bank to pour the stream back out. Their clothing will be dampish for the day.

Neil, like me, has water issues to confront. He too trembles. Seven years before this trip, he watched both his younger brother and best friend go down in Lake Roosevelt, the reservoir formed of the Columbia River below Grand Coulee Dam.

Near the burg of Keller the boys were hand-paddling inner tubes of tractor tires, three of them, to reach an island the dam had exposed. Mid-channel a wicked wind arose. The tires were stripped from their grip, sent rolling end over end, and they were left with nothing to trust but muscle power. Neil, a weight lifter and football player then, urged the others to work the water hard, he called to them to keep the faith, but no amount of urging could give them strength and warmth to stroke to shore. They cried out several times and then surrendered, "almost peaceful," Neil said, to hypothermia and fatigue.

My tortured imagination tells me that this is probably how Braden drowned. Wisely Neil did not try to rescue his drowning kin. The drowning swimmer often drowns the one who would save him. Panic sets in. It could have been that Jim, Braden's partner, who had broken his legs in a motorcycle crash two years before, was flailing and Braden tried to help him. Maybe both of them were dashed unconscious on the cliffs.

A month has passed. It's April 12. To get some rest, I turn to memories of him.

My son was intrepid enough to travel the West with me in a series of low-budget adventures. In an Oregon desert I cooked raw oysters over a juniper fire. That bummer of a supper never slowed his appetite. Those oysters quivered on his plate. They were snotty and chewy, charred and underdone, but he ate them and said I was a good cook.

Another time, beside a tent high in Nevada, at Great Basin National Park where millennia-old bristlecone pines grow, a herd of beef cows came thundering into our camp and almost flattened him. He was scared. He wet his pants. At least that's what an old photo shows. But he slept there with me in that tent, and as I remember he slept well.

He also rested on a thin canvas cot, spindly with aluminum legs, beside me for a week in Deary, Idaho, while we cared for a farm and eighty acres. Each night before we got in bed, we watched the mountains turn purple and heard the great-horned owls hoot. Then we checked each other's scalp for ticks that helped themselves to suppers of our blood.

There was another time, another long drive, all the way to Disneyland, sleeping at campgrounds and eating fast food. The first night in that plastic province we had some fish at a restaurant and took turns heaving at the motel toilet till after midnight. The next day he was cheerful enough to mug for my camera beside a wax-museum figure of Mr. T.

And we had dangerous times together—like driving the North Cascades Highway and hitting a mule deer that nearly crashed through the car windshield, like colliding with a runaway pickup wheel that disabled our Honda wagon on Interstate 5. After dark on foot we crossed those busy freeway lanes, southbound and northbound alike, holding hands and running hard and dodging cars, to reach a lighted rest stop on the other side.

Sleep returns after two months; it ravels back my tattered sleeves. In Bellingham we hold a memorial service. At that service Braden's friends and family speak. I stand up and speak, unsure at first if I can pull it off. My four-year-old son, Reed, takes the hand of his sobbing aunt and looks her in the eye. He and Braden had swum together.

Now it is July. Vicki says she hopes he won't be found—skeletal, decayed—rather that he be left alone. I agree, if only for her sake. Let him stay in Puget Sound, cushioned by seaweed, rocked by storms and tides. Finding him would be an irruption of the organic cycle. Instead we parents will erect a bench above the beach. That bench will warn off the ill-equipped, the innocent, the invincible. And it will honor our sons.

barry lopez

Not all human impact on nature is destructive. In simple yet fully descriptive language, Lopez recounts his surprise at discovering an ancient *intaglio* in the California desert—a stone picture created by turning over or clearing rock—and notes that such constructions are a part of nature, and just as vulnerable to destruction. Like other features of the landscape, the stone horse suggests to Lopez the whole epic sweep of human history—as well as one particular moment, one particular horse.

the stone horse*

The deserts of southern California, the high, relatively cooler and wetter Mojave and the hotter, dryer Sonoran to the south of it, carry the signatures of many cultures. Prehistoric rock drawings in the Mojave's Coso Range, probably the greatest concentration of petroglyphs in North America, are at least three thousand years old. Big game-hunting cultures that flourished six or seven thousand years before that are known from broken speak tips, choppers, and burins left scattered along the shores of great Pleistocene[1] lakes, long since evaporated. Weapons and tools discovered at China Lake may be thirty thousand years old; and worked stone from a quarry in the Calico Mountains is, some argue, evidence that human beings were here more than two hundred thousand years ago.

Because of the long-term stability of such arid environments, much of this prehistoric stone evidence still lies exposed on the ground, accessible to anyone who passes by—the studious, the acquisitive, the indifferent, the merely curious. Archaeologists do not agree on the sequence of cultural history beyond about twelve thousand years ago, but it is clear that these broken bits of chalcedony, chert, and obsidian, like the animal drawings and geometric designs etched on walls of basalt throughout the desert, anchor the earliest threads of human history, the first record of human endeavor here.

* From *Antaeus* (Autumn 1986), "On Nature" issue.
[1] A geological epoch lasting from one million to twenty thousand years ago, during which primitive man first appeared on earth.

Western man did not enter the California desert until the end of the eighteenth century, 250 years after Coronado brought his soldiers into the Zuni pueblos in a bewildered search for the cities of Cibola.[2] The earliest appraisals of the land were cursory, hurried. People traveled *through* it, en route to Santa Fe or the California coastal settlements. Only miners tarried. In 1823 what had been Spain's became Mexico's, and in 1848 what had been Mexico's became America's,[3] but the bare, jagged mountains and dry lake beds, the vast and uniform plains of creosote bush and yucca plants, remained as obscure as the northern Sudan until the end of the nineteenth century.

Before 1940 the tangible evidence of twentieth-century man's passage here consisted of very little—the hard tracery of travel corridors; the widely scattered, relatively insignificant evidence of mining operations; and the fair expanse of irrigated fields at the desert's periphery. In the space of a hundred years or so the wagon roads were paved, railroads were laid down, and canals and high-tension lines were built to bring water and electricity across the desert to Los Angeles from the Colorado River. The dark mouths of gold, talc, and tin mines yawned from the bony flanks of desert ranges. Dust-encrusted chemical plants stood at work on the lonely edges of dry lake beds. And crops of grapes, lettuce, dates, alfalfa, and cotton covered the Coachella and Imperial valleys, north and south of the Salton Sea, and the Palo Verde Valley along the Colorado.

These developments proceeded with little or no awareness of earlier human occupations by cultures that preceded those of the historic Indians—the Mojave, the Chemehuevi, the Quechan. (Ex-

---

[2] Francisco Vasquez de Coronado (1510–54), Spanish explorer of the region that is now the southwestern United States, searched for the seven cities of Cibola, fabled for their wealth.

[3] Mexico acquired much of the present U.S. Southwest after the Mexicans won their independence from Spain, but lost this territory to the United States in the Treaty of Guadalupe Hidalgo in 1848 at the conclusion of the Mexican War.

tensive irrigation began actually to change the climate of the Sonoran Desert, and human settlements, the railroads, and farming introduced many new, successful plants into the region.)

During World War II, the American military moved into the desert in great force, to train troops and to test equipment. They found the clear weather conducive to year-round flying, the dry air and isolation very attractive. After the war, a complex of training grounds, storage facilities, and gunnery and test ranges was permanently settled on more than three million acres of military reservations. Few perceived the extent or significance of the destruction of the aboriginal sites that took place during tank maneuvers and bombing runs or in the laying out of highways, railroads, mining districts, and irrigated fields. The few who intuited that something like an American Dordogne Valley[4] lay exposed here were only amateur archaeologists; even they reasoned that the desert was too vast for any of this to matter.

After World War II, people began moving out of the crowded Los Angeles basin into homes in Lucerne, Apple, and Antelope valleys in the western Mojave. They emigrated as well to a stretch of resort land at the foot of the San Jacinto Mountains that included Palm Springs, and farther out to old railroad and military towns like Twenty-nine Palms and Barstow. People also began exploring the desert, at first in military-surplus jeeps and then with a variety of all-terrain and off-road vehicles that became available in the 1960s. By the mid-1970s, the number of people using such vehicles for desert recreation had increased exponentially. Most came and went in innocent curiosity; the few who didn't wreaked a havoc all out of proportion to their numbers. The disturbance of previously isolated archaeological sites increased by an order of magnitude. Many sites were vandalized before archaeologists, themselves late to the desert,

[4] A region in southwestern France, site of numerous prehistoric caves.

had any firm grasp of the bounds of human history in the desert. It was as though in the same moment an Aztec[5] library had been discovered intact various lacunae[6] had begun to appear.

The vandalism was of three sorts: the general disturbance usually caused by souvenir hunters and by the curious and the oblivious; the wholesale stripping of a place by professional thieves for black-market sale and trade; and outright destruction, in which vehicles were actually used to ram and trench an area. By 1980, the Bureau of Land Management estimated that probably 35 percent of the archaeological sites in the desert had been vandalized. The destruction at some places by rifles and shotguns, or by power winches mounted on vehicles, was, if one cared for history, demoralizing to behold.

In spite of public education, land closures, and stricter law enforcement in recent years, the BLM estimates that, annually, about 1 percent of the archaeological record in the desert continues to be destroyed or stolen.

2

A BLM archaeologist told me, with understandable reluctance, where to find the intaglio. I spread my Automobile Club of Southern California map of Imperial County out on his desk, and he traced the route with a pink felt-tip pen. The line crossed Interstate 8 and then turned west along the Mexican border.

"You can't drive any farther than about here," he said, marking a small X. "There's boulders in the wash. You walk up past them."

On a separate piece of paper, he drew a route in a smaller scale that would take me up the arroyo to a certain point where I was to

---

[5] A Nahuatl-speaking people who in the fifteenth and early sixteenth centuries ruled a large empire in what is now central and southern Mexico.
[6] In this sense, spaces where something has been omitted or has come out, a gap, a hiatus.

cross back east, to another arroyo. At its head, on higher ground just to the north, I would find the horse.

"It's tough to spot unless you know it's there. Once you pick it up . . ." He shook his head slowly, in a gesture of wonder at its existence. I waited until I held his eye. I assured him I would not tell anyone else how to get there. He looked at me in stoical despair, like a man who had been robbed twice, whose belief in human beings was offered without conviction.

I did not go until the following day because I wanted to see it at dawn. I ate breakfast at four A.M. in El Centro and then drove south. The route was easy to follow, though the last section of road proved difficult, broken and drifted over with sand in some spots. I came to the barricade of boulders and parked. It was light enough by then to find my way over the ground with little trouble. The contours of the landscape were stark, without any masking vegetation. I worried only about rattlesnakes.

I traversed the stone plain as directed, but, in spite of the frankness of the land, I came on the horse unawares. In the first moment of recognition I was without feeling. I recalled later being startled, and that I held my breath. It was laid out on the ground with its head to the east, three times life-size. As I took in its outline I felt a growing concentration of all my senses, as though my attentiveness to the pale rose color of the morning sky and other peripheral images had now ceased to be important. I was aware that I was straining for sound in the windless air, and I felt the uneven pressure of the earth hard against my feet. The horse, outlined in a standing profile on the dark ground, was as vivid before me as a bed of tulips.

I've come upon animals suddenly before, and felt a similar tension, a precipitate heightening of the senses. And I have felt the inexplicable but sharply boosted intensity of a wild moment in the bush, where it is not until some minutes later that you discover the source of electricity—the warm remains of a grizzly bear kill, or the still moist tracks of a wolverine.

But this was slightly different. I felt I had stepped into an unoccupied corridor. I had no familiar sense of history, the temporal structure in which to think: this horse was made by Quechan people three hundred years ago. I felt instead a headlong rush of images: people hunting wild horses with spears on the Pleistocene veld of southern California; Cortés riding across the causeway into Montezuma's Tenochtitlán;[7] a short-legged Comanche, astride his horse like some sort of ferret, slashing through cavalry lines of young men who rode like farmers;[8] a hoof exploding past my face one morning in a corral in Wyoming. These images had the weight and silence of stone.

When I released my breath, the images softened. My initial feeling, of facing a wild animal in a remote region, was replaced with a calm sense of antiquity. It was then that I became conscious, like an ordinary tourist, of what was before me, and though: this horse was probably laid out by Quechan people. *But when?* I wondered. The first horses they saw, I knew, might have been those that came north from Mexico in 1692 with Father Eusebio Kino.[9] But Cocopa people, I recalled, also came this far north on occasion, to fight with their neighbors, the Quechan. And *they* could have seen horses with Melchior Diaz,[10] at the mouth of the Colorado River in the fall of 1540. So, it could be four hundred years old. (No one in fact knows.)

I still had not moved. I took my eyes off the horse for a moment to look south over the desert plain into Mexico, to look east past its head at the brightening sunrise, to situate myself. Then, finally, I

[7] Hernando Cortés (c. 1485–1547), Spanish conqueror of Mexico, conquered in 1521 the Aztec capital city of Tenochtitlán, which was located on an island in Lake Texcoco, where Mexico City stands today. Montezuma II, ruler of the Aztecs, had welcomed Cortés to his capital on November 8, 1519, and the Spanish stayed there, holding him hostage.

[8] The Comanches, who often attacked settlers on the southern U.S. plains until the last of them were settled on a reservation in 1875, were known as the finest native American horsemen of the West.

[9] Kino (1644–1711) was the most famous of the seventeenth-century Spanish explorers and Jesuit missionaries in what became the U.S. Southwest.

[10] Diaz, one of Coronado's officers, explored the Sonoran Desert and the delta of the Colorado River in 1540.

brought my trailing foot slowly forward and stood erect. Sunlight was running like a thin sheet of water over the stony ground and it threw the horse into relief. It looked as though no hand had ever disturbed the stones that gave it its form.

The horse had been brought to life on ground called desert pavement, a tight, flat matrix of small cobbles blasted smooth by sand-laden winds. The uniform, monochromatic blackness of the stones, a patina of iron and magnesium oxides called desert varnish, is caused by long-term exposure to the sun. To make this type of low-relief ground glyph, or intaglio, the artist either selectively turns individual stones over to their lighter side or removes them to expose the lighter soil underneath, creating a negative image. This horse, about eighteen feet from brow to rump and eight feet from wither to hoof, had been made in the latter way, and its outline was bermed at certain points with low ridges of stone a few inches high to enhance its three-dimensional qualities. (The left side of the horse was in full profile; each leg was extended at ninety degrees to the body and fully visible, as though seen in three-quarter profile.)

I was not eager to move. The moment I did I would be back in the flow of time, the horse no longer quivering in the same way before me. I did not want to feel again the sequence of quotidian events—to be drawn off into deliberation and analysis. A human being, a four-footed animal, the open land. That was all that was present—and a "thoughtless" understanding of the very old desires bearing on this particular animal: to hunt it, to render it, to fathom it, to subjugate it, to honor it, to take it as a companion.

What finally made me move was the light. The sun now filled the shallow basin of the horse's body. The weighted line of the stone berm created the illusion of a mane and the distinctive roundness of an equine belly. The change in definition impelled me. I moved to the left, circling past its rump, to see how the light might flesh the horse out from various points of view. I circled it completely before squatting on my haunches. Ten or fifteen minutes later I chose another view. The third time I moved, to a point near the rear hooves,

I spotted a stone tool at my feet. I stared at it a long while, more in awe than disbelief, before reaching out to pick it up. I turned it over in my left palm and took it between my fingers to feel its cutting edge. It is always difficult, especially with something so portable, to rechannel the desire to steal.

I spent several hours with the horse. As I changed positions and as the angle of the light continued to change I noticed a number of things. The angle at which the pastern carried the hoof away from the ankle was perfect. Also, stones had been placed within the image to suggest at precisely the right spot the left shoulder above the fore-leg. The line that joined thigh and hock was similarly accurate. The muzzle alone seemed distorted—but perhaps these stones had been moved by a later hand. It was an admirably accurate representation, but not what a breeder would call perfect conformation. There was the suggestion of a bowed neck and an undershot jaw, and the tail, as full as a winter coyote's, did not appear to be precisely to scale.

The more I thought about it, the more I felt I was looking at an individual horse, a unique combination of generic and specific detail. It was easy to imagine one of Kino's horses as a model, or a horse that ran off from one of Coronado's columns. *What kind of horses would these have been?* I wondered. In the sixteenth century the most sought-after horses in Europe were Spanish, the offspring of Arabian stock and Barbary horses that the Moors brought to Iberia and bred to the older, eastern European strains brought in by the Romans. The model for this horse, I speculated, could easily have been a palomino, or a descendant of horses trained for lion hunting in North Africa.

A few generations ago, cowboys, cavalry quartermasters, and draymen would have taken this horse before me under consideration and not let up their scrutiny until they had its heritage fixed to their satisfaction. Today, the distinction between draft and harness horses is arcane knowledge, and no image may come to mind for a blue roan or a claybank horse. The loss of such refinement in everyday conversation leaves me unsettled. People praise the Es-

kimo's ability to distinguish among forty types of snow but forget
the skill of others who routinely differentiate between overo and tobiano pintos.[11] Such distinctions are made for the same reason. You
have to do it to talk clearly about the world.

For parts of two years I worked as a horse wrangler and packer
in Wyoming. It is dim knowledge now; I would have to think to remember if a buckskin was a kind of dun horse. And I couldn't
throw a double-diamond hitch over a set of panniers—the packer's
basic tie-down—without guidance. As I squatted there in the desert,
however, these more personal memories seemed tenuous in compar-
ison with the sweep of this animal in human time. My memories
had no depth. I thought of the Hittite cavalry riding against the
Syrians 3,500 years ago. And the first of the Chinese emperors,
Ch'in Shih Huang, buried in Shensi Province in 210 B.C. with thousands of life-size horses and soldiers, a terra-cotta guardian army.
What could I know of what was in the mind of whoever made this
horse? Was there some racial memory of it as an animal that had
once fed the artist's ancestors and then disappeared from North
America? And then returned in this strange alliance with another
race of men?

Certainly, whoever it was, the artist had observed the animal
very closely. Certainly the animal's speed had impressed him.
Among the first things the Quechan would have learned from an
encounter with Kino's horses was that their own long-distance run-
ners—men who could run down mule deer—were no match for
this animal.

From where I squatted I could look far out over the Mexican
plain. Juan Bautista de Anza[12] passed this way in 1774, extending El
Camino Real into Alta California from Sinaloa. He was followed by

---

[11] The two color patterns for this breed of horse. The overo have white spreading irregu-
larly up from the belly, mixed with a darker color, and the tobiano have white spreading down from the back in clear-cut patterns.

[12] De Anza (1735–88), later governor of new Mexico, explored the route to California,
founding San Francisco in 1775.

others, all of them astride the magical horse; *gente de razón,* the people of reason, coming into the country of *los primitivos.* The horse, like the stone animals of Egypt, urged these memories upon me. And as I drew them up from some forgotten corner of my mind—huge horses carved in the white chalk downs of southern England by an Iron Age people; Spanish horses rearing and wheeling in fear before alligators in Florida—the images seemed tethered before me. With this sense of proportion, a memory of my own—the morning I almost lost my face to a horse's hoof—now had somewhere to fit.

I rose up and began to walk slowly around the horse again. I had taken the first long measure of it and was now looking for a way to depart, a new angle of light, a fading of the image itself before the rising sun, that would break its hold on me. As I circled, feeling both heady and serene at the encounter, I realized again how strangely vivid it was. It had been created on a barren bajada[13] between two arroyos, as nondescript a place as one could imagine. The only plant life here was a few wands of ocotillo cactus. The ground beneath my shoes was so hard it wouldn't take the print of a heavy animal even after a rain. The only sounds I heard here were the voices of quail.

The archaeologist had been correct. For all its forcefulness, the horse is inconspicuous. If you don't care to see it you can walk right past it. That pleases him, I think. Unmarked on this bleak shoulder of the plain, the site signals to no one; so he wants no protective fences here, no informative plaque, to act as beacons. He would rather take a chance that no motorcyclist, no aimless wanderer with a flair for violence and a depth of ignorance, will ever find his way here.

The archaeologist had given me something before I left his office that now seemed peculiar—an aerial photograph of the horse. It is widely believed that an aerial view of an intaglio provides a fair and accurate depiction. It does not. In the photograph the horse

---

[13] A broad slope of debris of rocks and gravel.

looks somewhat crudely constructed; from the ground it appears far more deftly rendered. The photograph is of a single moment, and in that split second the horse seems vaguely impotent. I watched light pool in the intaglio at dawn; I imagine you could watch it withdraw at dusk and sense the same animation I did. In those prolonged moments its shape and so, too, its general character changed—noticeably. The living quality of the image, its immediacy to the eye, was brought out by the light-in-time, not, at least here, in the camera's frozen instant.

Intaglios, I thought, were never meant to be seen by gods in the sky above. They were meant to be seen by people on the ground, over a long period of shifting light. This could even be true of the huge figures on the Plain of Nazca in Peru, where people could walk for the length of a day beside them.[14] It is our own impatience that makes us think otherwise.

This process of abstraction, almost unintentional, drew me gradually away from the horse. I came to a position of attention at the edge of the sphere of its influence. With a slight bow I paid my respects to the horse, its maker, and the history of us all, and departed.

A short distance away I stopped the car in the middle of the road to make a few notes. I could not write down what I was thinking when I was with the horse. It would have seemed disrespectful, and it would have required another kind of attention. So now I patiently drained my memory of the details it had fastened itself upon. The road I'd stopped on was adjacent to the All American Canal, the major source of water for the Imperial and Coachella valleys. The water flowed west placidly. A disjointed flock of coots, small,

[14] Gigantic lines from an unknown civilization are laid out geometrically on the thirty-seven-mile-long Plain of Nazca in southern Peru.

dark birds with white bills, was paddling against the current, forag-
ing in the rushes.

I was peripherally aware of the birds as I wrote, the only movement in the desert, and of a series of sounds from a village a half-mile
away. The first sounds from this collection of ramshackle houses in a
grove of cottonwoods were the distracted dawn voices of dogs. I
heard them intermingled with the cries of a rooster. Later, the high-
pitched voices of children calling out to each other came disembod-
ied through the dry desert air. Now, a little after seven, I could hear
someone practicing on the trumpet, the same rough phrases played
over and over. I suddenly remembered how as children we had tried
to get the rhythm of a galloping horse with hands against the thighs,
or by fluttering our tongues against the roofs of our mouths.

After the trumpet, the impatient calls of adults summoning
children. Sunday morning. Wood smoke hung like a lens in the
trees. The first car starts—a cold eight-cylinder engine, of Chrysler
extraction perhaps, goosed to life, then throttled back to murmur
through dual mufflers, the obbligato music of a shade-tree mechanic. The rote bark of mongrel dogs at dawn, the jagged outcries
of men and women, an engine coming to life. Like a thousand vil-
lages from West Virginia to Guadalajara.

I finished my notes—where was I going to find a description of
the horses that came north with the conquistadors? Did their manes
come forward prominently over the brow, like this one's, like the
forelocks of Blackfeet and Assiniboin men in nineteenth-century
paintings? I set the notes on the seat beside me.

The road followed the canal for a while and then arced north,
toward Interstate 8. It was slow driving and I fell to thinking how
the desert had changed since Anza had come through. New plants
and animals—the MacDougall cottonwood, the English house spar-
row, the chukar from India[15]—have about them now the air of the

---

[15] A gray-and-black partridge introduced into dry parts of the western United States
from India.

native born. Of the native species, some—no one knows how many—are extinct. The populations of many others, especially the animals, have been sharply reduced. The idea of a desert impoverished by agricultural poisons and varmint hunters, by off-road vehicles and military operations, did not seem as disturbing to me, however, as this other horror, now that I had been those hours with the horse. The vandals, the few who crowbar rock art off the desert's walls, who dig up graves, who punish the ground that holds intaglios, are people who devour history. Their self-centered scorn, their disrespect for ideas and images beyond their ken, create the awful atmosphere of loose ends in which totalitarianism thrives, in which the past is merely curious or wrong.

I thought about the horse sitting out there on the unprotected plain. I enumerated its qualities in my mind until a sense of its vulnerability receded and it became an anchor for something else. I remembered that history, a history like this one, which ran deeper than Mexico, deeper than the Spanish, was a kind of medicine. It permitted the great breadth of human expression to reverberate, and it did not urge you to locate its apotheosis in the present.

Each of us, individuals and civilizations, has been held upside down like Achilles in the River Styx.[16] The artist mixing his colors in the dim light of Altamira;[17] an Egyptian ruler lying still now, wrapped in his bysses, stored against time in a pyramid; the faded Dorset culture of the Arctic;[18] the Hmong and Samburu and Walbiri of historic time;[19] the modern nations. This great, imperfect stretch of human expression is the clarification and encouragement,

[16] Achilles' mother dipped him in the River Styx, holding him upside down by the heels, to make him invulnerable and hence immortal.

[17] A cave in northern Spain with Old Stone Age drawings of animals.

[18] A culture in Greenland and the Canadian eastern Arctic that flourished between approximately 800 B.C. and A.D. 1300; it is not certain exactly when or why Dorset culture disappeared, although the artifacts that remain give an idea of its nature and its daily life.

[19] The Hmong, also called Miao or Meo, are mountain-dwelling peoples of China and Southeast Asia; the Samburu are a tribe in Kenya; the Walbiri are aborigines of the desert in central Australia.

the urging and the reminder, we call history. And it is inscribed everywhere in the face of the land, from the mountain passes of the Himalayas to a nameless bajada in the California desert.

Small birds rose up in the road ahead, startled, and flew off. I prayed no infidel would ever find that horse.

john hales

This piece deals in powerful images and sense impressions, tying them together: a grandfather's Enfield rifle, used to kill in WWI, stock still slippery with oil; the warmth and scent of two teenagers in the back of a parent's station wagon; the bloody yet clinical disassembly of a boy's first kill, a buck. The year is 1968 in Utah, and as the Vietnam War draws closer, Hales gives us a fine-grained portrait of "the legacy of growing up Mormon and American."

love, war, and deer hunting

1

I remember my first real deer hunt, the year I turned sixteen and was allowed by state law and local custom to finally carry a rifle and kill a deer, as somehow entirely adolescent, unlike any deer hunt I'd been on before. In my memory, the hunt begins and ends with my girlfriend. We'd met that Friday morning as we did every school day, at her locker after second period, where she wished me luck and gave me the kind of quick dutiful kiss a suburban housewife might send a husband off to work with, and I ran from the rest of the school day with my two friends (who were also embarking on their first hunt) across the ROTC parade ground to the jeep I'd left in the parking lot. We drove south from Ogden through Salt Lake City and Provo and then through a series of increasingly smaller towns huddled against the Wasatch Mountains where they'd been placed by Brigham Young a century before, turned eastward at Nephi, a small town named in honor of a heroic character in *The Book of Mormon,* followed ever-narrower dirt roads high into the mountains and found a campsite.

We woke early on opening day, and late that morning I shot a deer. I remember nearly all the details of the actual shooting, but after that it's hazy. I know I gutted the deer—a young buck—and with some difficulty hauled it over my shoulder up a long steep hill to the jeep, and drove us all back to Ogden, but I can recall little of the long afternoon that followed the killing. What I remember most

178

clearly involves driving to my girlfriend's house, helping her on with her coat against the cold of the open jeep, and driving her to my house where she admired the deer I'd killed, hanging head down from a rafter in the garage, still slightly warm to the touch and dripping an occasional drop of blood.

That's how I remember the beginning, middle, and end of that first deer hunt. I remember my girlfriend, the details that surrounded my shooting the deer, and I can picture with remarkable clarity the rifle I'd killed it with. I'd borrowed the rifle—an ancient British Enfield .303, still slippery with preservative and heavy with military sights and other attachments designed for the trenches of France and the outposts of the British Empire—from my grandfather, but other than this distant patriarchal presence, and the fact that I'd borrowed my father's jeep, elders were strangely absent from my first real hunt, an important rite of passage for Mormon boys normally presided over by older men—fathers and grandfathers, uncles and family friends—who would provide the stories, make the jokes, and supervise the ritual of smearing the boy's face with the blood of his first kill. I'd been a spectator on a half-dozen hunts like this, accompanying my father, my older brother, and other hunters, learning the ways one stalked and then skinned his kill, looking forward to the time I'd be inducted into this society of hunters according to the old rules.

Although I'd missed my chance that year to experience the more formal rites of initiation, there were two hunts yet to come, two more opportunities to insinuate myself into the tradition: the next year's hunt, this time with my father, my older brother, and several family friends, when I'd shot my second and final deer, a doe, with a sporterized Springfield 30.06 I'd bought from a friend who'd just learned his girlfriend was pregnant; and the third hunt, when we'd finally gotten it right according to the conventions of deer hunting in Utah. That year, three generations of Hales men—my grandfather, my father, and me—joined in stalking deer in the mountains of northern Utah. From a distance, this hunt might have looked traditional, even tribal, the passing on of cultural lore and wisdom. In a way, it was.

The grandfather who joined us on that third hunt was the grandfather I'd borrowed the Enfield from, my father's father, a professor of physics at Brigham Young University. He'd purchased the rifle at least twenty years earlier for reasons no one in the family could remember. My grandpa Hales had never fired the Enfield, never even unwrapped the heavy brown paper it had been sealed in when it had been retired shortly after its service in the original war to end all wars. This grandfather was not an Army surplus kind of man. Unlike my other grandfather, my mother's father who had fought in two wars, my grandpa Hales had never worn a military uniform, let alone carried a weapon in war. As far as I know he had never even been on a deer hunt until we'd made it multigenerational on that last hunt, three deer seasons after I'd shot that first deer with my teenage friends, a year after shooting my second and last, the year I'd decided to give up hunting for good.

So of three generations of Hales men who went deer hunting that third year, only one of us—my father—actually carried a gun. In this inversion of tradition, it was the family patriarch, my grandfather, who was experiencing his first deer hunt. I was the youngest, yet had decided to stop hunting, and was instead walking some kind of late-1960s line between embracing nonviolence and participating in a cultural event I continued to value deeply; and my father was hunting for reasons that remain mysterious to me. Of that hunt, I remember that my father succeeded in shooting a deer, and I remember that during the long night before opening day, my grandfather twice had to leave the warmth of the pickup camper to relieve himself. The second time, noticing that I was awake, he leaned over to me and said, with only a glimmer of smile visible in the dark: "It's awful being old."

2

Two years earlier, that late autumn of my sixteenth year, my first deer hunt, I found myself camped then not with my grandfather or father or any other elder prepared to preside over my initiation into manhood (during his first hunt, my older brother had not only gotten the blood treatment on his forehead and cheeks; he had been forced by an older hunter to take a few bites of the liver of his still twitching deer), but with two friends from my neighborhood who were also hunting deer for the first time, and were also without their fathers. I was hunting with a borrowed rifle, my grandfather's Enfield, because I'd somehow arrived at the week of my first deer hunt without a deer rifle of my own. I'd spent a year attempting to track down exactly the right one, reading *The Shooter's Bible* and visiting every gun and pawn shop in Ogden, enjoying the process so much that I never found my way to an actual purchase. My father, who had recently completed an even longer process of building a sporting rifle out of a surplus Swedish Mauser, remembered that an unwrapped British Enfield had been stored in his father's garage. I drove the one hundred miles to Provo, had dinner with Grandpa and his second wife—my grandfather had been dissuaded from following my grandmother too soon to their plot in the Provo cemetery by this short pleasant woman who kept bringing plates of food to our table—and after dinner he found the rifle in the garage, wrapped like a corpse, aromatic with the competing smells of oil and decay.

I drove back to Ogden, unwrapped the Enfield, and fought discouragement as I held the heavy, slippery thing in my hands and rubbed off as much of the grease as I could, wiping it down with paper towels and rags soaked in the solvents and oils I used to clean my .22. I managed to bring a little luster to the dark metal parts that eventually revealed themselves, but the stock had been soaking up grease for half a century and it remained a little oily in my hands, still giving off smells of petroleum, gunpowder and, I imagined, the soggy trenches of wartime France. I was still intensely aware of that complex odor even as I squeezed off the round that tore into the hide and bone of my first kill.

It was a strange shot. I'd been walking slowly and as quietly as I could manage across a steep hillside toward a promising spot near the head of a ravine when I'd caught in the corner of my eye the quiet unmistakable flash of mule deer, below and almost behind me. I stopped, peered down through the steep aspen-shaded grove, and watched with an unforeseen degree of patience and focus as seven mule deer walked slowly but purposefully below me, their gray-brown backs moving single file through the tall grass and sagebrush where the hillside flattened a little on its way to becoming a meadow. It felt a little like an ambush. The deer had no sense that I was there, waiting above them concealed like a sniper in brush and quaking aspen; they were doing the kind of milling around that deer are driven to during deer season, when they've been understandably spooked by the sudden appearance of half the male population of the cities and towns of Utah, men who on Friday afternoon pitched tents and parked trailers alongside usually empty dirt roads, bedding down in the deer's territory for reasons I imagined deer wondering about. If the deer were puzzled by all this traffic on Friday, they were completely overwhelmed by the activity that commenced at sunrise Saturday, opening day, kept on the move by what I imagined to be the sounds of war, random echoes of gunfire near and distant.

I surprised myself with my calm. I flipped off the safety and watched over the long barrel, waiting for a glimpse of antlers, waiting for the clearest shot through the buckbrush and the white aspen trunks, finally taking serious aim at the last deer in the line, one I was pretty sure was a buck. I lined up the sights and deliberately aimed low, somehow able to remember what I'd heard over the years about the need to set your sights just below the kill spot when shooting downhill.

I also managed to remember what I'd learned only a few hours earlier that morning when I'd sighted in the rifle against a target I'd drawn on a cardboard box and set up against a hillside close to where I'd parked my father's jeep. Examining the pattern of holes in the cardboard, I'd learned that the sights were off a little: The barrel sent the bullet to a place just left of the spot indicated by the sight. The tweaked sights were fresh in my memory because I'd committed the almost unpardonable sin of heading into the woods on opening day without having sighted in my rifle. I'd picked up the Enfield from Grandpa only the weekend before, and I'd spent one evening cleaning it, taking it apart, and running live rounds through the chamber to make sure it fed properly and wouldn't jam in the heat of battle. Then, with the ammunition safely back in its box, I had dry fired it over and over again, taking aim against imaginary targets in my bedroom, trying to get a feel for the bolt action, the resistance of the trigger, the view over the elaborate military sights, the weight and balance and the fit of the heel plate against my shoulder. But I'd never actually fired it until opening day.

The week had been busy; there was school, and my after-school job sweeping out classrooms at the elementary school down the street from my house, and of course there was my girlfriend, with whom I'd spent every evening after dinner. Each night I'd drive to her house with my textbooks and homework and we'd concentrate earnestly together for an hour or so, touching shoulders over our work, getting closer and closer until we were doing the kind of touching that took us to the couch downstairs in the family room, where we'd frustrate each other for a few hours in our struggle to stop short of what our religion told us was of ultimate and eternal importance. Although we'd been dating for more than six months, we'd finally admitted that we were in love with each other, and we'd begun moving in a direction that was new for both of us, touching each other in places and in ways that until that fall we'd only wondered about, our hands moving above and then under clothing, finally releasing buttons, sliding zippers, our kisses following the slope of our necks to shoulders and throats and the bare skin under our shirts, our hands inching farther and farther below our loosened belts. We were discovering how our bodies worked, moving against each other in ways that worried us afterward and prompted no little discussion about guilt and control and just where we were in that dark murky area this side of the one specific act that we knew was wrong.

This was new to both of us. I was sixteen and she was a year younger, both of us kept relatively innocent until now less by our youth than by the proscriptions of our religion and the comfort and conventionality of our middle-class homes, and so we were discovering something new, it seemed, each time we moved to the couch in her family room. We were coming to understand something about physical and moral release at the same time we were learning control, exploring the boundaries between negotiation and surrender, keeping somehow a cool center of calm in the heated storm of urge and skin, discovering an ability to be ultimately responsible that I still wonder about and sometimes regret.

I probably should have postponed work a few hours and driven directly from school to the familiar abandoned gravel pit above Ogden Valley, a place distant and rural enough for us to shoot high-caliber rifles safely, equipped with a crude table made of old fence-posts and a row of railroad ties stacked a hundred yards away against an eroded dirt backstop. Weeks earlier, in the last warm days of an Indian summer, I'd helped my friends sight in their rifles, nestling their beautiful civilian guns into sandbags, treating their rifles with the calm and precision necessary to evaluate the accuracy of the sights, to experience as if under laboratory conditions the kick, to examine as if from a distance the science involved in firing live rounds of large-caliber ammunition.

I knew that in preparing for a deer hunt—especially your first carrying a firearm, when you don't really know how you'll react when the sudden view of the deer and the surge of adrenaline hit you at the same time—it was important to experience the actual firing of the specific rifle you'll carry into the woods, to feel the way the physics actually play out in practice, the action of the bullet's trajectory and the reaction of the butt against your shoulder, the explosion taking place less than an inch from your cheek pressed against the smooth wood of the stock, the sharp crack of the bullet, the smell of powder and fire, the practical application of the theoretical equation of shooting a gun. But a late afternoon in the mountains meant a night sweeping out classrooms, and I didn't want to give up even one evening with my girlfriend, this week of all weeks—it was that simple.

So I was fortunate to encounter the deer later in the morning of opening day, after I'd discovered how badly off the sights were. My friends and I had tried to do the right thing—deer hunting wisdom proclaimed that most deer were shot during the first hour of dawn on opening day of the season, and even though none of us could remember anybody we knew actually bagging a deer before 8 A.M., we were determined to be at the stands we'd located the day before, when we'd hiked around after setting up camp, locating likely spots alongside deer trails, near saddles and ravines that (the theory went) would funnel deer into walking a slow parade across our sights.

Even though we were on our own, we had no trouble remembering what older hunters had intoned on earlier hunts and in conversations around family dinner tables. I think we had mixed feelings about being out there alone, enjoying as any teenagers would the luxury of not being watched by grown-ups, yet missing the many benefits age and experience brought to something as logistically complicated as a deer hunt. We were responsible kids, and our parents trusted us to not shoot each other, but we were still only sixteen years old and were a little flaky on details. For example, none of us had brought a watch, and so we slept nervously, not knowing whether the darkness outside the tent indicated midnight or 5 A.M. We erred on the side of caution, not wanting to make this first mistake on the first deer hunt of our lives, and therefore endured an excruciatingly cold slow sequence of hours, hours that seemed even longer for our not being able to actually count them.

We shivered in the dark, looked forward to the emergence of the sun with a longing that bordered on pagan, squinted into the long, gray half-light trying desperately to see those deer that we were sure would arrive eager to lay down their lives for our emerging manhood, but no deer came. After a couple of fruitless solitary hours, we rejoined each other at the jeep according to plan, discussed our failure and considered our options. We decided to drive up the road a ways, higher up along the ridgeline, following a second piece of deer hunting theory we'd learned from our fathers: Unless there's snow to keep them down, nervous deer head uphill. Now in no real hurry—we were sure we'd missed our best chance—we warmed ourselves in the morning sun, sitting on the tailgate of my father's jeep and eating the peanut butter and jelly sandwiches our mothers had made for us, then decided to shoot a few rounds in order to remind ourselves of why we were there and, in my case, to see if my rifle's sights lined up.

Handling the Enfield was a military experience: There's no other way to say it. Wiping off the cosmoline had brought to light a configuration determined by wartime necessity, not mere sport. The Enfield's barrel and receiver were enclosed in a reddish-brown stock, scratched and dented by hard use and then softened by its fifty-year oil bath, and most of the many attachments and accessories had only military function for explanation: swivels and gray metal loops for attaching the shoulder strap, the heavy steel wings that protected the front sight and served to reinforce the bayonet mount beneath. Even the stock itself—running from butt to front sight—was intended to provide a good grip as its original owner, I imagined, against all common sense heaved himself out of a trench and into the line of fire.

I noticed that I handled my rifle differently from the way my friends handled their civilian Winchesters and Remingtons. The Enfield's configuration invited a more casual grasp and less concern about protecting the ornamentation that set off my friend's rifles, the beautiful but vulnerable checkering on their elegantly finished stocks, the polished blue steel of the barrel gleaming beyond the forestock, the gold bead of the fragile front sight—or, on one friend's rifle, the expensive optical complexity of the scope. My rifle had been thrown into trucks, dragged down rutted roads, perhaps—I imagined—dropped to the ground by a man whose flesh was that instant torn by a bullet sent by someone else's rifle, a piece of equipment similarly designed by the enemy to survive treatment at once careless and intimate, without real value until that moment of ultimate use.

Of course, most of my understanding of this rifle's story was pure imagination, the details served up by the endless stream of World War II movies that by the late '50s and early '60s showed up with monotonous regularity on morning and afternoon television, films in which platoons of young men of carefully varied ethnicity and social class—rural and urban, several with no education, some with money, most with wives and girlfriends of either the faithful or unfaithful variety—all carried their weapons in the same way, with regard for their utility and necessity but with a complete disregard for cosmetics. Of course they slept with them, but they were neither substitutes for women nor icons of manliness. In these movies, the bonding was with the other men in the squad, a collection of contentious individuals who in the first half of the movie became beloved comrades, a single unit created by Hollywood only to be whittled away relentlessly through the movie's second half by the skill of passionless enemy snipers, anonymous machine gunners, or by mortar rounds hurled from enemy emplacements that could only be taken out by artillery or by fighter-bombers that never came when they were most needed.

The rifles they carried were appliances, the tools of their trade, and I remember that these men paid attention to them only between battles, cleaning them finally when they had the leisure to talk about everything more important: the recent dead, the particular hellhole they'd be sent next, the wives and girlfriends who waited for their return.

I'm certain that the moment of my political awakening came when I finally recognized the difference between the war movies of my youth and the evening news of my teenage years, the televised real-time narrative of the Vietnam War. Those earlier movies taught me how wars should be fought: athletic and wholesome American boys charging with their dependable Springfield rifles in the direction of robotic German machine gunners or maniacal Asians, unkempt but handsome kids throwing grenades like hookshots. We learned from these movies how to cradle our rifles in the crooks of our arms as we moved on our knees and elbows like spiders toward the machine gun nests of our warplay, moves we eventually played out with live ammunition in the foothills above our houses as we moved uphill toward piles of rocks we'd imagined to be dangerous foreign soldiers; rocks, trees, and beer cans we'd take out with our .22s when we were old enough to be allowed to shoot real bullets but not old enough to fully understand just how dangerous those bullets really were.

So I'd begun learning about war from afternoon movies and from mornings carrying my .22 rifle into the foothills above Ogden, shooting birds and snakes, and at cans and bottles we'd make believe were enemy soldiers foolishly exposing themselves above their fortifications. Later, about the time I stopped playing war with my friends, I was required to play war in public school, learning military strategy and weaponry in a classroom, my texts actual U.S. Army manuals. In 1967 I entered the tenth grade, the first year of high school and the only year I was destined to spend in the uniform of my country. ROTC was required of all sophomore boys instead of physical education, for reasons that must have had to do with the buildup in Vietnam—it had been an elective the year before, enlisting only those volunteers we termed "RO puds" and considered pathetic, needing a uniform to compensate for low IQs or bad skin. But all the males in the sophomore class were drafted that year, and on the first day—after we were issued uniforms and brass to be worn, freshly pressed and polished, each Wednesday—we were given our own personal weapons, to be disassembled and cleaned regularly, to be marched with weekly and to be bonded with throughout. We were given five minutes to memorize the rifle's serial number, and punished throughout the year with push-ups if we couldn't pronounce that sacred number on command.

These were serious weapons: M1s, straight from World War II and the Korean War, displaced from service by the slightly more evolved M14 and, eventually, by the dinky little M16, a weapon smaller than some of the pellet guns I'd owned, a rifle that seemed to have more in common with my Ruger .22 than my grandfather's Enfield. My personal M1—serial number 5369464—was heavy, seemingly bigger than I was, credible beyond question. To present the rifle for inspection—to pull the bolt back, offer up the open chamber to a theatrically serious officer (usually an eleventh-grader pathetic enough to re-enlist) and after an inspection that never failed to disclose some grime somewhere, to snap the bolt closed once again, quickly withdrawing your thumb from the narrow chamber at just the right moment to avoid suffering the embarrassing broken fingernail and blood blister we called "M1 thumb"—was like opening a bank vault, examining the silver glow of your wealth, then slamming the thick door shut. You felt all that heavy metal sliding on invisible beads of grease, closing with groundshaking abruptness, machined steel turning and locking into secure place, keeping safe what was most important in life.

We were never actually allowed to fire our M1s, only to pull the trigger in a dry fire after we'd cocked the rifle for cleaning and inspection, the light quick snap we invariably called a dry hump when officers weren't around. The parody of maleness that was the ROTC depended a lot on sexual innuendo, at least as much as the world of the boys' locker room we had expected to spend our sophomore year snapping towels in. We were required to chant suggestive lyrics as we learned to march in formation—"I know a girl in Tijuana; she knows how but she don't wanna"—and the cadet unfortunate enough to refer to his M1 as a "gun" paid for his error by standing before the assembled troops, and whatever civilian students were walking across the parade ground on their way to smoking cigarettes in the parking lot, and shouting at the top of his lungs: "This is my weapon!" he'd scream, holding out his M1; "This is my gun!" he'd yell, pointing dramatically to his groin; "This is for shooting! This is for fun!"

We understood that all this was stupid and juvenile, aware in only the most superficial and joking ways of the complexity of the connection we were exploring between all that weaponry and the clumsy embraces with girls in the back seats of cars driven by friends old enough to have driver's licenses, gropings of hands and tongues after school and church dances that however frustrating we complained they were, still felt pretty good. We thought dry humping was a kind of sex, not yet understanding what it really was, the fully clothed bumping up against that spot where sexual urges met cultural imperatives, the awkward pressing of nerve endings hard against the proscriptions and guilt that were the legacy of growing up Mormon and American.

These were the experiences that prepared me for shooting a deer with my grandfather's Enfield: war movies, pellet guns, my Ruger .22, the M1 placed in my care by Ogden High School and the United States of America, a gun I could field strip, blindfolded, in fifteen seconds, and flip from vertical rest to shoulder rest to present arms with a precision I both mocked and felt an unaccountable joy in performing. Although I hadn't developed an equal degree of familiarity with my grandfather's Enfield, I recognized the smell of military grease and gunpowder and felt even the connection with death and war.

I'd imagined my M1 at Iwo Jima, at Chosin Reservoir, and I pieced together a similar story behind the Enfield. I imagined a man relieved to have survived the trenches serving out the remainder of his enlistment in a British armory greasing and wrapping the rifle carelessly, consigning it to a crate to be warehoused in anticipation of the next war, in which I believed it did not serve. It was for some reason important for me to believe that my grandfather's rifle had avoided service in World War II, the war of my father and uncles. I imagined that the British had sealed the rifle right after my grand-father's war, barely cool from all the shots I'd imagined it had fired, sometimes unaimed over the trench walls toward the place they believed the enemy to be, sometimes aimed with cool precision at a man's profile less than a hundred yards across a muddy and barbed wired no-man's-land.

This image of a man crumpling to the ground took hold of me at the exact instant I pulled the trigger, firing the Enfield for the first time against the target I'd traced on a cardboard box, weighed down with rocks and set about a hundred yards from the jeep that morning in early November, my first deer hunt. My grip on the stock felt for a moment like someone else's, and my hands seemed to understand easily the fussy complexity of the military rear sight, a ramp that flipped up to adjust for long distance, with knurled knobs you turned to compensate for what the ROTC manuals referred to as "windage."

I somehow knew, along with I'm sure the man who had shot this particular rifle before me, that this elaborate aiming device was the result of pure theory, the invention of officers in the planning and procurement part of the army, men who had the luxury to believe that war consisted of shooting someone several hundred yards away under conditions that allowed you to pick an individual enemy soldier from among the rocks or trees, to estimate just how close to a mile he was away from you, to read the scale inscribed on the ramp, to twist the necessary knobs to a precise point, to know just how much wind moved the air between you and the individual you'd targeted. I understood as I sighted my grandfather's Enfield that you either shot in the general direction of the enemy with a kind of defensive haste that rendered all that precision meaningless, or you peered over the open sights that revealed themselves when the ramp was folded out of the way, seeing not just an outline in enemy colors, but a person, close enough and careless enough to have revealed to you the intimate details of his face and upper body.

In other words, if the man was close enough for it to be personal and particular, close enough for you to actually see the individual human being you'd sighted, he'd be close enough for you to use the quick and dirty logic of the open sights. So after fooling around with what my friends and I referred to as the mortar sights, designed to lob rounds over the top of Mount Nebo to take out the enemy fifteen miles away in the small Mormon community of Nephi, I took aim over the open sights, lined up the foresight with the V of the sight near my eye. After a chilling second of imagining a human being fall into line with the rifle—an immediate and certain understanding that this very rifle had ended a human life—I squeezed off a shot that rocked me backward a little and planted a buzzing alarm deep in my ear.

By sighting on the plate-sized circle I'd drawn on the box and shooting a magazine full of shells, I was able to discover that at one hundred yards the immovable sights were inclined to the right of where the bullets were sent. I knew this from the reasonably tight pattern of bullet holes to the left and just outside the target, and through an understanding that I could honestly blame the sights because I was a good shot. I'd been shooting cans, birds, snakes, and even printed targets for years with pellet guns and .22s. I'd taken my girlfriend into the foothills to shoot my .22 a few weeks after we'd begun dating—believe it or not, a rather routine feature of teenage courtship in Utah. I'd tried to impress her with my ability to knock over a row of cans quickly and efficiently with my semiautomatic Ruger, and I'd loved the fact that she hadn't flinched as she fired off a few rounds herself. I was good enough on the ROTC firing range—also with .22s—to be awarded the only medal I'd managed to earn during my sophomore year in the Army. I had the theory down, and had practiced the bracing, breathing, and squeezing motions until they were second nature, actions I no longer had to think about. I'd been killing skillfully, if mostly vicariously, for years.

So when that moment came a few hours after firing at the cardboard target, I pretty much knew where to aim, and I was able to squeeze off the shot almost exactly where I wanted it. I lined up the broad battered V of the rear sight with the blunt stub of metal at the muzzle and placed this intersection where I'd imagined the heart to be, looking down on the back of the unsuspecting deer, correcting for the variables of motion and elevation and sighting error and squeezed the trigger. The deer fell in its tracks, thrashing a little but going nowhere, the shot entering the rib cage just to the right of the spine, tearing a jagged hole in the side of the heart that emptied a gallon of thick red blood into the deer's lungs and belly, drowning him from inside.

3

Earlier that morning, at that moment when I'd decided that this particular Enfield had taken a human life, these words took shape in my head: this gun has been fired in anger. The words came directly from my other grandfather, my mother's father, my grandfather Danvers, a man who had fought in two of his country's wars and who employed those exact words whenever he expressed his contempt for fellow veterans who were stupid enough to confuse the military and the civilian through membership in the American Legion. This grandfather believed that no man who had actually seen blood spilled in battle would do anything other than try to forget his war experiences the moment armistice was signed; therefore, the veterans who joined the VFW and the American Legion must not have, as he put it over and over again, "heard a gun fired in anger." One of the several ironies of my first deer hunt is that my rifle had been provided by my grandfather Hales, the grandfather who neither hunted nor had fought in war. My grandfather Danvers, who had undoubtedly killed actual human beings and had himself been wounded in battle, didn't hunt either, and wouldn't allow any firearms—rifles, bb guns, or even cap pistols—around his house, on his property, or even in the houses of kids his children played with. He hated guns. He thought they had one use: killing people. He didn't necessarily object to killing people, assuming it had to be done—a staunch Cold Warrior, he believed, for example, that Castro's Communist minions needed to be driven out by force of arms—but killing for sport just didn't add up.

He made this sound pretty simple, but his life revealed to everyone around him that it was much more complicated, that the truth be told, killing in war didn't finally add up for him, either. Like Enfields and M1s, Grandpa had done his duty in two wars. At seventeen, he'd lied about his age to fight in the Spanish-American War, leaving his girlfriend—my fifteen-year-old grandmother—in the small farm town of Plains City, Utah, writing letters that followed him to a part of the world neither of them had, until then, known existed; and twenty years later he'd left this same woman and their four children on a miserable farm in northern California in order to fight in World War I, where he'd been knocked unconscious by an exploding artillery shell, wounded just badly enough to have spent a day immobilized in an ambulance feeling the blood drip onto his chest from the man dying in the stretcher above him.

Awake, my grandfather explained to me that war was a case of doing what needed to be done, then getting on with your life. Asleep, distinctions like that disappeared, and his peacetime nights often erupted into nightmares of war. The details of these dreams and their effect on my grandparents' lives seldom made it directly to the ears of their grandchildren, but we overheard enough to gather that it was his first war—the year he'd spent in the service of taking the Philippines away from the Spanish empire in order to assemble from its pieces a more enlightened American empire—that provided the specific landscape of his night horrors. We learned that the fighting there had been hand-to-hand in a dark, wet jungle, that he'd seen throats cut, comrades mutilated, that he'd not known whom to trust, which was friend or foe. The specific colors and textures of my grandfather's nightmares were filled in for me through the 1960s with sparse details overheard from whispered conversations between my grandmother, my mother, and my aunts, details fleshed out with stories and images I'd absorbed from movies of the war in the Pacific. My grandfather's story was ultimately brought into focus for me through the televised film footage and *Life* magazine photo spreads that brought home the war in Vietnam, until finally in my mind it was a Southeast Asian jungle the boy who would become my grandfather fought his way through, and I finally saw in my imagination shadowy men in the black pajamas of the Vietcong—citizens of that very country we had come to save—who dropped from trees to silently slit the throat of the boy who in boot camp had become my grandfather's best friend.

My grandfather's experience taught me something about war that was far too complex to unravel. I didn't learn to hate war or even fear it—this was the early '60s, the height of the Cold War, the beginning of what looked to be the uncomplicated liberation of South Vietnam from the claws of communism—but I did learn to fear my grandfather. Some of my earliest memories involved my taking pains to not make any loud noises around him, especially while he was asleep. I eventually learned that my grandfather and grandmother slept in separate bedrooms because several times, finding himself in his dreams trying to survive in the jungle of his teenage war, my grandfather finally awoke to observe as if from a distance his large hands frozen tight around his wife's throat, understanding just in time that he'd not known the difference between the enemy of his youth and his wife, the woman he'd loved—with a passion we understood was rare—for more than sixty years, since the last decade of the last century, when they'd been teenagers together in a small Mormon farm town.

Senility eventually drove him completely into his past at the same time it brought him calm days and finally dependably comforting dreams; about the time I was old enough to begin wondering about what all this meant, my grandfather began emerging from his long naps wearing his olive green WWI military tunic, which still fit him remarkably well, the high collar buttoned crisply around the loose folds of his neck. He sat with the dignity of military erectness, taking no notice of the life that went on around him in his living room, the nieces, nephews, grandchildren, and neighborhood children that moved in and out of my grandmother's care. When he talked about politics, it was often about a world that didn't appreciate America's essential goodness, and the Filipinos, the Cubans, and the Vietnamese became exactly the same person, a friend that insisted on behaving as an enemy. Occasionally I'd stop by my grandparents' house on my way back from hiking or playing war in the foothills, and I always remembered to hide my .22 in the garage behind the house, understanding at least this much: that my grandfather Danvers hated guns of any kind, and would allow none in his house.

So my grandfather Danvers, who at great cost to his later mental health had killed his fellow human beings, owned no weapons, and would have punished any child of his who brought one home. My grandfather Hales had spent World War I as a graduate student (like my grandfather Danvers, he'd left his young family to provide for themselves for the duration, but he'd deployed himself to the University of Chicago), and World War II as a civilian researcher studying rain forest meteorology in Panama for the edification of the Army Air Corps. This grandfather owned an Enfield, still greased and mummified for peacetime, in his garage, waiting apparently for me, his grandson, to borrow in order to discover what it felt like to shoot something the size of a human being. Later, when I was agonizing over the philosophical and practical consequences of deciding that I would not allow myself to be drafted and sent to fight a war I believed was immoral, Grandpa Hales was the one person in his by then huge family to offer support. We talked about it from time to time, but I remember in particular one afternoon when

I'd driven the two hours from Ogden to Provo to spend a few hours in his den, almost exactly two years after I'd driven there for the specific purpose of borrowing the Enfield.

This conversation was particularly difficult for both of us because by then my resistance to war had become part of a larger revolution in my life that also involved my leaving the Mormon Church, the first and only of his many children and grandchildren to do so. But we'd focused our conversation that day on the morality of killing, the futility of war as a way to resolve political conflict. He'd learned something important from the bitter disappointment of World War I's aftermath, the failure of the League of Nations, the rise of fascism from the wasteland of military victory—a lesson the children of the next generation, my parents' generation, had not been old enough to grasp—and he was appalled by the waste and carnage, the profound inhumanity, of what he understood war to be.

My other grandfather, a man who'd experienced—even contributed—to the carnage, hated it deep in his brain, but defended it as a necessary evil he'd sign up for again. My grandpa Hales thought that perhaps a good person had reason to avoid killing his fellow man in war, even with the blessing of his church and country. He said he'd have to admit that while he'd been fortunate to avoid participation in the world wars his life encompassed, and although he believed that World War II had been that rarest of occurrences, a just war, nevertheless, he believed that a moral person might choose to leave the country or even go to prison rather than obey a law he found immoral. He mentioned the regret many of his physicist colleagues felt in facing the consequences of work that, however well-intended and theoretically elegant, had led the world to the brink of nuclear destruction. He noted that many of the most faithful and fearless Mormon men of the last century had served time in the Utah Territorial Prison, choosing to violate federal law rather than renounce God's law and betray the sanctity of their marriages to plural wives. He remembered that his own polygamist father—my great-grandfather—had fled for a time to Arizona Territory rather than choose between going to prison or obeying the law, an act that would have betrayed both his conscience and his family. My Grandpa Hales said he'd learned this much: A man should listen carefully to what his conscience told him. Life was sacred, he said, and unjustified violence against a human being was close to the ulti-mate sin, second only to denying the truth of the Holy Ghost.

This conversation took place only two years after I'd borrowed the Enfield, killed the deer, cut its throat, and sliced open its belly, drenching myself in the warm blood puddled in the chest cavity and with my hands and knife emptying it of everything not antler, hide, or meat, and then carried the lightened carcass across my shoulder to the jeep I'd borrowed from my father. Two years later, a few weeks after that afternoon I'd spent talking to my Grandpa Hales about war and conscience, I decided that I'd try not hunting at all. I'd already given up the more casual killing of birds and rabbits, and I'm not sure why the decision to stop hunting deer took so long. To-day, as I consider the difficulty of this decision, I begin to under-stand just how deeply rooted deer hunting was in who I had grown up to be. I didn't believe then, and still don't, that hunting was in-herently immoral, or that shooting a deer was in the same category as dropping napalm on a Vietnamese village. But I came to the con-clusion that it would help me develop a keener and more sincere pacifist self, and I knew that I had the support of my grandfather Hales.

Whether I had the support of my grandfather Danvers was a question made no less relevant by the fact that he'd been dead for four years. He had known in a place near the core of his being just what war can do even to those fortunate enough to survive its hor-rors, and although his war experiences had finally driven his wife from their bed, I was pretty sure that he'd have had even less sym-pathy for my decision regarding Vietnam than for those slackers down at the American Legion hall, veterans whose continued cele-bration of their war years proved simply that they must not have seen death or killed for their country, nor even heard a gun fired in anger.

It had all happened pretty fast, a period spanning three deer hunts, a little more than two years. While it is true that an entire generation came to political consciousness during the Vietnam War, those of us born in the middle years of the baby boom found ourselves scrambling up an increasingly precipitous learning curve. I was a high school junior when the first details were revealed concerning the My Lai massacre; my graduation from Ogden High took place a few months after the Cambodian invasion and the shooting of American students at Kent State. My urgent teenage reading of Thoreau, Martin Luther King Jr., and Mahatma Gandhi (I learned that the specific rifles Gandhi had stood unarmed against had been British Enfields), my attendance at demonstrations and teach-ins at the University of Utah, my helping to organize a not particularly well-attended protest at my high school during the second Moratorium—these experiences led me in all kinds of directions, toward the consideration of all the usual questions. I learned that Vietnam was a bad war, but were all wars? I understood that killing Vietnamese people in the name of their liberation was wrong, but was all killing? As I moved in the direction of pacifism, as I underwent draft counseling and considered the options of Canada, federal prison, or conscientious objection, I considered the various ways one comes to understand that it is wrong to kill.

Perhaps because I'd been a good boy all my life—religious, generally trying to do the right thing, consistently struggling to understand what was true and what wasn't—I wanted my answer to these questions to come to me in a way that was sufficiently weighty, a kind of revelation that would be deep and spiritual, if not precisely religious. I wanted this to be something more than a merely political decision. I didn't want to become a pacifist in the way one might become an auto mechanic or a Rotarian; I wanted to discover that I already was one, that I simply hadn't yet discovered this fact about the real me. I wanted to peel back the layers of 1950s anti-communist indoctrination, Republican parenting and the particularly intense dialect of patriotism spoken by Mormons (mostly, I came to believe, in order to atone for all those early years of defiance against federal laws banning polygamy) to reveal myself to be a genuinely pacific person. I longed for a pureness of heart that came from deep within, an understanding of the sacredness of life that transcended reason and theory, a soul whose electric circuits were charged with a positive attraction to living things and a negative repulsion to killing, a spirit that understood spontaneously and profoundly the ultimate connectedness of all life.

This is who I wanted to be, but the boy who killed his first deer was who I actually was, and I've spent my life stuck with him. Before that first deer, I'd killed fish, birds, snakes, and even squirrels and rabbits, but the deer I'd shot looked at me with eyes the size and depth of a human's, and I couldn't lie to myself about what I'd thought as I'd straddled the breathing, bleeding, paralyzed deer, pulled his head back by the six inches of antler and pulled my knife through his throat in a half-circle motion I'd seemingly known all my life. It was easy. I was calm, driven neither by bloodlust nor sadness nor regret, recognizing keenly what we had in common but not being distracted by it. The deer I'd shot—a young buck—weighed as much as the boy I'd been only a few years before, and there was no way to deny the consciousness that slowly left his eyes as they lost focus and glazed with death.

I'd heard stories about this moment, and I understood to what extent my culture examined this experience with an eye toward determining the dimensions of the boy's character. I'd met a boy in ROTC who told me as we spent fourth period practicing the disassembly and cleaning of our M1s that he'd killed his first deer the weekend before, with his .22, in the mountains above Ogden, completely out of season, without a license and for no reason other than he and his friends had been there with their rifles, and there it was. He described to me a frantic aftermath, an almost hysterical excitement that led them to kill the wounded deer with their knives (they'd unloaded their three .22s into the thick hide of the deer, bringing the deer down but not mortally wounding it) and then to mutilate it, cutting the animal into ragged pieces and leaving the carcass for whatever scavengers remained in mountains so near to a city. He actually giggled as he explained to me what they'd done. It was clear that something primal had kicked in, something disgusting and irresponsible, yet credible in a way I could neither dismiss nor understand. I was uncomfortable with the passion that had taken charge, transforming poaching—the simple breaking of a law—into something genuinely out of control.

I'd also heard a lot of stories about what we called "buck fever": hunters overcome by a kind of excitement in the moment they'd encountered their first deer that caused them to forget everything they'd ever learned about aiming and shooting. I knew a man my father's age who, no matter how many deer he'd eventually bring home or whatever else he would accomplish in life, would always be the teenage boy who had emptied his rifle into the ground a yard away from his boots, thinking he was shooting at a deer standing only twenty feet away but actually achieving—his friends joked—a pretty good pattern in the mud at his feet, even if it was a long way from the killing spot he thought he was aiming at. According to this pathetic story, the deer was so stunned by the boy's ineptitude that it waited calmly in place while the man attempted to reload, dropping cartridges in the mud, trying to force bullets backward into the magazine and flipping the safety on so that even when he'd succeeded in reloading and then chambering a round and finally lining up the deer, his sights, and sufficient calm, he found the trigger unresponsive, somehow disconnected from what needed to be done, a mystery never under the spell of buck fever to be solved.

Finally, the story went, another hunter from his group arrived at the scene and calmly shot the animal, putting both the deer and his friend out of their misery. A person who had encountered this kind of insanity was both the source of much communal humor and

201

an object lesson in character, and not necessarily bad character. Mormon doctrines of blood atonement and state-sanctioned executions by firing squad aside, the culture I was raised in did not like to think of itself as bloodthirsty, and I believe that while none of us looked forward to discovering that we weren't effective killers of deer, some of us felt a sort of unaccountable respect toward those for whom killing did not come easily.

There is another story, much rarer in Utah than either stories of ritual mutilation (this is the same culture, after all, that believes hanging a coyote carcass across one's fence provides a level of protection against further predation) or buck fever, the person who learns with his first kill that he isn't a killer, and never kills again. One of the most important adults in my life was a man who owned a small farm in Ogden Valley, not far from the abandoned gravel pit where we'd practice shooting our rifles, a man who worked a regular job in Ogden so he could support a small herd of horses and live in a beautiful place in the mountains. He was a good Mormon and a political conservative, and he accepted equally and without judgment the sensual pleasures along with the necessary barbarities of farm life, the horsebreakings and castrations and sometimes unavoidable spurrings and whippings of animals he loved. Of all the Mormon men I knew, he was the most conversant with what was both wild and beautiful in nature, and he was one of the few men I knew who didn't hunt. We spent hours talking about all kinds of weighty subjects as we hauled hay and afterward rode horses in the foothills above his farm, and given the times, questions concerning the morality of killing came up over and over again. When I'd press him on apparent inconsistencies in his views regarding hunting, he'd talk around the topic, never exactly explaining why he didn't hunt.

For one thing, hunting was woven so completely into the fabric of Mormon life in Utah that to criticize deer hunting was close to questioning the legitimacy of the Prophet. Mormon men went hunting. It was almost that simple, even though it was well known that deer hunting provided perhaps the only opportunity, as well as the only implicit permission, for more than a few Mormon men to break the Word of Wisdom, to pass a pint bottle around the camp-fire and to inhale cigarette smoke, either from your own smuggled cigarette or the Mormon elder's next to you. This man could see some dangerous questions rising in me, could see the way they were outlining a core of resistance against the values and assumptions with which I'd been raised, toward a stretching that would lead to a complete and tragic break with Mormonism, and he took pains to avoid criticizing the faith and the culture in which he wanted me to find a place. It was this tendency in me—an inclination he spot-ted long before anybody else did—that wouldn't allow him to quite approve of my chasing one of his several daughters, an intermittent romantic interest that neither of us finally pursued past a school dance and a little necking in the hay truck.

So this man intended no criticism—either explicit or implicit—of hunting or of hunters. He didn't much like guns, he said, giving none of the usual reasons involving safety or even the inevitable bul-let holes that riddled his rural mailbox. One day when I pushed him for an explanation, he said finally that hunting just wasn't him. He had tried it when he was young, he said, and had left it there, in his youth, along with cars he'd traded in and clothes that hadn't quite fit.

By the time I'd reached eighteen, I came to understand that hunting wasn't necessarily me either, but not in the way I really wanted it to not be me. Occasionally, I'd tell myself that hunting was part of a script handed to me at birth that I was still performing, al-most without my cooperation or assent, a series of events that in-cluded certain rites of passage: baptism by immersion at eight, the priesthood at twelve, an after-school job at fourteen, and a deer tag at sixteen. My father hunted, but for reasons that still aren't clear to me. He'd worked years rebuilding the Swedish Mauser into a beau-tiful sporting rifle, and he enjoyed driving the jeep on mountain roads, but no one looked less at home beside a deer carcass than my surgeon father, whose weekday cuttings into human flesh took place in the inner ear, a fastidious and almost bloodless exercise accomplished under a microscope. When he said over the years that he wasn't disappointed when he'd sometimes failed to bring home a deer, I actually believed him. But he hunted, as did my brother, who embraced hunting as enthusiastically as my father did awkwardly, almost to the exclusion of everything else. We came to depend on his yearly deer hunting success in the hills behind Mount Nebo (he was famous in our neighborhood for consistently bagging his deer with only one shot from his Model Seventy Winchester, and the buck he brought home always carried a significant rack of antlers), and his commitment to hunting would be only temporarily interrupted by his mission call, which placed him in Brazil hunting converts to the Mormon Church during the year I'd killed my first deer. I'm not sure any decision a child makes in the context of a culture that mixes family, religion, and landscape so completely can be an actual decision. I was a Mormon boy, turning sixteen, therefore I hunted.

But it was a little more complicated than that. I genuinely liked shooting things. I liked guns; I liked their smell, their heft, the functional beauty of their machinery, a simplicity of operation that contrasted so completely with the complicated uncertainty of my adolescence: a contained, directed explosion, an immediate and unambiguous translation of will into effect. I loved the hunt itself: I looked forward each year to building a camp out of canvas tents and Coleman lanterns, talking and joking quietly around the campfire, riding in open jeeps along rutted dirt roads, a vaguely military experience that involved holding your rifle's muzzle pointed carefully upward as you bounced through the crisp mountain air, breathing the exhaust that mingled with the smell of dust and dead leaves. I'd enjoyed hiking with my father and brother through the quaking aspen and sagebrush of late fall, locating stands alongside game trails, tracking deer in the snow that some years blanketed the ground.

And I loved how merely the anticipation of hunting made me feel: I'd spent that Thursday evening with my girlfriend, the night before I'd gone hunting with my friends, and there was a kind of glow I imagined over both of us, a feeling that the whole question of age that had dogged me through my life, my never being old enough for whatever I wanted most to do, would achieve some kind of resolution by the time I'd return Saturday night, in time, we hoped, for the dance our church held for its teenagers every other weekend. We both understood that I'd come back to her different somehow. I think we both hoped that what was so confusing for us night after night might be made a little more clear.

So the why is difficult to figure out. What I do know is exactly how I felt when I'd realized that I'd managed to kill a deer. I'd been a little surprised by my cool, proud of my skill and happy to realize that the deer was down for the count, that I wouldn't have to chase this animal all over the flanks of Mt. Nebo, and when I scrambled to the side of the dying buck—having even had the presence of mind to unchamber the cartridge I'd a few seconds earlier had the presence of mind to chamber after my one shot, in those short moments before it became clear that I'd followed in my brother's footsteps, that one shot would be enough—it was mostly a case of doing what I'd learned needed to be done: Slice the throat to make death certain and to drain blood from the carcass; cut off the musk glands embedded in the hair and flesh in the fold of the rear legs; begin the cutting open of belly and chest to empty the body of what spoils the meat.

As I completed these necessary operations and began making room in my mind to consider what all this meant, I felt something completely unexpected. Years later I would wish that this unexpected thought would be regret, that I would find out that hunting wasn't me in the deepest sense possible, that killing a deer was too close for comfort, too inconsistent with my emerging understanding of the oneness of all life. In later years I would imagine other reactions, the responses that would have come to a person better than myself: tears, sadness, thoughts of sin, plans for redemption. I would even come to wish that I'd felt some kind of terrifying lust, a loss of control, a glimpse of the dark and sordid underbelly of human life that could serve as a kind of morality tale, a revelation that would guide me in a more enlightened direction, a narrative that recognized another kind of sin, a knowledge of an evil within me, the necessary control of which might provide a direction for my life. Even an exaggerated and unseemly pride would have been something better to feel than what actually came over me, anything deeper, more profound than the feeling that presented itself: relief.

Relief. The closer I came to finishing the chores that accompany the killing of deer, the more the feeling of relief washed over me. I'd done it. I'd killed my deer; now I could relax and enjoy myself. I wouldn't have to make excuses, wouldn't have to explain exactly why I hadn't been able to do the very thing a sixteen-year-old Mormon boy needed most to do. I'd be able to say that I'd killed a deer, yes it was a buck, it was an appropriate distance—a hundred yards was just far enough away to require skill; we all knew that luck starts to become a factor beyond that distance, no matter how much talent is required to get the shot in the ballpark. Until that moment, I hadn't realized just how thoroughly my mind had been turning over these explanations, how much space had been taken up by the sense of expectation, of consequence, of the need to explain myself.

I instantly understood a couple of things: I knew that next year, I'd shoot the first deer, doe or buck, I managed to lower my sights on, because it was the having done it I was after, not what specifically I'd bring home, and that's exactly what I did. The next year— the fall of my senior year, the year I began to consider from a more distant perspective what deer hunting meant in the grand scheme of things, how it related to militarism, imperialism, the original sin that is violence in America—I shot a doe, the first deer I saw, the last living thing besides trout and horseflies I would ever kill.

I would have my own rifle by then, another weapon from World War I, a bolt-action Springfield 30.06. I'd buy this beautifully sporterized rifle from a friend, a boy I'd grown up with who just a few months after my first deer hunt had gotten the news that his girlfriend was pregnant and that he would be getting married right away. He needed the money, of course, and he told me his hunting days were over.

The swords-into-plowshares absurdity of this equation has dawned slowly upon me over the years. I didn't point out that we both knew he would certainly go deer hunting the next year, either with a borrowed rifle or a less expensive one; that, in fact, the importance of providing for one's family by bringing home venison was a permutation of deer hunting ideology in Mormon culture that came with marriage, fatherhood, and responsibility. But at the time it seemed very simple: I gave him $150 for a rifle we both somehow believed was a luxury under the circumstances he couldn't afford, something he wouldn't be needing for a while. What we didn't quite understand was the part selling the rifle played in the rushed rite of passage that was a forced teenage marriage.

Anyway, I gave him the money, he mournfully handed over the rifle, and the next evening my girlfriend and I brought the gift of an electric frying pan to the wedding reception, a collection of Mormon friends and relatives who gathered upbeat but disapproving in the local church social hall, arranging themselves around my Sunday-suited friend and his new wife attired in the nonwhite of her pale yellow prom dress, the experience leaving me with my own rifle, military yet refitted in the civilian wardrobe of a beautifully abbreviated and checkered walnut stock, freshly chromed bolt and blued barrel, and sights that adjusted only to what might be expected during the hunting of deer. My friend's misfortune—for that was what we all understood it to be—also left my girlfriend and me with a more practical perspective from which to consider the boundaries of skin and touch we'd been exploring during the months before and after my first deer hunt, a new level of gravity lightened only by our joke about what might result from our escalating activities in her parents' "family room."

4

I was the only one of the three of us to see a deer, let alone shoot one, that day, and diplomacy required that I keep my discovery—that we hunted only so that we could be finished with hunting for the year—to myself. We hauled the deer home in the jeep, hoisted it from the rafters in my garage, and after I'd dropped off my less fortunate friends, I drove as naturally and unconsciously as a salmon heading upstream to my girlfriend's house, to tell her my good news and to retrieve her so I could show her the deer I'd killed. It was late afternoon, close to sunset, and we had a date for a couple of hours later, the church dance I was afraid I'd miss if things got complicated in the mountains, but part of the deer hunting experience seemed necessarily to involve driving to her house in the jeep, knocking at her door still wearing my blood-encrusted sweatshirt and still smelling of gunpowder, viscera, and the musk glands I'd so conscientiously sliced from the deer I'd just killed.

I'm a little embarrassed today, of course, to speak of the excitement I'd felt standing bloodstained on my girlfriend's front porch, ringing the doorbell, explaining with appropriate modesty to her approving father (who was not only a hunter himself, but had let me know in clear if indirect words that he knew pretty well what homework we'd been accomplishing downstairs on the family room couch) how I'd gotten lucky: a buck, one shot, close to a hundred yards, an old Enfield almost too long, too heavy, and too greasy to aim with any authority at all.

Her hair was still damp from the shower she'd taken after an afternoon of playing church basketball with the girls in her ward. Nevertheless, I helped her on with her coat, and would have opened the door to the jeep if there'd been one, so gallant I felt, and as we drove through the cold November evening to my house I explained everything except the relief I'd felt: one shot, my calmness and control and efficiency, my first deer.

I remember the words I used, but only in retrospect do I finally hear what they actually communicated, even if I find it impossible to understand how it all seemed to add up to something so innocent, so happy. I was telling her that I was a killer, a good one. I'd killed skillfully, coolly, clinically, and I'd encountered no difficulty in slicing this animal's throat, piercing with my knife the tough hide of the belly, not even repelled by the cascade of bright, hot blood that flowed over my thighs, the voiding of the deer's urine and excrement, the necessary cutting away of testicles and penis. I didn't tell her the other discovery, the relief, the understanding that I had done it, and was off the hook for a year, that whether or not I'd wanted to kill the deer, I was genuinely happy to have done it. I also didn't tell her that there was still a lot I didn't understand about what I'd done, something at the eye of the storm of feelings I had right then driving us to my house, more complex even than those unexpected feelings of relief, something that would explain why it was so important for me to show her the animal I'd killed, why I was so happy.

Because the scene in the garage carried me beyond relief into something I still don't quite understand. I liked showing the deer to her for reasons that are pretty ripe and murky, and she seemed to like seeing it. She really did. I thought so then, and I still think so, even though I should know better than to have imagined then or now that I understand anything about what she thought or felt, a fact I was reminded of recently in a graduate seminar I was teaching in the literature of nature and wilderness. We'd finished reading some essays by women articulating a feminine view of the relationship between humans and the natural world, and to restore some kind of context, to take the class a little further from the theoretical world of the essays we'd read, I briefly described the scene in my garage. I recalled the pride I'd felt, and I explained what had seemed to me at the time her obvious admiration for my accomplishment.

Even though I was careful to employ a mocking and ironic tone in relating this story, the women in the class rolled their eyes. They laughed out loud. One student took a stab at locating my experience in the anthropological context we'd discussed earlier in the semester, the need for females to secure mates that could be depended on to bring home game, an impulse that may well have survived the development of agriculture, the ascendancy of the women's movement, and the invention of pizza delivery, but that student was pretty much shouted down, and several women explained to me what should have been obvious to me even then: of course she seemed happy, impressed, elated. It was her job. A fifteen-year-old girl, in Utah, in 1968? Give me a break. She was even less in touch with her feelings than you were, if that was possible. She was standing by her man, forcing her true reactions underground in order to pursue one of the few options open to her. You were her boyfriend, they told me, laughing, as if that explained it all.

Of course these women were right. They had the advantage of having grown up female, and several women who were my age had been in exactly this girl's place at that precise moment in history. These women spoke with the insight and credibility that resulted from intervening years of increasing self-awareness, a broader sense of history and context, as well as in some cases decades of bad marriage, single parenthood, and the reading of feminist theory. On the other hand, I still can't help but think that it's more complicated than that, that my girlfriend's motivations and reactions were at least as complex and ultimately unknowable as mine.

Whatever its meaning, the scene is something I just can't get past: I'm sixteen, she's fifteen. I'd had my drivers license for about four months. We'd been falling in love with each other for a little longer than that, talking as much as we could in that restrictive and self-conscious culture about the way we felt about each other, expanding the range of our touching, finding in the smells and textures of each others' bodies something overwhelming, something both frightening and liberating. We'd made a kind of love in the back of my parents' station wagon, on the couch in her family room, during a hike to a waterfall in the mountains above our neighborhood; we'd been publicly affectionate during the slow dances at a number of school and church dances and at least one prom. We were pretty well matched: we were good kids, both guilt-ridden, sometimes equally awkward and embarrassed and ironic about the lengths we'd go to stay clothed and virginal, sometimes both of us giving in, just loving the smells, loving the hard and soft places on each other's bodies, sometimes coming very close to losing ourselves.

And here we are: She's happy that I didn't panic or screw up. She's somehow proud of my ability to put emotions aside and find the heart through all those aspen leaves, through moving muscles and skin, to be distracted neither by adrenaline nor tenderness. She puts her arm around my bloodstained sweatshirt and pulls me close alongside her, all the time admiring the carcass hanging in my garage, strung up by a rope tied around a stick of wood sharpened on each end to pierce the skin between the bones of the deer's rear legs, spreading the legs apart to more efficiently cool the meat, blood somehow still dripping from its nose and expanding a dark pool on the garage floor, eyes still open wide and glazed over. She touches the stifled attempt at a full rack of antlers, laughingly says "a buck" in a way that is both mocking and affectionate, telling me that she knows that it is important to me and maybe to her too. She holds the Enfield for a moment, a rifle still smelling of death in Europe a half century before and the smoke of more killing that afternoon, before putting it down as something too heavy, too serious, for the mood we're in. We remember our date an hour away, silently anticipate the public touching in the church's social hall, and later, in the back of my parents' car, the anguish of physical permission and denial, of losing and then regaining control. After propping the Enfield in the corner of the garage and turning out the light, I drive her back to her house, kiss her chastely on the lips at her front door and return home to shower, to wash the blood from my hands, my hair, the back of my neck.

lucy wilson sherman

In this unabashed ode to goats, Sherman explores the complex relationship that can grow up between animal and owner, and the way that relationship can satisfy in ways human ones sometimes cannot. In the course of her essay, each of Sherman's seven goats emerge as fully-drawn characters, with quirks, love lives, life histories—and even a curious kind of wisdom.

learning from goats

"... a symbiotic relationship with ruminants opens an unguarded back gate to Eden ..."

JIM CORBETT, *Goatwalking*

When I was a kid, my mother was so busy and so often harried I thought she didn't love me. Sometimes I used to feign illness in order to be permitted to stay home from grade school. I thought, What if Mother looks up from her housework on this particular day and turns, lovingly, in my direction between the hours of 8 A.M. and 3 P.M., but I am in school?

As a rebellious, sexually adventurous teenager, I got Mother's attention, all right. But finally I gave up the whole struggle and became just like her, so for all these years since I've had the inner comfort of knowing Mother would approve of my incessant busyness.

You'd be amazed what I can accomplish before 9 A.M. on an average day. You'll never find me just sitting around. I am constitutionally unable to watch daytime TV; I'm not even sure it's OK to watch TV at night. My daughter and my sister, independent of one another, each gave me the book *Meditations for Women Who Do Too Much* by Anne Wilson Schaef. Naturally, I haven't made the time to read it straight through. God forbid Mother or I ever simply stopped, sat down, and for a moment accomplished nothing. Some urge from within that was not on our daily TO DO list might well up, or worse, nothing might. How would we know we existed? To be on the safe side, we never sat down.

I married, completed college, began a career as an alcoholism counselor, attended graduate school at night, maintained a home, and raised a child. When Mother thought my daughter needed a sibling, she suggested that if it were another girl I name her Belinda. But instead my husband and I divorced, and I had my tubes tied. It wasn't until many years later, when my new husband, Henderson, and I moved to a farm in northeast Pennsylvania, that we were given two baby goats, and I had the opportunity to name my first kid Belinda.

Mother, who has been dead for twenty-one years now, would have liked Belinda. They are really very similar, both ladies, both thin and fastidious about their appearance. Mother never wore slacks in her entire life; Belinda, for her part, finds it unpleasant to step into water. Both have long thin noses. And an expression of disdain finds their faces a congenial surface upon which to reside.

But of Belinda's love I am certain; she's never too distracted for affection. She discreetly positions herself next to me whenever possible. I can comb her endlessly, although she's not fond of any roughhousing. She'll step aside and wait for me to calm down or transfer my exuberance to her big brother, Capricorn, a gentle, somewhat bewildered buck. Like all the goats, Capricorn is mesmerized by my stroking. He sways slightly in a trance, but if I stop, takes his big front hoof and paws at me till I continue. He is a big boy and this sometimes results in bruises. It's best to keep on stroking or get up and call it a day.

I name these goats, nickname them, and then re-nickname them with names that play upon their original nicknames. While one doesn't take too many liberties with Belinda's name—Linda B'Linda or just a backward LindaB—Capricorn doesn't seem to mind Corny Two Shoes or Sweet Corn at all.

For a few years, Capricorn impregnated Belinda each fall when she came into heat, and the dear girl produced, for our amazement and delight, dancing baby twins each spring. We kept the first generation, born the following year, and named them Ivy, as in "little lambsy divy" and GG, for Gray Goat, a take-off on the name we gave our farmhouse when we first saw it in 1985, the Gray Ghost.

The gestation period for goats is five months. They go into heat in the fall and are supposed to give birth in the spring. But because our girls have always bedded down right beside their buck and therefore get pregnant as soon as the first heat is upon them, "spring" births always seem to land during a bitterly cold week in February. One baby was even born on a cold night before Christmas. We called him Billy Bejinks because Mother used to say it was as "cold as Billy Bejinks." I don't know who Billy Bejinks was or where the expression came from, but my daughter and her husband have further edited it. When they're shivering, it's "coooold as Billy!"

Capricorn knocked up his daughters Ivy and GG when they came of age. I'd read in my goat books that incest is OK as an animal husbandry technique to encourage desirable traits. With us, it was not for genetics but on account of what we saw as the friendliness of keeping all the animals together, and because of the impossibility of housing a pawing, moaning, thrashing male goat apart from the objects of his desire. However, after a dozen or so offspring we decided to bring in a new stud just to keep things on the up and up.

We sold as pets all the baby goats that were born after GG and Ivy, but we enjoyed the privilege of spending two early spring months with each set of newborns, the only creatures I know of who literally jump for joy when they're only two or three days old. Apart from watching them prance sideways down the hill when they are a week old and able to join the others on our daily walks, there is nothing more delicious than cuddling on one's lap a ribcage as thin and fluttery as a bird's, tucking the tired legs up under its soft, furry little body, and kissing the face of a dozing baby goat.

Henderson and I resist using the proper names for the animals we've met in the country. It would sound pretentious and formal for me to call Belinda a doe and Capricorn a buck and the kids, kids. A bitch is an awful name for a female dog. So a cow is a cow, as is everything else out there in the farmer's field, male or female. (I've been told but I keep forgetting what a heifer is, or a steer. I believe these names refer to the state of the animal's reproductive organs: either she has not yet become pregnant or he has had his testicles lopped off so as not to get her pregnant.) In my lexicon it's all very simple: boy animals are boys and girl animals are girls. But I suppose my anthropomorphizing might amuse the local farmers who rightly look upon their barn inventory somewhat less fatuously.

The only goat we actually bought was Sweet William, a purebred Alpine, to be the new husband of our girls so that we didn't carry this incest thing too far. We bought him from a neighbor farmer whose name is Bill, and as I was considering wildflowers as a category of future names and boy goats are called billys, I thought this name apt. However, it was a pretty limp-wristed name for the buck who was to be our main stud for the next four years.

He was the first and only goat we imported, and we found ourselves shocked and cringing at the bad luck that befell him once Belinda perceived him to be a threat to her girls, who, like him, were adolescents. Belinda, the light of Sweet William's eyes, the replacement for the mother he'd just lost, his future bride, tried to break Sweet William's bones. Sweet would moon around after Belinda from a distance, hoping she'd notice him. She noticed him all right and charged, again and again, bashing him sideways against the fence so hard we heard the slam at the house. She'd swivel, rear up and charge again. She was possessed with the idea that Sweet William should die right there in the goat yard. All he wanted was her love.

Finally, as he inevitably gained on her in size, her will to kill him flagged, and miraculously that fall she let him mount her. They've been inseparable since. However, I do not think we can extrapolate from this any parallel to human male/female relations.

We had to castrate Capricorn because Sweet William, younger, bigger, and now the herd queen's main squeeze, tried to eradicate him. Once again the sounds of foreheads thudding together rose to the house, and appalled, we watched as they even drew blood.

The vet came one late spring day and tranquilized a humbled Capricorn, who stood, legs apart and swaying, while the vet injected Novocain into the testicle area and, when it had taken effect, sliced down the scrotum to expose what looked like huge veined eyeballs. He gathered the two eyeballs in his left hand, pulled them down firmly and sliced through the cords with which they were attached to the body. I don't remember much blood. Then he sliced off the bottom of the now empty scrotum, left it unstitched, and when it healed it just hung there, a tiny reminder of Corn's former prowess. For several days afterward Capricorn walked gingerly, his back legs slightly apart.

I may resist using the proper nouns for livestock, but I'm enough of a farm girl to appreciate an opportunity to recycle. I threw the dogs one testicle each and watched, intrigued, as they chewed them right up.

From the coupling of Sweet William and GG came Daisy, whom we nicknamed Daisy-May (and Daisy-May-and-Then-Again-She-May-Not). She was an exceptionally affectionate little goat, and Henderson relented and said we could keep her. The next year, all four girls delivered babies; all babies went to good homes. But now I began to feel that allowing our girls to become pregnant year after year might not be good for their bodies, and I suspected that, even with my head-over-heels amore for those of the caprine persuasion, the goat population of Susquehanna County would eventually peak: the pet market would be saturated and we'd be trucking the babies to auction just prior to Easter and Passover where they'd be bought up by Greeks and Jews, we were told, and eaten as the holiday treat, chevron. This time Sweet William stood legs apart, trembled and walked gingerly for several post-op days.

Mating season, while offspringless, occurs each month now. The girls go into heat and Capricorn is best advised to show no interest. Sweet William's still herd buck and spends his days in a miserable frenzy sniffing the girls' bottoms, hanging his mouth under their stream of urine, lifting his head, pulling back his upper lip so it comes closer to his nostrils to better smell the odor of their urine, and then suddenly, out of the corner of one eye, takes notice of poor, innocently-standing-by Capricorn who gets charged and flattened.

On one winter walk, Sweet was busy sniffing and empty-humping his girls and Capricorn, although minding his own business, must still have seemed like a threat. I was walking ahead, goatherd, minding my own business too when Sweet charged Corn, who bolted, looked back in surprise at Sweet, and without watching where he was going, charged right into me. My legs flew straight up, at right angles to my body. I hung a few seconds in mid-air before landing, sharply, on my bottom in the snow. The blow floored me, knocking my teeth together, immediately banging out a migraine, hurting my feelings unreasonably, embarrassing me, and causing me to look around nervously to see if my awkward mishap there in the woods had been spotted. Of course we were quite alone and the heartless goats, used to blows of this sort, ignored me and kept on cramming white pine needles down their throats as fast as their smug, lipless lips could work.

Out of all this coupling, productive and not, out of all the hours feeding and milking goats in the barn and making cheese seven months out of every year, and just before SW gave up his balls, came the best-loved little goat princess ever born at Gray Ghost Farm, my own bottle-fed, breast-fed if I could have, lovingly hand-nursed four then two then one and now, sadly, no times a day, my own last-of-the-lot, light-of-my-life, Rosemary. I was considering herbs as a name category when she was born. Her brother, whom the mother, Miss Ivy, did not leave to wither, the fat, warm, well-licked Basil, eventually went to auction. Rosemary came to bed with me.

What else could I do? We checked the barn as soon as we got home from Cape May after my daughter's twenty-ninth birthday, and found Basil doing well beside his bemused mother. But off near the milk stand, squished against the cold wall of the shed, was a wet and trembling jumble of bones, and it was a girl. Girls are more desirable because they give milk, obviously, don't become as big as boys, and don't pee straight into their own mouths if the opposite sex is near and in heat. Besides, I like a goat in bed with me, under the electric blanket.

I put down a towel, naturally, should she pee, but with death on its way, all systems are down and you have to worry first about cold, and then something to put into the little body before something can come out. I'd read goat books, which served mostly to terrify me into assisting at births when I really wasn't needed, but because of their advice, I'd frozen some of last year's colostrum. We thawed it, and with a large plastic syringe, squirted tiny amounts between Rosie's locked jaws. She'd given up hope and was calling it a rather cold and unenviable day. We weren't.

We got her to agree with us. We took her out of my bed (if we were lucky her little system eventually would work) and placed her on a towel on an electric heating pad with a moisture-proof cover in a big cardboard box at the foot of my bed. During the day she gathered strength as I forced more and more colostrum down her throat. We moved her in her box to the shop where I work, so I could cuddle her on my lap and give her ever increasing portions of colostrum and then milk from her mom. Finally she agreed to suck. Then suddenly she sucked with such certainty she swept the bottle out of my hand!

By the second day she was standing. By the third, standing and walking were no big deals. By the fourth night, when we went to bed at 10 P.M., Rosie in her box, I in my bed, Rosie stood right up in her box, head tilted smartly over the side of the box, indicating she was ready to play. I called Henderson. "I don't think Rosie's a house goat anymore." He took her to the barn. My sleep matters to me.

Of course she bellowed, but somehow managed to find enough warmth among the others to get through the night; her mother never has recognized her and I am proud to be the only mother Rosie's ever known.

I am unabashedly head-over-heels in love with goats.

But about Rosemary in particular I am rhapsodic. In the barn, it's Rosemary May and Rosie May and Rosie Pay and Rosie Posie Mosie Dosie Bosie May until I nauseate even myself. We have a hugging and kissing bee each morning after I milk. Rosie, now a one-year-old chunky adolescent, jumps up on top of the feed bin and leans forward, all in one motion, against my body which is simultaneously there, arms open to gather her in. She licks the salt off my neck and cheeks and I pummel and scratch her and gather up her thick skin and hair in folds and look for itches which all goats have along their sides and backs and which they can't reach with their teeth. When I do her armpits, her licking tapers off as she concentrates on the pleasure, her amber eyes close to slits and she leans into my chest for balance so that if I stepped backward suddenly, which I never would, she'd topple.

I kiss goats on their mouths. Occasionally, I get mouth sores which Henderson says is from kissing goats. Then he says I have goatitis. I don't care. I'm intrigued by their mumble mouths, lipless mouths, like llamas. They have only bottom teeth in the front. Top and bottom in the back, for grinding, but only bottom ones in the front and smooth gums like a baby on top. They only need bottom ones for biting off leaves and bark. In my work with alcoholics in Philadelphia, I knew men without top or bottom teeth, all pulled by the welfare system which figured one dentist visit once and for all is economically prudent. I have secretly recoiled from the toothless mouth. Now I have been right up in that toothlessness looking for the cud, and on goats, toothlessness is a most charming and sensible dental arrangement. I am gaga over goats.

I keep trying to catch a glimpse of their cud, but so far haven't been able to. I'm fascinated by their cud, or rather, what I'm really fascinated by is a creature that thinks to chew its food again, being a bolter of food myself who scarcely chews it the first time. I cannot imagine a life placid enough to chew my food twice. I get the food in as fast as possible, as much as possible in one sitting, and I'm off. Ruminants teach me about patience.

Together Belinda and I learned to milk. Now I'm a pro. I sit down right next to each goat on the milk stand, my cheek against her side, her sweet hay smell in my nostrils and reach under with soap and a warm washcloth and clean her udder. She's having her grain. I squeeze her teat just so and squirt milk into the container. But doing four goats takes so long I need to listen to books on tape or time my milking to correspond with *All Things Considered* on public radio not to be bored. I am not, as you see, a meditator.

My daughter found a book for me called *Goatwalking*. She inscribed it, "For my Mother, the goat." The author, Jim Corbett, understands why being with goats frees one from responsibility for carrying the relationship, which humans do with dogs, for instance. "Unlike pets, goats never seem to think they're human, but they tolerate physical differences and allow properly behaved human beings to become fully accepted members of the herd." It is my wish to become so properly behaved. Under a section titled "Doing Nothing," he writes: "Being useless uncovers despair . . ." and his discovery exposes my compulsive need to be busy.

I moved to this farm twelve years ago, tired and close to an edge. For years I have held up the earth with my shoulders, and I've had the migraines to prove it. It's been my job to see that between friends there are no misunderstandings. I am the cause of a party's failure (and its success as well, I might add). I am the cause of the automobile breaking down, the source of any pain in my relationship with my daughter. I longed to live close to things that were beyond my domination, beyond even the thought of domination, things that could get along without me, like mountains and trees. Like goats.

During the long hours of the day when I'm inside working, the goats are getting along fine without me. I gaze out at them through the window. They're all chewing their cuds or peeing, often simultaneously. They doze, heads hanging. They are caught in the moments of their life as I am never able to be. Like the mountains around them, they are implacable, steadfast, steady and present.

They have something eternal running through them which is not of my making or my maintaining. That is a big relief.

Goats are concentrating, unconsciously, on the flavor of the grain, the saliva in their mouths, the grinding of their stomachs and the returning of the cud. They are certainly not accomplishing anything. They are, let's face it, grand meditators, and that's what I want to learn from them. To learn to focus, to concentrate so narrowly I forget myself in the moment and am unselfconscious.

I always resolve to stay longer in the barn, brushing the goats. But it's too close to not getting anything accomplished and I'm up and off, promising to spend more time tomorrow. Yet, when I can pull myself down, sit down on the milk stand with wire brush in hand, all are takers. They gently offer me their noses and throats and press against each other to get closer to my hand. Seven big bodies jockeying to be groomed—Belinda, Capricorn, and Sweet William and their children Ivy, GG, Daisy, and Rosemary. All my children, too. This press of life catches me up in its immediacy and I am lost for just a minute in getting my hands and forearms and elbows to touch each warm, breathing, beloved body in as many places as I can reach and kissing as many cheeks and noses and yes oh yes lips as I can and being as much a goat myself as I can be.

I still haven't spent a day or even a few hours up on the hillside, in a chair, with the goats, even with some distractions like books to ward off the demons of uselessness which arise from my central fear that if I quiet down too much I'll find I don't exist at all.

This summer, however, I might chance it.

mark doty

In this bittersweet piece, Doty uses several metaphors—
nesting, rebuilding, gardening—to consider the lengths
both animals and humans will go to carve out a safe
space in the world. As he points out, however, "no place
is protected" from death, and his efforts to deal pro-
ductively with his partner's HIV diagnosis becomes
part of this domestic reflection. Like the birds of the title, nesting can be an effort to hold back death—and a
celebration of life.

house finches

Spring has opened its big green hands.

Yesterday I noticed that there was actually shade, beautiful greenish shade, under the box alder tree beside my kitchen. The shadow of leaves appeared against the white clapboards of my neighbor's garage; how long since I've seen the shadow of leaves, one of those things that vanish all winter, though we seldom notice that they've gone until their reemergence. The first buds of the three-foot crabapple I planted three summers ago have opened.

But the new season's surest evidence is the presence of two house finches, little, rose-throated gray birds who've begun to nest in a climbing rose that scrambles up the wall beside my bedroom window. All morning they perched on the points of the fence pickets, threads of straw and grass hanging from their beaks, before they'd dart out of view. Going out to the garden, later, to take the dogs out for a noontime walk in the woods, there was a hurried rustle and then two arcs so quick as to be almost unseeable out of the thickening green of the rose's tumble of briers. There, half-made, was a fragile cup of ocher, its form apparent even though it wasn't yet solidly built, light still shining through the bowl which would, in time, support the eggs.

House finches: I love the warmth and domesticity of the name, and their habit of nesting up against the walls, in any sort of shelter or pocket that will protect them. The first ones came from China, fifty years ago, brought to New York City as pets; freed, they established themselves in the East across a territory that grows wider over the years. I've known them before, and probably that's part of why they seem to me the real heralds of spring, their appearance that announcement of the new season which is the one to be believed, the one to be celebrated.

The other pair I knew was in Vermont, back when whatever shadows darkened our horizon were the ordinary ones—jobs, money, how to make the best of our lives—those things that are momentous, but come to seem luxurious considerations when illness fills up the stage of a life, or two lives. In those days we lived in a ramshackle thirteen-room Victorian house in Montpelier. I'd gotten a grant from the Massachusetts Artists Foundation, just before we left Boston to come north for a teaching job for me. The generous foundation gave me a check for $7,500, a princely sum for us, and we decided to use it as a down payment for a house, since property in the north was cheap then. Even at the low prices of 1985, what we looked at was far beyond our means; we were despondent and about to give up when our realtor drove us past the flat-roofed, down-at-the-heels New England version of an Italian villa, its handsome form abused by a sea of mustard paint trimmed in chocolate brown. Yellow and brown, for some reason, is a traditional combination in Vermont's working-class neighborhoods. There was a For Sale sign on the rickety picket fence, which had been forced to wear the same shade of chocolate.

"That?" the realtor said when we asked. "Oh, you don't want to see that house. That ought to be torn down." Which was really all we needed to hear, contrary creatures, scavengers, aficionados of barn sales and other people's attics that we were. And it did turn out to be like a barn sale, really—except that we bought the barn, for twenty-nine thousand dollars. It had no insulation, an antique wood-fired furnace that consumed whole cords of timber in a wink, and period plumbing of unquestionable authenticity. Whether the flat roof was a concession to poverty or the Italianate fashion I never knew, but in the course of one Vermont winter the absolute madness of the idea became clear. Snowfall after snowfall meant shoveling the roof, and as soon as there was a bit of a thaw ice dams pushed at the spongy old roofing material until the melting water began to drip, and then to cascade, into our bedroom.

But all that was down the road. First the sellers, Clayton and Rita, taught us the intricacies of the furnace, the mysteries of a kerosene-burning stove. Rita worked in a clothespin factory and made all Clayton's meals; he gathered mushrooms and cut firewood, though I never saw him do anything but sit at the kitchen table and smoke. They sized us up in five minutes, and seemed perfectly happy to accept us as a couple, especially once they'd figured out that Rita could talk to Wally about where to shop while Clayton told me about maintenance, shoveling, plumbing—men's work. He'd even make jokes about the fussy concerns of wives, winking at me and nodding in Rita and Wally's direction.

Once Clayton and Rita vacated for their new house, we found ourselves alone in thirteen rooms of linoleum concealing wide-plank floors, cheap lumberyard paneling covering up layer upon layer of wallpaper roses. The house had long been inhabited in the manner of poor Vermonters who made do, got by, put a patch on what broke. It had been a long time since that house had gotten any serious attention; had it *ever* gotten serious attention? But it didn't matter a bit how much work confronted us, or that the renovation would turn out, eventually, to be unfinishable work—what mattered was it was ours, a great rambling dream of a house, eccentric, temperamental, rife with character, capable of being profoundly loved. And we were thrilled; the house was ours to rescue, to uncover, to inhabit, to play with, a piece of the world on which to make our mark.

For the five years we lived there—in which time my hands, or Wally's, must have touched every surface of that house, inside and out, as we painted and plastered and stripped and cursed, built and caulked and wept—every penny we could make went into the house. Mustard and chocolate gave way to a creamy colonial yellow, white trim, and blue shutters; the town paper suddenly carried an article about "the rising tide of gentrification." In a while it had a rainproof roof shielding new insulation, new chimney linings, a huge soapstone woodstove big enough to defeat—almost—the bitter Januaries of the snow queen. (Bobby or Lynda, visiting, used to wrap up in layers and layers; he in sweaters, she in kimonos and tunics and a plethora of scarves.)

And we bought a new pair of storm doors, beautiful ones, which brings me back to the finches. The house had a narrow double front door, still sporting its figured brass hardware, patterns half-obscured now with a hundred years of paint—handsome doors, but not very practical ones, since it was impossible to effectively block their drafty cracks and seams. For a while we sealed them off with plastic, six months of the year, and then it seemed time—the rest of the house was at least *that* much ready—to use the front door as it was meant to be used. At a salvage company I found just the right thing—for the proverbial arm and leg, but it was grant money, and it was for our *house*. O the rationalization that justified many an expense we couldn't afford, many an hour spent in the hard folding chairs of auctions, many a Saturday rooting in some collapsing barn! Just the right thing was a pair of oak doors, multipaned; they were french doors, really, but with the right varnish and framing they made the most splendid storm doors imaginable. It was the storm door raised to the level of art, and so the entryway of the house took on its proper dignity, a happy transition from the outer world to the inner one. At Christmas they were best, decked out and inviting.

It's true the invitation was mostly to ourselves, and for a few good friends at the college where I taught, since we fit into our little Vermont town none too well; we were the only out, gay male couple in the whole place, and though we were thoroughly accepted by the town's liberal community (that overlayer of exiles that make Vermont culture tolerable) we were strange new creatures to the urlayer of native Vermonters who made up the town's human bed-rock. And who, significantly, made up most of our neighborhood. Our house wasn't cheap just because the floors sagged; it took us a while to learn what people meant by that insistent talk about *location*.

But we had a world for ourselves there, and one very real advantage to living with a window designer was that he could make *anything* look good—the right arrangement, a little fussing with the details: splendor! The high ceilings accommodated a huge tree at Christmas, thus making use of the ornaments Wally had been squirreling away for a lifetime, souvenirs of other people's childhoods collected at a decade of yard sales: Bohemian glass beads strung into crystalline snowflakes, great garlands of shimmering glass, an under-tree world of ancient toys. The big granite cellar was perfect for the universe of display props Wally used for store windows. For me, a realm of gardens, borders of perennials out front (against the now properly white picket fence, every new picket of it cut with my own hands) and herbs and vegetables out back.

And doors to deck. One Christmas we made boxwood wreaths from a cutting I took from the ruins of a formal rose garden at the college; one hung on each of the gleaming oak doors. They looked so classic, and lasted so long, that by early spring they were still hanging there, plain without their ribbons and trim, cheerful and promising—qualities that Vermonters need desperately, suicidally, in February and March.

This is where the house finches come in. I noticed that every time I opened the door there'd be a buzz of winged activity, something hurrying through the branches of the wide old lilac. And every time we'd come home, a parallel commotion. Soon we saw what the fuss was about, which was the house these two new colonizers had made for themselves, a woven bowl of grasses and straw nestled into one of the wreaths, built against the glass. At eye level! We stopped using the front door right away, and rigged a system of reflective plastic film inside to allow us to watch, quietly, from the front hallway, our tenants about their work. Their long work, it turned out, weeks of sitting, the male coming and going, leaving and returning with food, and then, miracles! A cluster of mouths and necks and awkward featherless gray about-to-be-wings writhing in the nest, a cup of pure and insistent hunger.

Once they'd all gone on, the nest having served its purpose, we considered saving it—but it was too well used a thing, too stained and too shit in. It made us happy to have been host, for our house to be home, even briefly, to some other life, some welcome and mysterious pulse of energy from the outer world. Where would the new finches go? The bird book said they fed in the wild, individually, in summer, then formed great flocks in fall. I liked to imagine a cloud of them, a storm of gray and rose.

I didn't think of the house finches again until this new pair showed up in the roses, spring incarnate, pulses of desire and intention. How little they'd weigh, if you could hold one, and how utterly intent they are on their purpose, possessed by their own green and burgeoning industry: to build, to nest, to rear. *We further the world, small as we are, little handfuls of feather and heartbeat; we make it go on.*

My friend Chris said that after his wife died, in winter, spring was painful for him, all the world but her—and him—renewing itself. I don't find that spring hurts. I am aware that my interior season is winter, the republic of bare branches, the austere structure at the heart of things. And yet I take pleasure in my garden, even if my heart's not in it the way it has been other years. In Vermont I gardened with a vengeance, that fire a part of my own imperative to make a safe home, to surround myself with a place to stand. And raise, unlike the birds, not young, but ourselves. And splendid lilies, monkshood, and delphinium, campanula and strawflowers and love-in-a-mist.

When we came to Provincetown, I loved my much smaller garden, a little cottage plot—infinitely more manageable, and small gardens actually are more likely to open into revelation than large ones; in the intricacy of a contained space the world opens, the way it does in a Cornell box. On the Cape the sea warms the air a bit in winters, and cools it in summers, so that the climate partakes of the marine, of English weather. Thus roses thrive, lavish and luxuriant sprawlers, and if the sandy soil is infertile it also makes for fabulous drainage. I've gardened joyfully here.

But this year, no rush to buy seeds, no pushing at the limits imposed by frost or cool wet nights. I am in no hurry, am no jubilant participant, although I am glad for spring to unfold.

And, I think, this greening does thaw at the edges, at least, of my own cold season. Joy sneaks in: listening to music, riding my bicycle, I catch myself feeling, in a way that's as old as I am but suddenly seems unfamiliar, *light*. I have felt so heavy so long. At first I felt odd—as if I shouldn't be feeling this lightness, that familiar little catch of pleasure in the heart which is inexplicable, though a lovely passage of notes or the splendidly turned petal of a tulip has triggered it. It comes back to me as if from a great distance, this old delight in the world. It's my buoyancy, part of what keeps me alive—and I realize suddenly I can't remember when I felt it last. It's a sort of feeling that doesn't want to be long examined; happy, suddenly, with the concomitant experience of a sonata and the motion of the shadows of leaves, I just want to breathe in that lightness, after it's been so long lost.

Something about this new sunlight and warmth begins to dispel something darker and colder in me. I have the desire to be filled with sunlight, to soak my skin in as much of it as I can drink up, after the long interior darkness of this past season, the indoor vigil, in this harshest and darkest of winters, outside and in.

So this afternoon I lay on a high hill, a dune at the top (and it seemed the heart) of the world, surrounded by blooming beach plums, the glazed new leaves of poison ivy. I lay against the warm body of the hill, a child, and there was some generous and laving quality about the sunlight that allowed me to let go, to let all of the tension and grief and chill sink out of me, into the sand, which was old enough and warm enough to hold it all. A few inches down the sand's still cool and moist, this time of year, but it's been busy drinking in the sun as well, and its surface glows and invites like human skin.

In the night it rained, and the wind blew hard, dislodging some canes of the climbing rose from the anchors that pin them to the walls. I think the finches' nest has been jostled; it seems more exposed, and maybe squeezed a bit, not quite so shapely. The birds are nowhere around; have they given up on this site already, subject to their implacable imperative, and moved on?

What a fragile thing a house is, though it doesn't seem so. All the energy we poured into the house in Vermont couldn't complete it; it was so big, and so needy, that I used to dream, even after five years, of part of the house falling away, the sloping floors gone their way at last, tumbling in the direction they'd always pined for. Or I'd dream of whole rooms I hadn't even discovered yet—rooms that, of course, needed immediate and serious attention. By the time I was just getting to some project I'd long postponed, I'd find that something done years before needed doing *again*. There was barely time to enjoy that particularly homosexual pleasure, décor; there was too much work to be done. Paint peels, plaster cracks, and gardens, of course, are the most ephemeral constructions of all.

What disappears faster than a garden without a gardener?

I learned just how fast and entire the loss of a garden is when we left Vermont. The back, private part of the garden was the last thing I studied, just before we left; I stood up on the deck above that geometry of paths and raised beds and looked down into the heart of it. It was a kind of externalization of something essential in me—is that what all gardens are?—and it had anchored me, mirrored me back, held me in place. I like the psalmist's phrase: a dwelling place; I didn't understand how intensely that garden had become a dwelling place for my spirit until I left it. Wally found me there, holding onto the railing we'd built ourselves, its turned spindles the salvage of some Victorian porch from a little town down the road. I *wanted* to go, and at the same time I knew I was taking leave, that moment, of some irreplaceable part of the history of my heart.

Not that I regret that decision, or have ever done so. We stayed in Vermont a year after Wally tested positive, reeling with the news at first and then beginning our accommodation to what Wallace Stevens called "the pressure of reality." "The more reality pushes against us," Stevens said, "the more the imagination is compelled to press back." He was referring to making poems, but it's also true that our imaginations went to work on a more pragmatic level. How was this news to fit into our lives? That mortal sword that hangs over all our heads hanging now a little lower, how were we to live? Wally was fine, then, physically, but his T-cell counts (vague marker that they are) weren't impressive ones, and we couldn't help but imagine versions of the future. In Vermont we felt as if our reality was exactly that—*ours,* not a shared sense of the world but an isolating otherness. My sense of what lay ahead, should we continue to stay there, was of a narrowing darkness and solitude, an increasing struggle against increasingly difficult demands. And how, someday, was I going to get in six cords of wood by myself?

A pair of friends, Chris and Brigid, offered to buy our house. It was easier to relinquish it to them—this would be their first house, too, and they brought to the prospect of owning it great eagerness, and a palpable love for the place, difficulties and all, which was what pleased me most. This wasn't entirely an easy house to love, ungainly and oddly laid out and, for all our five years' efforts, presenting inexhaustible prospects for the next energetic dwellers.

And so we let it go. As well as the grief I felt, abandoning my garden, and the groundedness it stood for, there was a real joy, an energizing quality in moving ahead. We were taking charge of the future, or at least a part of it. The test results had seemed to take the future away from us; letting go of our old life, pouring our energies into getting ourselves to a new place, was a way of wresting a bit of that control back. We all put up with less appealing aspects of the present for the sake of a future we anticipate later on. An HIV diagnosis calls the wisdom of such deferral into question. What were the pleasures we wanted now? How did we want to use our time together?

That autumn of our move, 1990, was one long golden extension of summer. We rented a house on the beach, in Provincetown, as far out toward the very tip of Cape Cod as it is possible to live. And because that autumn and winter were one of the mildest in memory, we felt we'd been given a radiant sort of gift, a season out of time, which seems to me now something suspended in amber: Wally and Arden on the beach, wrestling or resting, while I am inside the house, my desk up against the window that looks directly out past them toward Long Point Light, our promontory's last, haunted outpost. Wally and Arden wading, further and further out, into the long mercurial wash of low tides, the tidal flats shimmering around these two smallest figures, tiny evidence of my love held in the silver expanse of the afternoon.

It was summer again before I saw the old garden in its new incarnation—for an old garden, without its gardener, isn't the same entity at all, but a new event in the world. I hadn't realized how much the garden reflected my own obsessive propensities to shape it, how much that shape had to do with some ideal garden held in my head, toward which the raw material of the real space would be trimmed, trained, and cajoled. Chris and Brigid, bless their hearts, were not gardeners—or was it that *their* garden was aligned toward some other ideal?

Though they took pleasure in the effort, it was clear that they weren't sure which things were noxious weeds, to be banished, which the perennials I'd introduced and then given years of assistance to. The garden, seen from the street, seemed newly a jungle, an over-the-top efflorescence, consequence of my own overplanting

235

gone mad. I had a visceral, physical response; I wanted to let myself in the gate and *weed*.

That response was, of course, about my not really having let the garden go. But the garden that was mine, I soon realized, was the interior one, the memory; the external garden had already become something else. What I saw as a particularly invasive, enormous weed might be, to the template of beauty which the new gardeners brought to their creation, the model of lush growth, a welcome wildness. Whatever, it was theirs now.

Until Brigid died, the following winter, in an accident on Route 2, the icy two-lane road she and I used to drive to work every morning. When Wally and I had put the house into Chris's and Brigid's hands, it was with a sense of their ongoingness, of the future ahead of them; it was clear they wanted to fill the big space with friends, animals, and, later, children. I was sidestepping a vision of my own future: lonely Vermont winter closing in, Wally sick and needing all the care I can give, no help, the dark little town around us, all the chimneys on its steep hills billowing white smoke and steam into icy and unforgiving air, our street going narrower and darker. Did I think we were sidestepping death, too? Perhaps our leaving when we did made Wally's life a little longer, I don't know. Certainly it made the last years brighter ones; I don't know how we'd have gotten through them without all the help and good company we found.

But I never thought it was Chris who would be widowed in the big house—a place for one person to get lost in, caught in the echoes of his own voice—instead of me. Sometimes I'd catch myself imagining death was determined to sweep someone away from that house, and that we'd somehow leapt out of the way, but that Brigid hadn't been able to.

The following summer the garden became something else entirely, and any sense of regret or nostalgia I had about it was subsumed into a kind of wonder at how the orders we make vanish so quickly, subsumed. The whole house seemed to go into a kind of accelerated decline; paint peeling, fence pickets snapped, the cream yellow of the clapboards (a Shaker sort of color, it had seemed to me when we chose it) dirtied with the soot of tired oil furnaces struggling to keep up. The building seemed to express the psychic life it held, as if it were grief's outer skin.

Chris lived there for a while, then rented out the house, but he eventually found the payments impossible, the burden of the place overwhelming—and so it went back to the bank, to his sorrow and relief. I haven't seen it now for a long time. I understand that some friends took various perennials from the garden, which is just a shining idea, now. Which, in a way, is what it always was, an idea given not flesh but leaf.

We did not rescue the house, as we'd thought we were doing, those years ago. Oh, we did for a while make it not merely habitable but lovely, maybe more so than it had ever been; even when it was brand new I suspect it was built to be workman's housing, and I doubt that love had been lavished upon its details. But the gleam of a loved house lasts only as long as he who loves it can keep polishing, keep occupying. What we did was to make for ourselves, for a while, a dwelling place, a deeply occupied zone in which to encounter and to recapitulate all our dwellings, a house deep enough, ours enough, to dream into. And then time swept us away, and in time took the house itself.

Did it? Perhaps now, repossessed, the place will be cheap enough again for somebody to come along flush and foolish enough with a sense of possibility, indifferent to the politics of location, with enough hubris to see some shining thing this sow's ear can become in time. Apartments? Offices, or the flat indignity of a parking lot?

The birds are flitting about in the box alder; in their hurry to nest, have they found another site? The need must push at them, requiring that they try again—a more protected place, this time. Though isn't it plain that no place is protected?

I enjoy the garden, this spring, but I don't feel that imperative to shape, perhaps because I see how quickly it blows away, how swiftly occupancy changes. I remember Wally talking, one afternoon in December, at a time when his speech or his ideas weren't always clear. I was rubbing his feet, which ached with cramps as they turned inward to point toward one another, his legs seeming to wither in front of us. Massage would ease the pains better than anything else, and so I was always at his feet, sometimes for a long time, a peaceful, steadying time to talk. "I wonder how many people," he said, "had their feet rubbed in this house?" I understood he was talking about how many people had been sick here, really, in our room, how many had died here, in this house's two hundred years. We knew that for most of this century one family lived here, and raised eleven children, enough people to generate generations of intensity, resonant moments and gestures of the sort that reverberate in a house. Before them, there aren't any records, but since maybe 1790 people have been holding this house, and being held by it. I felt that Wally was experiencing himself, that moment, as part of that history; he was joining a community. As we did, in fact, when we bought this place, and set to work on it—just in time, as it turned out, to make a home around us for the onslaught. We had just enough time to do the essential things, to make the house feel like ours. This house is actually small enough for me to finish—someday—the projects we started. I love to be here in storms, when the low-slung roof sheds water, and I can feel the gravity of the big beams holding the roof down, as they always have, as perhaps they did when they were part of some ship. We became part of the life of the house, one which seems to stand, to go on. When I was rubbing Wally's aching feet, did the dead of this house come and stand around him?

At seven this morning—a clear and resonant day, an aura of freshness and possibility around everything—there was a commotion in the roses: the birds, back at work. The nest looks larger, as if they've gotten an early start today on reinforcing it, trying to build something capable of withstanding the wind. I've been out to look at it, from a distance I disciplined myself to maintain. They've anchored it with soil in the bottom, the action of wise engineers.

Contagious persistence: the will to inhabit, to make, out of whatever is offered, a dwelling place.

diane ackerman

Diane Ackerman turns her famous talent for lush, yet scientifically accurate, description to detailing a close encounter few people ever get to experience—swimming in the ocean with a right whale and her baby. Ackerman's piece is extraordinary not only for the way she portrays the everyday lives of whales, how they appear almost human—but for the way she considers how we might appear to whales.

from *the moon by whale light*

For hours, I sat quietly and watched the busy nursery bay. Fang rolled onto her weighty side, and her baby nursed. Then the baby got rambunctious and strayed a little too far. Mother lowed to it in a combination of foghorn and moo, calling it back within eyeshot. From time to time, Fang submerged slowly, her tail hanging limp and loose, trailing one tip of a fluke in the water. She made burpy sounds, with occasional moans, and I think she may have been napping.

When a whale sleeps, it slowly tumbles in an any-old-crazy, end-over-end, sideways fashion, and may even bonk its head on the bottom. Or it just lies quietly, looking like a corpse. When it rises again to breathe in the midst of sleep, it comes up as slow as a dream, breaks the surface, breathes a few times and, without even diving, falls again slowly toward the bottom. Right whales sometimes sleep in the mornings on calm days in Argentina, and some of them seem to be head-heavy, with light tails. The result is that they fall forward and their tails rise out of the water. Humpbacks are rarely visible when they're sleeping, because they're less buoyant and usually sink fast. But the behavior of right whales is easy to study, because they're at-the-surface whales. They're so fat that they float when relaxed, and they spend a lot of time with their backs in the air. When they're asleep at the surface, their breathing rate drops tremendously, they don't close their nostrils completely between breaths, and so some-times they snore. In fact they make marvelous, rude, after-dinner noises as they sleep. When they wake, they stretch their backs, open their mouths, and yawn. Sometimes they lift their tails up and shake them, and then they go about their business. Often, they sleep at the surface so long on calm days that their backs get sunburned; and then they peel the same way humans do, but on a big, whale-size scale. The loose skin from their backs falls into the water and becomes food for birds. When they breach, they shed a lot of loose skin as they hit the water, and seagulls, realizing this, fly out fast to a breaching whale. Not much skin sheds from the tail. The gulls know that, and when a whale is merely hitting its tail on the water, they don't bother with it.

A gull swept down, pulled a piece of skin from Fang's back, and Fang, in obvious pain, shook her head and tail simultaneously, flexed almost in half, then dove underwater. The gull flew to another pair of whales nearby, attacked them, and went off. A bizarre habit had developed among the gulls in this bay. Instead of waiting for the whales to shed skin, they landed on the backs of whales and carved the skin and blubber off. Two species of gulls—the brown-headed gulls and the kelp gulls—yanked off long strips of skin and set up feeding territories on the backs of their own particular whales. When Roger first started studying right whales at Valdés Peninsula, he noticed that only brown-headed gulls were peeling the skin off the backs of sleeping, sunburned whales. Soon, however, the kelp gulls not only learned this technique but also began carving holes in backs. The result was that whales like Fang were pitted with craters made by gulls. When a gull landed on a whale's back, the whale panicked. This year there were fewer whales in the bay, and Roger thought the kelp gulls might have been chasing them away, to bays where kelp gulls don't yet know the tricks.

Juan appeared at the edge of camp, on foot, apparently hiking in from a walk to a neighboring bay. By the time I got back to the main house, he was just arriving, wearing shorts, a T-shirt, and a knitted hat.

"Tired?" I asked with an inflection that said, *I really hope you aren't.* "Want to go find some whales?"

He grinned. "Just let me get a Coke, then *vamos*."

I put on a leotard and tights and began crawling into a half-inch-thick wetsuit that included Farmer John overalls, a beaver-tail jacket, boots, gloves, and a hood. There was so much neoprene in the suit, trapping air, that I'd need to wear weights around my waist to keep from bobbing on the surface.

Juan tugged on a thick wetsuit and boots, and we went down to the beach, where Minolo joined us in the *Zodiac*.

Heading north along the bay, we came upon two mothers and calves, but the mothers were naturally protective of their calves and hurried them away. We wanted to find a young adult. Juan had been collecting loose skin for Judy and then going into the water to photograph the heads of the whales it came from in order to identify them. I hoped to join him. We searched for an hour but found none in the mood to be approached. Finally, we headed back toward camp and, coming around a bend, discovered Fang and her calf still playing. We cut the motor about two hundred yards from the whales. Juan and I slipped over the side of the boat and began to swim toward them, approaching as quietly as possible, so that they wouldn't construe any of our movements as aggressive. In a few minutes, we were only yards from the mother's head. Looking down, I saw the three-month-old baby beside her underwater, its callosities bright in the murky green water. Slowly, Juan and I swam all the way around them, getting closer and closer. The long wound on Fang's flank looked red and angry. When her large tail lifted out of the water, its beauty stunned me for a moment, and then I yanked Juan's hand, to draw his attention, and we pulled back. At fifty feet long, weighing about fifty tons, all she would have needed to do was hit us with a flipper to crush us, or swat us with her tail to kill us instantly. But she was moving her tail gently, slowly, without malice. It would be as if a human being, walking across a meadow, had come upon a strange new animal. Our instinct wouldn't be to kill it but to get closer and have a look, perhaps touch it. Right whales are grazers, which have balleen plates, not teeth. We did not look like lunch. She swung her head around so that her mouth was within two feet of me, then turned her head on edge to reveal a large white patch and, under that, an eye shaped much like a human eye. I looked directly into her eye, and she looked directly back at me, as we hung in the water, studying each other.

I wish you well, I thought, applying all the weight of my concentration, in case it was possible for her to sense my mood. I did not imagine she could decipher the words, but many animals can sense fear in humans. Perhaps they can also sense other emotions.

Her dark, plumlike eye fixed me and we stared deeply at one another for some time. The curve of her mouth gave her a Mona Lisa smile, but that was just a felicity of her anatomy. The only emotion I sensed was her curiosity. That shone through her watchfulness, her repeated turning toward us, her extreme passivity, her caution with flippers and tail. Apparently, she was doing what we were—swimming close to a strange, fascinating life-form, taking care not to frighten or hurt it. Perhaps, seeing us slip over the side of the *Zodiac,* she thought it had given birth and we were its young. In that case, she might have been thinking how little we resembled our parent. Or perhaps she understood only too well that we were intelligent beasts who lived in the strange, dangerous world of the land, where whales can get stranded, lose their bearings and equilibrium, and die. Perhaps she knew somehow that we live in that desert beyond the waves from which whales rarely return, a kingdom we rule, where we thrive. A whale's glimpse of us is almost as rare as our glimpse of a whale. They have never seen us mating, they have rarely if at all seen us feeding, they have never seen us give birth, suckle our young, die of old age. They have never observed our society, our normal habits. They would not know how to tell our sex, since we hide our reproductive organs. Perhaps they know that human males tend to have more facial hair than females, just as we know that male right whales tend to have more callosities on their faces than females. But they would still find it hard to distinguish between a clothed, short-haired, clean-shaven man and a clothed, short-haired woman.

When Fang had first seen us in the *Zodiac,* we were wearing large, smoked plastic eyes. Now we had small eyes shaped like hers—but two on the front of the head, like a flounder or a seal, not an eye on either side, like a fish or a whale. In the water, our eyes were encased in a glass jar, our mouths stretched around a rubber tube, and our feet were flippers. Instead of diving like marine mammals, we floated on the surface. To Fang, I must have looked spastic and octopus-like, with my thin limbs dangling. Human beings possess such immense powers that few animals cause us to feel truly humble. A whale does, swimming beside you, as big as a reclining building, its eye carefully observing you. It could easily devastate you with a twitch, and yet it doesn't. Still, although it lives in a gliding, quiet, investigate-it-first realm, it is not as benign as a Zen monk. Aggression plays a big role in its life, especially during courtship. Whales have weapons that are equal in their effects to our pointing a gun at somebody, squeezing a finger, and blowing him away. When they strike each other with their flukes in battles, they hit flat, but they sometimes slash the water with the edge. That fluke edge could break a person in two instantly. But such an attack has never happened in the times people have been known to swim with whales. On rare occasions, unprovoked whales have struck boats with their flukes, perhaps by accident, on at least one occasion killing a man. And there are three reported instances of a whale breaching onto a boat, again resulting in deaths. But they don't attack swimmers. In many of our science fiction stories, aliens appear on earth and terrible fights ensue, with everyone shooting weapons that burn, sting, or blow others up. To us, what is alien is treacherous and evil. Whales do not visualize aliens in that way. So although it was frightening to float beside an animal as immense and powerful as a whale, I knew that if I showed her where I was and what I was and that I meant her no harm, she would return the courtesy.

Suddenly, Juan pulled me back a few feet and, turning, I saw the calf swimming around to our side, though staying close to its mother. Big as an elephant, it still looked like a baby. Only a few months old, it was a frisky pup and rampantly curious. It swam right up, turned one eye at us, took a good look then wheeled its head around to look at us with the other eye. When it turned, it swung its mouth right up to my chest, and I reached out to touch it, but Juan pulled my hand back. I looked at him and nodded. A touch could have startled the baby, which might not have known its own strength yet. In a reflex, its flipper or tail could have swatted us. It might not have known that if humans are held underwater—by a playful flipper, say—they can drown. Its flippers hung in the water by its sides, and its small callosities looked like a crop of fieldstones. When it rolled, it revealed a patch of white on its belly and an anal slit. Swimming forward, it fanned its tail, and the water suddenly felt chillier as it stirred up cold from the bottom. The mother was swimming forward to keep up with it, and we followed, hanging quietly in the water, trying to breathe slowly and kick our flippers as little as possible. Curving back around, Fang turned on her side so that she could see us, and waited as we swam up close again. Below me, her flipper hovered large as a freight elevator. Tilting it very gently in place, she appeared to be sculling; her tail, too, was barely moving. Each time she and the baby blew, a fine mist sprayed into the air, accompanied by a *whumping* sound, as of a pedal organ. Both mother and calf made no sudden moves around us, no acts of aggression.

We did not have their insulation of blubber to warm us in such frigid waters and, growing cold at last after an hour of traveling slowly along the bay with them, we began to swim back toward the beach. To save energy, we rolled onto our backs and kicked with our fins. When we were a few hundred yards away from her, Fang put her head up in a spy hop. Then she dove, rolled, lifted a flipper high into the air like a black rubber sail, and waved it back and forth. The calf did the same. Juan and I laughed. They were not waving at us, only rolling and playing now that we were out of the way. But it was so human a gesture that we automatically waved our arms overhead in reply. Then we turned back onto our faces again. Spears of sunlight cut through the thick green water and disappeared into the depths, a bottom soon revealed itself as tawny brown about thirty beet below us, and then the sand grew visible, along with occasional shells, and then the riot of shells near shore, and finally the pebbles of the shallows. Taking off our fins, we stepped from one liquid realm to another, from the whale road, as the Anglo-Saxons called the ocean, back onto the land of humans.

kurt hoelting

Hoelting speaks both as a commercial fisherman and as a man who has spent a lifetime learning about the ecological and cultural heritage of the Northwest. Hoelting links his unfulfilled childhood dream of catching salmon in Puget Sound with the sweeping ecological changes that have made salmon rare in those waters, and that continue to threaten the environment. Any ecological plan for the future, Hoelting warns, "must include wild salmon, if we want it also to include children who dream."

dreaming of salmon

I grew up by the shores of Puget Sound, dreaming of salmon. My childhood summers were spent on Liberty Bay, in a cabin near Poulsbo. It's where my strongest memories were wrought. Winters were passed somewhere in the confusion of the city. But with school's ending each spring, we made a beeline for the cabin, and life began again. From earliest memory the waters of the Sound pulled me to them as inexorably as the tide.

There was magic in those waters, and nothing held more power in my imagination than the elusive salmon. My father worked in the city right through the summer and had no interest in fishing, so I did the best I could, drop line in hand, working my way up the ladder from bullheads to sea perch to dogfish—always dreaming, dreaming of salmon. I read books about salmon, drew pictures of them in fine detail, plotted endlessly and fruitlessly to lure one onto my hook. My brother was almost always with me when we went in search of salmon. Yet only once, in all those youthful summers, did we actually approach our quarry. Trolling a spinner behind our rowboat, with dusk coming on, my brother hooked what could only have been a salmon. His pole nearly jumped from the boat, line singing off the reel. In one majestic run, the fish stripped the reel, snapped the line, and was gone.

To this day, the memory haunts me. It's part of the enduring lore of our family.

We never did catch a salmon in Puget Sound. Nor did we suspect how many had already been lost. No one told us about the Elwha River kings that commonly reached one hundred pounds, or the Quinault River sockeye that were coveted by Indian tribes in trade up and down the coast, all gone. We didn't hear tales of Graywolf pinks, Soleduck summer coho, Satsop steelhead, Skokomish chums. No one was there to tell us.

We knew little, and understood less, about the true stature of salmon in the ecological and cultural heritage of our region. But we knew our own yearnings. And the tenacity of our efforts to catch a salmon for ourselves, however futile, was testimony to the power of this astonishing creature. Our lives were shaped in part by the strength of the encounter, even if this encounter occurred only in our imaginations. Years later, as a college student working on a salmon seiner in southeast Alaska, I finally caught salmon myself. I also witnessed the spectacle of wild salmon returning to their streams in huge numbers. In a place far to the north, I caught a glimpse of the lost legacy of my native Puget Sound. Year after year, through college and graduate school, I left the Sound to head north for the salmon-rich waters of Alaska during the summer, "just one more time."

Somewhere along the way I figured out that this annual migration was my life, not merely a prelude to a "real" job in the city.

This summer will be my twenty-fifth season fishing in Alaska. The passing years have done little to diminish my enthusiasm for catching salmon or for being present at the return of the world's last great wild runs. But I am more reflective now, more aware of the tragic ironies that pit one region against another, healthy runs against threatened runs, wild salmon against their genetic stepcousins from the pen. These ironies offer themselves now as a metaphor for our times, a poignant case study in our efforts to rethink the place of human beings in the natural world. For me, the contrasts are jarring. The last two seasons in Bristol Bay, for example, have each seen returns of over forty million sockeye salmon, making them the first and third largest runs on record. When the Bristol Bay Fishery dies down in late July, I travel to the southeast

Alaskan panhandle to purse seine for pink salmon. With returns of over fifty million pinks the last two seasons, these numbers are breaking century-old records at just the time when once-great runs to the south are sliding toward extinction, and coastwide closures are being ordered in a desperate attempt to save them.

My own life is divided between two worlds, one to the north, one to the south, one of plenty, one of want. I am framed by the contrasts, unsettled by the collision of opposites. For years I have taken for granted the necessity of traveling long distances away from home to find what was once the heart and soul of my own region. I have become intimate with the waters of Bristol Bay and southeast Alaska, while remaining a stranger to Puget Sound itself, even though more of my time is spent here than in Alaska. With the eclipse of salmon in the Northwest, the region slides toward economic irrelevance. Never mind that Microsoft is busy producing millionaires, and Boeing is filling the earth's skies with ever larger jets. The salmon are gone, and with them goes the biological and cultural bedrock that has held the region together since the retreat of the last ice sheet.

The cultural historian Thomas Berry has observed that our sense of the divine is linked inextricably to the diversity and splendor of the natural world. Nature provides the raw materials, the primordial context out of which all imagination grows. As the exterior world shrinks and decays, so goes the seed stock of natural inspiration. Perhaps it is our capacity for wonder that is the final victim of an unbridled devotion to progress. What does it mean to our collective imagination to gaze out on waters emptied of wild salmon? What does it mean to have scattered the cloud of witnesses—bear, wolf, orca, eagle, seal—who gathered so faithfully each year through the centuries to celebrate the salmon's return? To my mind, nothing can ever replace salmon in the religious imagination of the Pacific Northwest. The poet Gary Snyder is on the right track. He has suggested that we prepare a Ten-Thousand-Year Plan for the management of our national forests. I propose a Ten-Thousand-Year Plan for the Restoration of Wild Salmon Runs in Puget Sound. It is a reasonable proposal, precisely because it offers a time frame that wild salmon understand. I'll believe we have a chance when such a plan is proposed not by poets and philosophers, but by engineers and politicians. We will have reason for hope when, as a people, we understand that our endowment of the future extends far beyond the pittance of time that is granted ourselves and our immediate offspring. That endowment must include wild salmon, if we want it also to include children who dream.

permissions

about the editor

Lee Gutkind, founder and editor of the popular journal *Creative Nonfiction,* has performed as a clown for Ringling Brothers, scrubbed with heart and liver transplant surgeons, traveled with a crew of National League baseball umpires, wandered the country on a motorcycle, and experienced psychotherapy with a distressed family—all as research for eight books and numerous profiles and essays. His award-winning *Many Sleepless Nights,* an inside chronicle of the world of organ transplantation, has been reprinted in Italian, Korean, and Japanese editions, while his most recent nonfiction book, *An Unspoken Art,* was a Book-of-the-Month Club selection.

Former director of the writing program at the University of Pittsburgh and currently a professor of English, Lee Gutkind has pioneered the teaching of creative nonfiction, conducting workshops and presenting readings throughout the United States. Also a novelist and filmmaker, Gutkind is editor of the *Emerging Writers in Creative Nonfiction* book series from Duquesne University Press, director of the Mid-Atlantic Creative Nonfiction Summer Writers' Conference at Goucher College in Baltimore, and writing mentor for National Public Radio.